Samuel Sullivan Cox

Orient Sunbeams

Or, from the porte to the Pyramids by way of Palestine

Samuel Sullivan Cox

Orient Sunbeams
Or, from the porte to the Pyramids by way of Palestine

ISBN/EAN: 9783337309992

Printed in Europe, USA, Canada, Australia, Japan

Cover: Foto ©ninafisch / pixelio.de

More available books at **www.hansebooks.com**

ORIENT SUNBEAMS

OR

FROM THE PORTE TO THE PYRAMIDS,

BY WAY OF PALESTINE.

BY

SAMUEL S. COX,

Author of "Buckeye Abroad," "Eight Years in Congress," "Winter Sunbeams,"
"Why we Laugh," "Free Land and Free Trade,"
"Arctic Sunbeams," Etc.

> "The changing seasons and the march of time,
> The trees, the flowers, the fields, the rivers, Thine!
> Heaven, earth and sea, in one harmonious chime,
> Hymn forth the Holy God—the Beautiful, Sublime!"
> —*Müller.*

NEW YORK
G. P. PUTNAM'S SONS
27 AND 29 WEST 23D STREET
1882

CONTENTS OF VOLUME II.

CHAPTER I.
The Upper Bosphorus—A Home of Healing and a Circle of Delight...   PAGE 1

CHAPTER II.
The Upper Bosphorus—Scenes and Associations.................... 8

CHAPTER III.
The Towers of Europe and the American College................... 22

CHAPTER IV.
The Upper Bosphorus—Prophecies of Turkish Decay—Giant's Mountain—Jason—Classic Scenes..................................... 37

CHAPTER V.
Excursion to the Ancient Ottoman Capital—Broussa and its Attractions 46

CHAPTER VI.
Constantinople and its People—Walls, Gates and Towers............ 56

CHAPTER VII.
Among the Churches and Cemeteries and Around the Walls of Constantinople 66

CHAPTER VIII.

Around Constantinople—Among the Dead—Fortune-Telling—Sacred Waters.. 76

CHAPTER IX.

The Old Seraglio—St. Sophia—The Old Greek Hippodrome—The Museum of Ancient Costumes—Among the Howling Dervishes... 85

CHAPTER X.

The Changes in the Turkish Capital Within Thirty Years—Dynasty and Dynamite—The Tombs of the Sultans..................... 104

CHAPTER XI.

The Ottoman Empire as seen beneath the Surface—Its Degeneracy—Its Corruption and Venality—The Dead Turkish Parliament—The United States and Turkey.. 117

CHAPTER XII.

Reception by the Sultan.. 135

CHAPTER XIII.

Constantinople—Other Changes in Thirty Years..................... 154

CHAPTER XIV.

Through the Dardanelles with an Irish Captain—Sea Coasts of Asia and its Dead Empires and Cities—Domesticities of the People—Arabs as Cattle Drovers—Jews Persecuted—Beirut reached........ 169

CHAPTER XV.

City of Smyrna—Waters of Poesy and Mythology—Ill-Fated Chios.... 192

CHAPTER XVI.

An Ephesian Day.. 206

CHAPTER XVII.

Ephesus—Her Divinities and her Divinity........................ 218

CHAPTER XVIII.

On the Way to Damascus.. 230

CHAPTER XIX.

Damascus—Its Wonders and Glories, Massacres and Mosques—Its Tombs and Walls—Its Apostolic Memories and Grave of Buckle.. 241

CHAPTER XX.

A Hebrew House in Damascus—Damascus Mirth and Music......... 262

CHAPTER XXI.

On to the Holy City—Jaffa—Latrone—Ramleh—Jerusalem.......... 271

CHAPTER XXII.

West Walls of Jerusalem—Jaffa Gate—Hebrew History—Jews and Their Wailing Place and Hope................................. 286

CHAPTER XXIII.

The Star in the East—What Bethlehem is to-day—Scenes of the Saviour's Birthplace.. 301

CHAPTER XXIV.

The Holy Places of Christianity—Olivet and Bethany—The Scene of the Ascension.. 316

CONTENTS.

CHAPTER XXV.

                                                              PAGE

The Holy Places of Christianity—A Sunday in Jerusalem—Tomb of David—The Crucifixion and Sepulchre 327

CHAPTER XXVI.

Site of the Temple of Solomon—Mosques and Moslems............. 339

CHAPTER XXVII.

A Walk on Holy Ground—The Soldiers, Pilgrims, Tourists and Money Changers—Round About Jerusalem—The Pool of Bethesda—A Visit to the Tombs of the Kings............................... 352

CHAPTER XXVIII.

Egypt's Faded Glories—Alexandria and Cairo—The View from the Citadel—A drive to Heliopolis—A Glance at the Pyramids....... 361

CHAPTER XXIX.

The Ancient and Modern Land of the Pharaohs—Visit to the Sphinx and the Great Pyramid of Cheops 373

CHAPTER XXX.

The Pyramids and Tombs... 387

CONCLUDING CHAPTER.

Boulak Museum—Farewell to the Nile 403

LIST OF ILLUSTRATIONS.

	PAGE
TOWERS OF EUROPE (ROMOLO-HISSAR)	Frontispiece
THE SULTAN'S PALACE	56
MOSLEM AT PRAYER	188
AQUEDUCT AT EPHESUS	216
THE CITY OF EPHESUS (FROM MOUNT CORESSUS)	218
RUINS OF EPHESUS	220
DIANA EPHESIA	222
GATE OF CITADEL. EPHESUS	224
WALL OF DAMASCUS	254
TOMB OF ABSALOM	324
THE HOLY SEPULCHRE	334
ASCENT OF THE PYRAMIDS	396

INTRODUCTORY CHAPTER.

THIS is a companion volume to "Arctic Sunbeams; or, From Broadway to the Bosphorus, by way of the North Cape."

It continues the story of a summer travel in 1881.

After a restful sojourn in the capital of the Turkish empire, it takes the reader through the holy places of Mohammedan, Hebrew, and Christian, to that land of old renown, Egypt. It indulges in observations upon the present condition of the empire of Othman, and its principal and most interesting dependencies. Within this shining crescent of travel, Ephesus, Damascus, and Jerusalem are of course included.

This volume, like its predecessor, photographs for the eye, rather than elucidates for the mind. The photograph does not disdain to picture the humblest hyssop on the wall; and it presumes to reproduce the wall itself, with its moats and turrets, sieges and histories.

From pine to palm, from pole to pyramid, from the midnight sun of the North to its beams in the Orient, the least as well as the greatest of objects have provoked reverent suggestions and enthusiasms, which, in the absence of sedate study, may afford recreation to the reader, as they did to the author.

FROM POLE TO PYRAMID.

CHAPTER I.

THE UPPER BOSPHORUS—A HOME OF HEALING AND A CIRCLE OF DELIGHT.

> "'*Twas a place to revel, to smother, to drown*
> *In a bliss inferred by the poet ;*
> *For if ignorance be indeed a bliss*
> *What blessed ignorance equals this,*
> *To sleep,—and not to know it ?*"
> —HOOD'S MISS KILMANSEGG.

IT is Sabbath morning on the European shore of the Bosphorus. Domiciled with our consul and minister, we are at home. "Interterritoriality" is the international doctrine and technical term, and we feel its solace in all its length ; for who could be more comfortable, after our long journey, than ourselves under the roof of our courteous consul, Mr. Heap, and his affable wife? Besides, is not General Wallace, the new minister, a friend of a score of years, and enjoying with us and his accomplished wife this novel and delightful life? As I sit at the balcony, somewhat barred, as in all these houses, I see protruding from his window the General's huge meerschaum. Its smoke, mingling with that of my *chibouque*, flies out upon the blue waves, to mingle with that of the steamers, which are plying up and down and reminding the Turk that there is a peculiar civilization not altogether born of his eastern clime.

We are twelve miles from Constantinople. The

heats and noises of the city affect us not. A fresh wind blows briskly through the opening, a mile above, where the Euxine begins its swift current through the Bosphorus to the Sea of Marmora (Propontis), the Dardanelles, and the Mediterranean. This current dashes across the bay, and its reflux, after it strikes our stony quay, makes perpetual seething and murmurous motion, to which the sough of the wind amid the trees and terraced walls adds its high notes. It is difficult to describe the peculiar effect of the sound of these waters as they rush in and play back. They remind one of the " Rip-Raps " on a moderate scale, in their irregular unrest, except that there is a sound not unlike that of a cataract or fountain in deep woods, begetting a drowsy hum, like that of multitudes of bees. We have no word to describe it exactly. The French have *clapotage*—a sort of melodious choppiness. Here, after wandering in harsh northern climes, and amid rougher scenes, we find repose, health, and transport.

Our home is situated at Therapia. Its very name has a medicinal origin, starting, however, like all the delights of the *materia medica*, with poison. Medea, daughter of the King of Colchis, where the sheep were folded which bore the Golden Fleece, fell in love with Jason, who took more interest in the fleece than his right of hospitality required. She was quite familiar with things a lady ought not to know, such as charms other than her own. Her magic was not that which is generally conceded to the sex. She used it to obfuscate the dragon that guarded the Golden Fleece. She thus became *particeps criminis* with Jason in the larceny. and fled with him across the Euxine, coming into this beautiful bay, and making, in part, the same journey which we ourselves enjoyed, the other day, in another kind of craft. Here Medea opened her magic box, looked over her drugs, and threw the perilous stuff ashore. The Greeks, for euphony (as we used to say in college), changed *Pharmakia* into *Therapia*, which the cooling airs and lofty hills attest to be a "proper name" for health and comfort. The village signifies a "cure." The primates of the Greek nation came here in early days to dwell, and all the ambassadors have hereabout their summer homes. Here my wife, following the Medean example, threw away her drugs, and received healing from the hills, winds, and waters. The myth, therefore, hath much meaning and comfort for us.

We never felt so much the kindness of old and new friends of our own people as now. There was no reason why we should have been so kindly received by our minister and consul. We were not of their party, but when one is abroad how minute party lines look. We were strangers to the consul, although his fame as a patriot in the war, and his long service as consul at Tunis, had made for him a notable record; but the sad experience which Americans are undergoing at home and abroad, as the consequence of the crime of a miscreant, drew us together for mutual sympathy. And is not this the very beatitude of neighborliness, without reason, or custom, or price? It springs forth like the very healing breath of home to give consolation. No amount of reluctance on our part could overcome the gentle urgency of our diplomatic friends and whole-hearted hosts. *Nolens volens*, we are at home and in measureless content. Not Long

Branch, Old Point Comfort, Newport, or Mount Desert can compare with this, our summer resort. The dog days do not affect it, and the dust and moil of active life are only a memory. The mongrel civilization which makes the city below seem coarse, even in the variety and colors of its phases, does not intrude here. No dervish whirls or howls, and no narrow streets contract our vision.

The Turks have a name for this delightful, dreamy existence. They call it "*Kef*." The word is produced, as an egg is, by warmth; for it could not be understood in Trondhjem or Stockholm. It conveys the idea of quiet, ease, coolness, and complete repose, physical and spiritual. The senses are just alive enough to enjoy the warm breath, mitigated by the cool zephyr and grateful shade, lulled in sensuous activity, only not apathy, by the sound of remote music or the lapse of refreshing waters. The Turk will have his "*Kef*" after his bath and with his pipe. He will have it a half day at a time. He will have it with the aid of fountains; or, if not that, with the bubble, bubble of the water in his *narghile*, as the cooled smoke rises through the long tube to his longing lips, which dreamily cleave to the polished amber. Given a *chibouque*, a blue sky, the musical waters of the Bosphorus, far from the noise of the going and coming of people, and a host like our consul, and a companion like our minister, and your entire family within ear-shot, and you have the "*Kef*" we keep in this Ramadan time upon the upper shores of the Bosphorus. The murmur of the waters not only makes music, but prismatic music—the spectrum and the gamut. The waters are as crystalline as brooks in July, "when we see each grain of gravel." They are deep enough for any craft, and so are called fathomless. It is only their beauty which is unfathomable. A hundred feet from the gateway of our house are these plashing waters, whose silver waves make prism and music in the morning light. On our right, to the north, sweep the green hills along the margin of the bay, at whose base are the summer palaces and beauteous gardens of the European legations and the opulent pashas. Here, too, is a village, which is itself a picturesque locality. These hills become less ornate as they approach the Euxine; and on the opposite shore, in Asia, where there is less moisture from the sea, the hills are denuded of trees and somewhat of grass. Peeping above them on either continent, you may perceive the white lighthouses and the towers of the castles where the Turk commands the entrance and exit.

This enchantment may not last long; for the steamers, with their black Cardiff coal-smoke, fling their dusky pennons against the blue sky. All about the bay and river ply, like fairy boats, the long, yellow caïques, rowed by oarsmen in red caps and white clothes. These boats seem, in the clear light and water, to be rather in the air than on the denser element. Their plash, as they clip the waves, is more musical than the songs the boatmen sing as they row. These songs remind us of the south of Spain and north of Africa. They linger in our memory, and have more sadness in their tones than melody. When once heard, they are never forgotten. They grate upon the ear and disturb the harmony of the "*Kef*." These oriental singers, whether Ottoman or Greek, Armenian or Arab, should cultivate the Goddess of Silence, who presides over Painting and Sculpture. They should not vocalize. The chant is fearfully vague and monotonous. The tune is a drawl, as unmusical as the muezzin. The key is sure to be wrong, and the tones nasal. It climbs by ragged, cragged spasms to the top of the chromatic scale, and, yelling discordantly there till exhausted, it drops into a melancholy and abysmal whine, out of which there is no resurrection. Happily the upper Bosphorus is rarely treated to these outdoor performances.

These caïques are sometimes as regal and gorgeous as our fancy desires. They are furnished with rich rugs, and upon their damask cushions sometimes sit the mystic goddesses of the harem, enveloped in many folds of colored silk or white muslin. It may not be out of place to say that we have been presented to two of these goddesses. Prudence forbids us to mention their names. As the consul and myself were walking on the quay, he was saluted by them from their boat. Hastening to his door, he found them making a call. They were the widow and a sister of a pasha, high in honor. They were appareled like Una, in celestial white, but through their *yashmak* of immaculate mull their features were easily seen. My wife was presented by Mrs. Heap, and found that they talked French with the best accent and elegant grace. Mr. Heap dared to enter the presence. This was too much for me. I asked audience also, and, by the beard of the prophet! was admitted. We all took tea together. They could not drink very well without dropping their veils. With curious look I gazed upon these Circassian faces, with their dreamy, beautiful eyes and pure alabaster skin ; in fact, I shook their lily-white hands at parting, and furbished up a French phrase or so as sweet as "syrups tinct with cinnamon," and then the vision vanished in the barge of beauty, and our "*Kef*" was renewed with double Orientalism.

We observed in the evening paper a notice from the police (not of this transaction, although it had to be *sub rosa*) that an order had been issued "to employ thick veils," and not the transparent subterfuges which these goddesses now use.

As these divinities depart, we seek the balcony to gaze at the shoreless Euxine through the gateway by which we entered into this enchanted place. There is no horizon but that of sea and sky. As we look, the offing displays ships in full wing, glittering in the golden light of the evening. It is impossible to look toward this illimitable margin, without a sense of awe, which takes us out of our human experience into the mysteries of the Unseen. Are these ships phantoms of a land of myths—dreams of poets of the golden age?

There are many golden associations here. Time has not tarnished them. Not that golden eggs are laid by the geese we see driven by Turks along the quay ; nor are the golden pippins of Hesperus sold along with the golden Choussa grapes; nor are the caïques of the Golden Horn as sumptuous as the golden barge of Cleopatra ; but there are memories of the Colchian sheep with the golden fleece, which reminded Hood of the golden age of farming, under a golden sun in the golden East!

CHAPTER II.

THE UPPER BOSPHORUS—SCENES AND ASSOCIATIONS.

> *'Tis time, alas—the mysteries and the lore*
> *I came to study on this wondrous shore*
> *Are all forgotten in the new delights,*
> *The strange wild joy, that fill my days and nights.*
> —MOORE'S EPICUREAN.

THERE is a road and a path below our window. The sights upon them, are peculiar to the Bosphorus, and serve not a little to break the beauty of the scene and to disenchant us of our *odalisque* vision. Three hags, of dirty attire, are sitting shoeless in the dust and muttering their plaints to each passer-by. Failing to get alms, they take a bite all round of bread and cucumber, varied with raw tomato, and then a sleep. They are aroused in a flutter of spite by a flock of a hundred geese, driven by three traders, who thus traffic along the bank. They are hardly settled in their former attitude, before a Turk, astride of a donkey, with enormous panniers, like wings, sweeps them out of the path; while the next moment the boatmen who are pulling around the curve, and against the current, a lighter, full of goods and fruits, disturb them again. Full tilt down the dusty road we perceive a small boy of a Mussulman, with a huge club, driving homeward two untractable animals of the same meek family of misery. Cries of fruit and vegetables arise upon the air, as their venders drag the provision boats along the wharf. In front of the different legations (ours excepted), a mile off, on the shore, are steamers, called *stationnaires*, which are used by the embassies. In them these ministers sweep down to the great city in pomp and circumstance; while near each are little tugs, which fly around as tenders to the bigger craft. Immediately across the bay there is a mountain, from which Jason looked upon the Euxine, before he ventured forth after that fabled fleece of gold. His name, in the Greek of his time, and thoroughly approved by the scholars here as authentic, is carved upon a pillar upon its heights.

This is not the only historic or traditional association with this central spot of our earth. Along these banks, and over these hills, and upon this stream what struggles have taken place between races and religions, fighting for this ground of vantage and seat of empire! Persian, Scythian, Goth, Greek, Latin, Genoese, Venetian, Turk, Russian, English, French, and Italian, with fleets and armies, striving by force to subdue and hold these places of power, and to settle not merely the position and condition of our races, almost from their genesis, and certainly in their exodus, but determining the relations of distant empires and colonies here at this one pivot of human movement. To-day the same uncertainty remains as to what people shall hold this key to empire. The old problem returns: " Shall the Ottoman still hold his own, or is it his own? Whose is it? Or whose shall it be?"

The day after we arrived at this our temporary

home, I made, with the minister, the circuit of this end of the Bosphorus. General Wallace ordered out the legation caïque. It is some thirty feet long. Three Turks, in their clean, white attire, from the stockings (for they were shoeless) up to their bare necks, pulled their six oars; while the stout and grave old "*cavass*" of the legation, Mehmet, with sword by his side and pistol in belt, took the helm, cross-legged and serene. The General and myself sat on soft cushions and smoked, like true believers, the "most virtuous of weeds."

Therapia is called, as I have said, "the place of healing," and, while, it is deserving that name, it might also be called the place for fighting. We did not take our *cavass* along for fear of a fight. The Turks are very peaceful now. The *cavass* is, however, always prepared. He is the successor of the *chaousch*, or janizary. When Constantinople was made almost untenable for strangers and Christians, by reason of this famous band, the custom arose of employing them at the legations for safety; and, when the janizaries were eradicated by Mahmoud II., the custom remained, the name only being changed. Mehmet has been the servitor of the United States for twenty years in this fighting relation. He goes with the minister and his family on every occasion. When Mr. Maynard was minister here, not long since, he made a trip into Thessaly, and, in some abstract condition of mind, wandered off up a mountain, twelve miles from the ship, in a very brigandish vicinage. He was missing for hours, and great solicitude was felt. Mehmet was nearly crazed. He wrung his hands and cried: "Oh! has it come to this, that I (Mehmet) should lose my minister? Allah! O Allah!

send him to me, and never more shall he go from my sight." Mr. Maynard appeared, and Mehmet was relieved.

What I meant to say was that these were belligerent waters. They form a splendid harbor, deep and broad enough for any vessel or conflict. Here was the theatre of sea-fights long before those between Venetian and Genoese. We skirt the shores of this bay, and cross in the teeth of the strong current and breeze which comes from the direction of the Crimea. We row over the waters which flash against the outer walls of a sultan's palace, and remark that every place has its soldiers on guard.

What exquisite palace of white marble is that on the Asiatic side, embosomed in trees and guarded as if it were a prison? That is also one of the Sultan's elegant homes. It is just now holding in gentlest durance the Sheik of the Kurds, who was found in rebellion against his sultanic majesty. Strange, is it not, that these Kurds are the very tribe from which Xenophon, in his retreat, received the hardest fighting? After several thousand years, its chief looks out, a prisoner in his "retreat," upon the thirty odd steamers which make the round of the Bosphorus every day.

Along these shores were once temples to Jupiter, Neptune, and Diana, and nine other divinities, who were appeased by the Greeks before they ventured over the Ægean and Euxine. The evidence of these shrines of piety has been found in Greek inscriptions of the period. In later days of the Greek Christian domination, these hills and the mountains behind them were covered with churches and monasteries; but the main attraction is the classic Greek remnants, which find verification in a thousand ways. The mosques, which superseded the churches, are of less interest, as, generally, the classic and Christian decorations are whitewashed or despoiled. From the promontory at the mouth of the sea to the Tower of Medea, which is now a lighthouse, and from Giant's Mountain to the βοῦς πόρος (the passage of the ox), from which comes the name of the straits, there is no more beautiful spot, according to natural attraction, than the old castle which the Turks made, to subdue the last of the Greek Empire.

At every turn General Wallace repeats his observation, as if it had not already made an indelible impression: "I tell you, sir, that this is only a Turkish encampment, head-quarters down at Constantinople. Soldiers everywhere. Why, our interpreter was in America the other day. He came back, and said he hadn't seen a soldier while there —four months. Didn't see a uniform; but here one sees hardly anything else."

Varying our talk with incidents of "Billy the Kid," just shot by the sheriff in New Mexico, and making our connection between the Orient which we observe and the Orient (through the Spanish-Moorish-Mexican race, which the General has governed so recently) which we have in America, making the *sheriff* and the *sheik*, the *alcalde* of California and the *caliph* of Bagdad fraternal in philology, we take a sharp turn around a point, into and within the "Sweet Waters of Asia," under the promontory of Lembos. There the euphonious Geuk-Soo makes its little stream reflect the Castle of Asia, built in 1393, by Sultan Bajazit, surnamed Thunder. It was built for the subjugation of Constantinople, and played its part in the action. Glancing up at its old walls and towers, here and there decked with vegetation, we espy two storks, looking proudly down upon us. The General's fingers itched for his gun. There was blood in his eye.

The picture was quite enchanting, as the evening was settling down upon the scene. When we passed up the "Sweet Waters" we observe lazy Turks fishing and eating; notice upon the shores a few eunuchs watching the odalisques, who are out upon the banks for a stroll, enveloped in their *yashmak*, which faintly conceals their features and their form.

Having surveyed these waters, we turn our boat out upon the Bosphorus and steer for the European side, keeping in view the large round towers of the Castle of Europe. They rise in superb grandeur above their battlements, and out of the surrounding wood and houses.

We pass over the very spot spanned many hundred years before the Saviour by the bridge of boats on which Darius, king of kings, with his 700,000 men, crossed for the conquest of the Scythians. But Darius is not the main attraction here; nor is it the fact that here the Bosphorus is swift and narrow; but above us is the most exquisite mediæval fortress extant. It is large, with winding walls and three grand round towers, and is celebrated as well for its strength and permanency as for its history. It was built in four months, under such orders as only a Mahommedan sultan could give, and under promises of honors beyond all the dreams of wealth. It was the head of that anaconda which Mahommed II. made to swing around and crush what was left of the Greek Empire.

Still further below the towers of Roumelia (or Europe) is a beautiful kiosk, built for some sultan, upon the site of a temple of the chaste Diana. Many houses are under the shadow of the towers, and below them is a cemetery, full of turbaned tombstones, of which but few seem to be cared for.

At this interesting point the narrowness of the river makes the " Devil's Current," and we summon some genii of terrible turbans and brown aspect to assist our boat around the rapids. The excitement of the pull is not great, as the wind is not aiding the current. Soon we pass beneath the throne of Darius, in the college-grounds on high, and from which his army was watched as it passed over to Europe. The present here combines with the past, for we are told by our helmsman :

" This is the palace of Young Turkey, or Reshid Pasha, purchased of him by the Sultan Abdul Assiz, for his daughter, who married Reshid's son."

Cypress groves are passed, and then we turn about the point which leads us into the Bay of Stenia. It is full of Grecian associations of the earlier day, which Constantine transmuted into Christian romance ; for here the " winged genius " which encouraged the Argonauts was transformed into the Archangel Michael. Palaces were here built and destroyed ; villages have come and gone ; maritime contests were here waged—Nature having fitted this bay as one of the grand theatres in this grandest of historic centres.

A few more dashes of the oar, and our tired men wipe the sweat from their brows, receive their stipend from Mehmet, and we are upon our own steps at our landing. There is no star or stripe flying over it. It is sad in our household, for the President is dying. The English embassy, near by, has its ensign saucily snapping at every breeze. Our own home is not as gay in oriental arabesque as the Persian palace which we have passed; nor does it look so mysterious as the silent houses and palaces, guarded by soldiers, along the route where the Turkish millionaires and rulers live; but we find it most attractive in its hospitality and its position.

Before the sun goes down, we stroll into its garden, and survey the round trip we have taken. Under a mountain ash upon our terrace, we look far out through the open door of the Euxine. The water seems more restless and fretful, almost worried, as it rushes down to find its barrier against the piers at our feet. Our garden is not without its hammock, out of which you may see, between the urns upon our balustrade, the active scenes and splendors of the bay and stream. Below us, on the street, carriages and equestrians fly by; and ladies, in bundles of many clothes, awkwardly shuffle, followed by black and white servants. One of the company's boats which flies the red flag with star and crescent, and makes its voyage from Galata Bridge to this point, flashes by, laden with its motley groups of passengers. A dozen fishermen are trying their luck along the shore. Every moment a caïque comes in sight, making for the village of embassies across the bay, which is surrounded, like another Como, with its manifold villas. For a moment the oriental loveliness is stained by the smoke of the steamer, only to brighten into golden lustre under the sinking sun. There is a gala at the Austrian legation. Its *stationnaire* boat is decked and gay with flags. It is the emperor's birthday, and we are promised an illumination to-night. The little yacht, bearing its Austrian colors, plies about in eager activity. These evidences of modern interests and people do not detract from the dreamy memories of the elder world, which pursue our eye and entrance our fancy, as we glance between the mystic pillars of that gateway to the north.

In the midst of these reveries I am unromantically called to tea. But does one need the "cup that cheers" in such a scene? I am oblivious in the intoxicating draught of pure air which is ever laden with freshness, the more enjoyable because in such contrast with our ruder Scandinavian and Russian experiences.

Preferring a higher and sweeter taste of life than tea and its inspiring talk, I wander into the garden on the southern side of our home. The magnolias are yet in bloom, and the evening air is freighted with the fragrance of the flowers in parterres and along the uprising terraces. Winding up amidst their paths, with walls of ivy and plats of flowers, we reach the uppermost and outermost wall of this enchanting garden.

These grounds were laid out by a Frenchman. They are called after his name, with the affix of "Folly." If they be as foolish as they were expensive, it illustrates the biblical phrase as to those who plant vineyards while others eat the fruit thereof. Clambering to the topmost wall, above the vegetable garden, I look out to the bare hills behind the terraced beauties, and then far off to the Asiatic mountains and to the battlements we have closely surveyed in our boat. The ranges of yellow and white palaces under the European hills across the bay are beginning to make magical their marble magnificence in the mirroring water, which is calming with the mildness of evening. Fancy is assuming or usurping the throne of reality. The Bosphorus becomes a telescope. From the eminence its valley is an iridescent tube, ground out by fire and clarified by water. With the license of a little more phantasy and a large map, there is larger view. Looking through the haze of distance, as it were a magnifying-glass or channel of vision, to the north-west, there is seen on one line, 350 miles across the Black Sea, Sebastopol, with its hills of battle and vales of culture. Looking south, we should see at the same distance as the Crimea, the snow and cloud of the Asian Olympus; while at double the distance we might peep, pigmy-like, between the huge legs of the Colossus at Rhodes, if the earthquake and the usurer had only left its brassy proportions astride the harbor; and discern still further on, into the desert of Africa, on the borders of Egypt, the oasis of Ammon, gladdening the heart of the *chronological* Bedouin with *dates* and his camels with water.

The illumination begins at the embassies, and the stars glisten doubly in sky and river. The scent of the flowers below rises, while the acacia, orange, and lemon furnish their foliage, fruit, and fragrance for the delightful picture. Around our feet are rare plants, whose names are unfamiliar; but the laurel, althea, verbena, and lavender are old friends. Upon the hills about, as thick as soldiers, rise the Lombardy poplars and funereal cypress, making as lovely a scene as ever wave washed, leaf beautified, or sun glorified. It is a scene where

> "The winds with wonder whist,
> Smoothly the waters kist,
> Whispering new joys."

No wonder the current of one's thoughts flows with the ceaseless tide below, unrestrained by no power save that "arbitrary Queen of Sense," by which, as those tranced, we are held in thralldom.

And to think that, amidst all these lovely scenes and floral delights, this splendid seat of temporal and religious power should be the favorite haunt of luxury and putrescence. Brothers may not now kill brothers who are too near the Ottoman throne; the mysterious Bosphorus may not now drown the too-froward odalisque; its waters may not now bring to the haughty Moslem the treasures of the Orient and the beauties of Circassia, or bear navies equal to those of powers further west, by which he is "guaranteed"; or, as "Eothen" has it about this restless river of divers and sinister memories, "it may not watch the walls of the Sultan's serail, or quiet the scandals of his court, or stifle the intrigue of his ministers, or extinguish his rivals, or hush his naughty wives one by one," or do these and other vast wonders of the Deep, without the world knowing it somewhat. But still this River of Revenge and its depths of despair have, within the few years since I saw it last, had stormy seasons, guilty eddies, desperate currents, noisy and noisome scandals, many a wreck of minister and sultan, and many a crime most foul, to turn its green "one red." Yet, with all these changeful phases, its current is still as clear as ever.

and it still trends toward the Propontis and the world without and beyond.

On our way to our legation to-day, were we not shown the palace where the last Sultan, Abdul Assiz, was said to be strangled, and the hole in the wall through which his body was borne for the examination? If this sultanic power be on the wane and no longer "crescent"; if its splendors are fading like evening out of the European sky; if many of the thousand crimes which link the Bosphorus with the execrations of mankind are as hideous as ever, they are certainly not as common or as impunitive now as when the "Magnificent" Suleimans ruled by a rod or a scimitar, a sack or a bow-string, and gave "fiat" from the furthest India to the gates of Hercules.

Yet I am painfully reminded by excesses in our beloved land, where a President lies hovering betwixt two eternities, that it is not for us to reproach others of scandals and assassinations. As the curtain of night is drawn over these scenes of outward loveliness—if, indeed, that be a curtain which is only a folded wimple, like that over the features of the Nourmahal—the stars come forth, not singly, but in multitudes, appareled in celestial light. The Orient hath, indeed, its compensations for excesses. My mind darts back to the Arctic Circle and its nightlessness. The stellar glories of these skies, like pearls at random flung, come to me in meditations that trail in mysterious awe after the constellations through this deep oriental heaven. A sweeter sonnet was never sung than that of Blanco White, wherein he describes Hesperus leading the hosts of heaven in the rays of the great setting flame, whose glorious canopy of light and blue make us blind to such countless orbs. His questioning is the philosophy of mystery—as he inquires why we should shun Death with anxious strife; for if Light can thus deceive, wherefore not Life? Is it not true that the stellar boss of Night contributes best to spiritual insight and foresight? I picture the consternation of those bold Vikings, for whom the sea had no terrors, when first they saw this heaven of night enveloped with stars; for those bold Norsemen, from whose ancient homes we are newly come, did not omit far-off Stamboul in their adventures. Nor did I wonder that men even from the land of Boreas, with its setless sun, here worshiped the infinite and uncreate God, the author of this heaven and its myriad hosts, and with pious earnestness bore its knowledge to the rocks and snows of Northland; for out of the heart of this Orient, as out of the eastern sky, and before the dawn of our physical advancement and science, the star of Bethlehem flamed in these nocturnal heavens, lighting the seers of other lands, besides those of the North, to the spot where lay the Babe of Bethlehem.

Thus musing I recalled the " tale of the Christ," which our gifted and gallant host has told in his " Ben Hur." It is a story of divine love. As I recalled it, the weird scenes of the desert of Judea came upon me with an all hail! hereafter. We bid them, though at distance, hail, as Hope lightens our heart and waves her golden hair. Thither we as pilgrims are tending.

There, under the infinite stillness of the eastern sky, the wise men of the East met to compare their inward experiences and enjoy their mutual ecstasies. Through their inner light of faith, and by the lambent flame which became a stellar focus of celestial promise they followed, star-led, till they found " the Christ."

CHAPTER III.

THE TOWERS OF EUROPE AND THE AMERICAN COLLEGE.

Revolution may change the face of nature and sweep nations from the earth ; custom and habit and exterior circumstances may change and pass away, but the inner life of man, with all its joy and hope and love and sorrow and care, remains the same in every nation and in every age—intensively active and grand and interesting.—BULWER.

WE have been three weeks and more in Constantinople. The time goes by as in a dream. Although the weather is hot, we have found comfort, both at Therapia and at the hotel in the city, which overlooks and is cooled by the Bosphorus and Golden Horn. The city is also a summer resort, with all the attraction of water and mountain aspect. Besides, it has the movement of clouds, smoke, steamers, boats and sails, and the unresisting flow of the stream, which here begins to contemplate a rush toward the Dardanelles through Marmora. To these is added in plain view, under the moon, now full, or under the brightest of sunlight, the domes and minarets which give to Constantinople its individuality among cities. The sounds which rise about us are those of the bells, for an active Catholic church is near, and there is much devotion within its walls; then the cries of venders, which after daybreak are incessant, or the clamor of the dogs baying at the moon or at a strange dog, or a canine chorus in full agony; or the metallic ring by night of the watchman's staff upon the stone pavements, or his startling alarm of fire, as he wends his way amidst the narrow lanes down the declivity to the shopping centres. Nor ought it to be forgotten, as one of the sounds now familiar, that we have each hour a salvo of bugle-music or of artillery from the forts on both sides of the Bosphorus, which indicates more than anything else that these seven hills of Byzantium are an encampment, realizing the Byronic lines that

> "The city won for Allah from the Giaour,
> The Giaour from Othman's race again may wrest."

Indeed, it is asserted and known that the Turks have always kept their archives packed in knapsacks, ready for a movement into Asia, believing that what the Koran records will take place, and that the Moslem "must go" to Asia, whence he came.

The most attractive spot on the Bosphorus, as well as the narrowest, is the three-towered "fortress of Europe." It is called Romolo-Hissar. It eternizes the fate and fall of the city. It is a perpetual object of admiration to the stranger, as he goes up and down the river. It is situated midway between the city and the legation at Therapia. One of the attractions near the spot is the American College, founded by Mr. Robert, of New York. Around this fortress and college live the professors. Among them is Professor Grosvenor, who for thirteen years has been teaching Greek, and has a responsible position in the direction of the College. I will not say that we are friends, because he happened to be of "my party." He is a clergyman, of the Congregational Church; but, be he what he may, it was my good fortune to meet him here for the first time in this Eastern World, though he declares that he has represented me in the world of dreams. This is the story he tells: He was in Faneuil Hall, in 1872, when Horace Greeley was running for President, and on the stand and about to speak, when the presiding officer demanded his name. He utterly forgot his own and gave mine, and was introduced with thundering applause. He proceeded to make a speech on the line of amnesty and brotherhood; and, when through, was received with congratulations so pronounced that he awoke. This was a strange psychological fact, related far off here by a gentleman of probity, who became thoroughly identified with another person, losing his own identity. Inasmuch as he had personated me so much better than I could myself, and had come to have a sort of property in me, we yielded to his invitation, and resolved to visit his home at the towers near the College.

Our boat-ride was as lovely as usual, and in an hour we were at our haven. Professor G. and his little son were there to receive us. My wife was soon seated in a palanquin, which two *hamals* took in charge—one before and one behind.

"Thus mounted, escorted by the gentlemen," says her journal, "we climbed the hill and reached the house. The ropes over the shoulders of the porters held the two ends of the poles in loops to either hand, and made the chair quite an easy method of riding, besides reminding me of my ascent up Mount Vesuvius. Poor fellows! They patiently plodded upward, and when they deposited their burden (only 125 pounds) on the hospitable doorstep, the perspiration was pouring from them. I was not allowed to pay an extra *piastre*, as 'they might be spoiled for other occasions.' "

We find a pretty garden, a sweet hostess, and a cordial welcome. The new matting on the floors gives forth a fragrant odor, and we comfort ourselves with the hope that it harbors no fleas, to which the Turkish rugs give overmuch welcome. Thus speaks the observant housewife of domestic objects, to which I never had an eye, single or otherwise; but I did observe in the household an abundance of books. Here I found every book which one might need to understand the decline and fall, the increase and rise of the nations which have come and gone along these shores. What a field for luxurious study is right here. The illustration of each epoch and incident graved by the finger of the Almighty on the hills and mountains, rocks and waters, is within our vision. The two million of composite races who people the places on each side of this river of the centuries are mostly the remnant of races whose old roads and ruts show the movements of men, as the rocks show the movements of glaciers. The fallen or disfigured columns which stand about these hippodromes of the past, the broken arches, crumbling aqueducts, dirt-filled cisterns, dilapidated palaces, and the half-hid courts of mosaic—these, as the existing inscriptions show, were once erected and made by great emperors, adventurers, or conquerors. They represent a population once dense, who lived upon these now fruitless, though once fertile hills and plains, which they then made gardens, and whose coasts furnished marts of commerce, the most magnificent in the world.

This home of our American professor is a charming place to visit. The house is built on an American pattern, for convenience. The garden is large, where, literally under his own vine and fig-tree, the professor may rest after his labors in the College, across the valley.

Before we were fairly settled, or had our first meal, we were with him in the great tower of the fortress, overlooking this classic and historic ground. To reach it, we did not require a palanquin, for it was nearly all down-hill, through narrow paved streets, past old mosques, deserted minarets, and tumble-down houses, now habited by a kindly people. Mrs. G. called them "peaceful neighbors." They were all Turks, for within the fortress live only the descendants of those who held it when Mohammed II. took the city. They hold these old houses by some feudal tenure. They cannot be dispossessed. There is a law, however, that when once the houses are destroyed by fire or otherwise then the grounds are to be cleared. At one point about the Professor's grounds a conflagration would be a blessing, for it would open a new and beautiful view to the Upper Bosphorus.

There are three of these immense towers in this extensive fortress. The largest and highest is that in our frontispiece. It is in good preservation, and is in constant demand for the pencil of amateurs, especially from the Bosphorus point of view. The stairway, with its thick walls, remains intact. Many rooms, once used for storage of provisions, are yet preserved, though of wood. The floors of the tower are going to decay. The tower has a diameter of 50 feet. It has in its gloomy side vaults and rooms. It is the very genius of safety as a prison or a refuge. It would seem as if its walls were invincible, at least, against the olden modes of assault. We get glimpses from its port-holes of the scenery about, as we ascend to its battlemented top, which is 250 feet above the stream. The College stands about on a level with the tower; and to the south and west the hills and mountains of Europe appear veiled in lustrous beauty. Below us, within the walls which climb the acclivity, turreted and winding, is the old Turkish village, with thick clusters of wooden houses; while far off, above Therapia and along the river to the gate of the Euxine, the superb villas of ambassadors and pashas glisten in the evening light.

"Here is a vulture's nest!" exclaims the Professor. And, sure enough, this bird of prey has made this tower his eyrie, and, like the Turk of earlier years, from hence has pounced upon weaklings below. We descend, after our exalted view, and have a pleasant dinner, which reminds our "housewife" of "the welcome by a minister-missionary at his home in the Piræus, some thirty years ago." "At eleven," says the journal, "we have family prayers, in which our host made kindly and touching mention of the guests under his roof-tree." We must confess, albeit in a public way, that the calamity which impends over the White House at home has made us Americans abroad more tenderly regardful of and toward each other in all the relations of life.

After descending from the tower, we ramble about the fortress and its paths. We are pointed out the home of a most learned pasha. He sometimes lives within this latticed and humble house. His *odalisques* are the old Sanscrit and other records of the past, to which he gives a devotion quite like that of his relatives in the days when Cordova had its Moorish university, and Spain was ennobled by Saracenic learning.

On leaving the fortress, my wife, with the habits of her sex, turned to look over her shoulder, and descried a mystic letter over its gateway. It was hidden beneath the dust of two centuries. The observant Professor had never seen it till now. He deciphers it as a Turkish monogram of the Sultan Mohammed II., who built the fortress. This discovery was received with satisfaction, and the lady was at once established as an applicant for a medal of the archæological associations. She had already discovered a thousand-year old pattern key in the old Greek church (now a mosque) at Eyoob. It was a labyrinth used in modern embroidery. If all other signs failed, it would fix the origin and quality of the building. Hence, we felt a double pride in our archæological angel.

This is an archæological age. Only the other day there were thirty-nine mummified Pharaohs found in nice linen and in lacquered coffins—kings, queens, and their children, including the veritable scriptural hard-hearted Pharaoh. Cases within cases, with papyri, preserved the body and fame of these dynasties of Egypt. One of the cases was broken into three parts; but the Egyptologists were enabled to make out that it was no less than Thothmes III., the great king of the eighteenth dynasty. Granite sarcophagi held these dead royalties, all sceptred. Sometimes sheets of gold were found enveloping the dead, very dead remains. Facial portraits and serpents, blue cobalt head-gear, and inscriptions in very fast colors were discovered, to illuminate the Egyptian darkness. The Boulak Museum contains these relics of remote antiquity. We hope to see them; and we have a right to see them, for has not one of our family found fame as an archæologist on the Bosphorus, which Pickwick, in his crude endeavor to decipher "Bill Sykes x his mark," could not attain? Coming out of the Flag-tower of the Great Fortress of Europe,—a tower upon which hung the destiny of two great races and religions,—the tower by which Constantinople was besieged—had she not discovered the magic letter over that gateway, and in Turkish script? Our learned friend, the Professor, at once said: "It is an M. You, Madam, are made immortal with an M. Your immortality shall go down with one 'M.'"

Mohammed II.! He that rode into the grandest church on horseback! Let Schliemann turn up all Troy for the decoration of his wife with the parure of Helen's head-dress; let him dig around to find the bones of the suitors for Penelope's hand, while Ulysses was a-wandering, and find, if he please, the very distaff with which she used to kill time; let Cesnola emulate Layard, and Newton and Wood emulate the archæologists of all ages; let Nineveh and Babylon, Baalbec and Troy, Thebes and Cyprus, Kertch and Jerusalem give to the living their dead secrets to bridge over the epochs of history—it remained for one of us, without delving or digging, with the inspiration of only a woman's curiosity, to discover the hidden magical M which makes complete the confirmation that Mohammed made this monumental magnificence to memorize his majesty. Besides, are we not from Ohio, within whose borders are now being found terra-cotta tablets, an alphabet, and zodiacal symbols, which bind the prehistoric period with our own, and the extreme East with the West?

What next may not a watching and wondering world expect from us? We visit Ephesus next week, Baalbec the week after, and Damascus and Jerusalem, and the sphinxes and pyramids before we leave the portals which lead to the earlier and eastern civilizations. No need for us to obtain firman or employ natives. We can sing to other genii of these old haunts of history:

> "Dig, dig, dig amid earth and mortar and stone,
> And dig, dig, dig among ruins overthrown;
> Spade and basket and pick and toiling Arabs ply,
> From breath of early dawn till evening shades draw nigh."

For without this labor the spirits of the vasty deep of the past answer our summons.

Seriously, what an exultant enthusiasm is there in discovering by patient research, reasoning, and digging, the characters of ruined races; and in their monuments their relict religions, dead constitutions, obsolete systems of order, and mysterious mazes of language. Minds like Gladstone perceive in such ruins the life of the *Juventus Mundi*. A good traveler, like Lord Dufferin, finds, as he related to me, in an old path of empire, on the shores of the eastern Mediterranean, the records of seven expeditions engraved upon the rocks, from Sennacherib to Louis Napoleon. Men test the soil for fruit, grain, gold, and iron, and by eye and chemistry find pleasure in these discoveries. Dust-delvers were never so busy as now. Soil cultivators of another kind seek for links in the chain of history. They find "pictured rocks," left by men, and chronic moral strata, before Carthage was, or Rome existed, or the revelations of Deity were vouchsafed to man.

We are up betimes, and I devour the books

which are the key to these positions in history. My first inquiry is as to this fortress. Its history is briefly this: In 1451, two years before Constantinople fell, when the Greek empire was honeycombed with corruption, Mohammed II., who was drawing his lines about its capital, and with much guile and cunning hiding his object, had constructed in forty days this triangular fortress, with its three towers. One of them is on the shore below, and the two others upon the hills. Khalil Pasha, a friend of the Greeks, known as the "associate of infidels," built the lower tower. The first Mohammed had already built the Castle of Anadolou, on the opposite side of the Bosphorus, and this Castle of Europe was to be its coadjutor in taking the city below.

The Greek emperor, whose family had held this point of greatness, commerce, and empire so long, could hardly believe that he would be so seriously menaced. He sent envoys to the Sultan, who sent them back with arrogant denunciations. Meanwhile the Sultan had collected his masons. He brought his wood from Nicomedia, now Ismed (to which there is now a railroad seven hours off), at the eastern end of the Sea of Marmora. He planned the fortress at the place where the waves are loudest, called Phonea, or the Echo, and endeavored to imitate by its shape the Arabic letters of the word Mohammed. In fact, the four towers together form the four letters in the name—M, H, M, D. The fortress being up and down, and scraggy generally, a good archæologist, like one of my family, could easily discover these Arabic characters in this higgledy-piggledy arrangement of walls and towers. This intelligent plan being settled upon, three generals (Khalil, Chakan, and Saricha) were assigned the duty of making the three great towers. Each of the 1,000 masons had to build two yards, while the workmen who answered to the call of "Mort!" were to hurry and cement the work. Greek churches were torn to pieces to furnish the material. The name of the lower castle was "Strait Cutter." It was built in three months, and was thirty feet thick. It commanded the river and levied tribute on all ships. Upon the big tower, which we ascended, guns were lifted, and stone balls of enormous size were thrown from them. All these monuments remain in such perfectness as to astonish the beholder.

Other memories are associated with the spot, "Here," said the Professor—"here is the most notable place in ancient or modern history. When Darius arrived upon the Bosphorus, the bridge was joined by which his army passed into Europe, or into Scythia, about 500 years before Christ. It is yonder, a little higher up, where the current is not so strong. The bridge of boats swung around from the Asiatic shore, under the eye of the Persian monarch. This spot here is yet called the 'Throne of Darius.' The rock, in the form of a throne, remained. It is now covered by the fortress. If the fort is ever torn down, the two columns of white stone will, doubtless, appear. The inscriptions upon them are in Assyrian and Greek, and contain the names of the nations over which Darius ruled."

"See here!" said I to the Professor, "is it not a heavy load of credulity for me to carry home—this army of 700,000 coming over here on a bridge?"

"The proof is in the history," he replied. "It says 70 myriads, and 10,000 to a myriad. Also 600 ships."

"How do you know the bridge was built?"

"Here it is," taking down his Herodotus. "We know that Mandrokles, of the Isle of Samos, was the bridge contractor. We have that in writing. See here! Book IV., 88th paragraph, original Greek. I will translate and write it down.

"'Mandrokles having built a bridge across the Fishy Bosphorus, dedicated a picture of it to Juno. By the execution of this design of Darius, Mandrokles gained glory for the Samoans and obtained a crown or reward.'"

"What did he send a picture of it to Juno for? Why not to Mars, or Minerva, or some other divinity?" I ask.

The Professor looked puzzled. At length he said:

"I have it! Mandrokles lived on Samos. You may know that Virgil says that Samos held Juno in especial regard, and this was a neat way of pleasing his fellow-citizens."

"Why," I ask, "does the inscription call this the Fishy Bosphorus? Is it because there are so many fishy stories?"

"See here! Don't try any of Mark Twain's snapperadoes on a young man like me, away from home. There is another Bosphorus, on the coast of Azof, and this is the fishy one. Why, I saw your wife fishing on it yesterday at Therapia, and you may see porpoises at play every day."

"Yes, and she caught four fish, two inches each in length. If Darius resorted to a miracle to feed his army on these fish, I can comprehend it. But a truce to scepticism. I swallow it, fish and all; for nothing is more marvelous than yonder American College on this historic hill. Let us make our visit to it."

The College is five stories, and substantial. It has an inner, well-lighted court and a mansard roof, giving air, as well as light, to each room. The students number about 200, and room in the building. One-third of them are Armenians, one-third Bulgarians, and the rest Franks, Poles, English, etc. We wandered into the laboratory and then into the library. The first book I opened was entitled "Religion of the East," with impressions of foreign travel, by Dr. J. Hawes, D.D., pastor of the First Church in Hartford, Conn. It was printed in 1845. It was rich in independent thought about this land of religions, and in devoted love to our own land. The first sermon has as its text: "The lines have fallen unto me in pleasant places." In it he repeats what has been upon our tongue ever since we began our journey, "Souls are ripened in our northern skies," exclaims this divine. After making his pictures of the meretricious splendors of the East, he breaks forth with rapture over "our own goodly land, with its mighty resources, its free institutions, its countless blessings—social, civil, literary, and religious—which pour around us the light of Heaven, to warm every grateful heart. America! God's last dispensation towards our world! This act passed, the scene closes, the curtain of time drops, and the glories of eternity are revealed.

The College has a museum in embryo, to which we were escorted by a daughter of Dr. Long, in the absence of her father, who presides over physical science; then into Dr. Washburn's rooms, who is the head of the College, and where the ladies dipped into the mysteries of Turkish embroideries, flowers, plants, and portières; and, after a beautiful view over the scenes below and the College grounds, which are assuming a park-like appearance, we return to our host's house and prepare for the descent to the landing.

While waiting for the steamer, the Professor smokes his *narghile*, while I watch the groups of Armenians, Greeks, and Turks, priests and laymen, fruit-sellers, boys and men, in every variety of costume and detail of raggedness.

Looking around at this rout of ragged rascals, gathered on the dock, we inquire if it be safe for Madam and the American women hereabouts.

"We never come down," she says, "except through the village. The cemetery yonder is a nest of danger."

"Did you ever think of putting these towers to any use—I mean strategetically?"

"Oh! yes," said Madam, the hostess having in view the protection of her boys, to say nothing of the husband, "we thought of making this tower a refuge in the time of the Russian War, in case of disaster or rapine. The College could have manned it."

Would it not have been a climax, to have had an American college holding the "Fortress of Europe" and the throne of Darius against the Russian Czar and his hosts?

Apropos of this was the conversation which the Professor held with a Persian ambassador. He was the kindest of men, and took care to make the cordialities between his once grand kingdom and the rest of the world. When he made a visit to the College, not long since, the Professor said to him:

"This spot must be most interesting to you, as

a Persian. Here was the marble throne from which Darius saw his army cross the Bosphorus."

"When was it?" he asked.

"Oh! some five hundred years before Christ."

"Ah! What did he come here for?" the minister asked.

"To make war on the Scythians."

"Just so," said the Persian. "It was well done. The Scythians had displeased us, hey?"

"Oh! greatly," said the Professor. "They presumed to exist, and were not tributary to Darius, king of kings!"

We leave these scenes of historic splendor and present squalor, pondering upon the great eventualities here once determined and to be determined. Is it not one of the most interesting spots of Europe? Not alone because here Europe almost touches Asia physically; not because the swarms of invaders and crusaders, Goths and Turks, have here crossed and recrossed; but because the spot is doubly distinguished by momentous events. Turn in your mind the strangest pivots of history—the destruction of Rome by the Gauls, the siege of Leyden, the discovery of America, the beheading of Charles I., the landing of the Pilgrims, the burning of Moscow, the battles of Cressy, Pultowa, Marston Moor, and Waterloo, Trafalgar, the Declaration of American Independence, the taking of the Bastile, and other signal events upon which world-wide policies have turned —yet you will not discover in them, each and all, such universality of significance as is here found to bridge over the ancient and modern worlds and the oriental and occidental civilizations.

CHAPTER IV.

THE UPPER BOSPHORUS—PROPHECIES OF TURKISH DECAY—GIANT'S MOUNTAIN—JASON—CLASSIC SCENES.

> *If one seeks*
> *More comprehensive scale, th' arithmic mounts*
> *By the Asankya, which is the tale*
> *Of all the drops that in ten thousand years*
> *Would fall on all the worlds by daily rain;*
> *Thence unto Maha Kalpas, by the which*
> *The Gods compute their future and their past.*
> —ARNOLD'S " LIGHT OF ASIA."

ONE of the pleasant excursions planned by our friends at Therapia was to the Giant's Mountain, opposite our home, with the Consul. The mountain is higher than it seems, and also steeper, so that much preparation is made for the ascent. Besides, as we go through an encampment of Turks on the Asiatic side, we propose, for safety, a large party. Major-Gen. Wallace, our Minister, with his revolver, was commander enough, and the wife of our Consul acted as commissary. Clever English naval officers brought in a little steam launch, and with the wives and others—young men and maidens—of the vicinage, we start across the Bosphorus, a gleeful party. Prof. Grosvenor is along to give us the classic associations.

On arriving upon the other side we perceive our conveyance. It is drawn by white oxen. It is called an araby. It is a springless, heavy, lazy concern, whose wheels are at every angle to the axle, and whose parts are tied together by ropes and wires. It will hold ten, but has no seats. We improvise cushions for the ladies out of shawls and coats, and the Turkish driver starts the team with his goad. It is an antique, and fills us full of effusive fun. The araby has once been gilded and carved. I apostrophize it:

> "I know not, I care not, if gilt's on that wagon,
> I'll follow its fortunes if it leads to the—Dragon.

It was a hot afternoon; and with only one equipage it looked as if many of us would have to walk the four miles to the summit. However, we found another rickety conveyance, and a horse with a yoke, with some red cushions inhabited by fleas. These insects kept us lively, and enabled us to enjoy the ruts of the mountain road. The road was over a plain—where old plane-trees, some of them thirty feet round, and hollow, kept guard, with soldiers and junketers around them. This plain is a favorite resort for Turkish families. Here, near one of the palaces, is the spot where the Sultan received the Empress Eugénie, and had the grand review of soldiers in her honor. Through an avenue of trees we slowly wended our way, following the brisk walk of the oxen. We met another araby of very regal style. It was "Araby the blest," compared with ours. It had an Effendi, with three Turkish beauties done up in white muslin. It was a bridal party on a wedding tour for the third wife. One woman looked like a mother-in-law, so cross she seemed when we gazed at her behind her fleecy yashmak. There were three wives, so the question of mother-in-law became complicated. However, it was a pretty sight, and one peculiarly Asiatic.

At length we are at the top of the Giant's Mountain. We find his grave and a cemetery under the shadow of trees, and a mosque and minaret. Some dervishes are there. They permit us entrance within the holy places in our stocking feet, and for a consideration. It seems that this is the burial-place of many soldiers who fell here in defense of Islam. It is also the spot where a holy pilgrim or priest is buried. His tomb is covered with small pieces of rags, signs of a good future and good health to those who leave them. We ascend the narrow, dark stairway, up the stony steps of the minaret. Every object in view from this point is of interest. Under our eye, to the west and across the blue water, the Latin crusaders under Count Raoul encamped, until they crossed into Asia. There, too, Godfrey de Bouillon had his ten thousand cavalry and sixty thousand infantry, ranging along the environs of the Propontis, from the bridge of Cosmedion, the point of the triangle of Constantinople which meets the Golden Horn, to this upper point of the Bosphorus. Here are old earthworks, made by the French engineers for the Turks against the Russians in the last century; and there are the pharos (lighthouse) and the promontories on the sea. Turning our back on the Bosphorus and looking to the east, or south of east, far off over the Sea of Marmora, to the cerulean mountain curves, we may see, without fancy or glass, the veiled beauty of the ragged defiles which streams and torrents have made. Through these passed Xerxes and his host. Through them also came Alexander. Out of them came

Orchan, the son of that Othman who founded the dynasty of the Turk, laying siege to Nicomedia, now Ismid, to which English enterprise and capital have made a railroad. Here began the march of that army whose janizaries were invincible. They rested not, until the beginning of the fourteenth century found them crossing into Europe, under the Thunderbolt Bajazit, scattering the combined armies of Hun, Goth, and Frank. Here was nursed that prowess in arms which cemented the foundation of those civil and bloody codes of the Moslem empire, whose crescent flag was seen by trembling Austria, not two centuries ago, at the gates of its capital, and to celebrate whose repulse in 1863 Austria is now raising monuments. Hence came the Othmans, Amuraths, Mohammeds, Suleimans, and Selims, who startled nations and made history from Venice to Vienna, and from Bagdad to Granada.

There is no standpoint more interesting than this for a review of the great struggles between the eastern and western civilizations. Yet now, as we gaze, how peacefully reposes the scene, where so many embattled millions marched. One can imagine the struggle of standards, the rush of javelins, the crash of charges, the iron tread of the mailed horse and rider, the dash of chariots and the neighing of steeds, the notes of bugle, the shouts of the knights leading their squadrons, the flash of lances, the waving of pennants, the *élan* of victory and the devastation of defeat!

But there are classic scenes beneath our eye from this minaret, as well as verities of history. Do you see those white, low houses beyond that village? There is the authentic spot where the harpies tortured Phineus. But above all in elevation and interest is the hill on which we stand, where the Argonautic heroes brought each their handful of soil, until the heap arose as a monument in honor of the expedition which makes the name of Jason immortal. The authenticity of these places, made familiar in the muse and tradition of Hellas, is vouched for by no less a scholar than our Prof. Grosvenor, who has made them seem at least absolute verities by confirmations.

"Do you not know," said Gen. Wallace, warming with these associations, "that there is a sensible view of Jason and his search after the golden fleece? There were golden sands in the mountain streams of that El Dorado. Not being adept in gathering the golden dust, like our New Mexican miners, these Argonauts soaked their fleeces in the water, which was stirred into auriferousness, and when the fleeces dried they flailed out the precious particles."

From this minaret can be seen the point of Heraclea, which was sighted by Peter the Great 182 years ago, day before yesterday, as he sailed down the Black Sea, under much Turkish distrust and against much opposition, to visit the city of Constantinople, which his descendants have not failed to covet ever since.

Upon this visit, and the longing of Russian ambition, have hung many great wars, only exceeded by those symbolized in the Turkish or Christian legend whose "four angels were loosed from the great river Euphrates." This has been interpreted to mean the rush of the Turkish hordes upon Europe. It was made out in some of the wise solutions of the "Revelation" of John the Divine, that the description of the cavalry, colors, and the "power of their tails," applied to the Mohammedan army; and that the text in Revelation ix. 15, they "were prepared for an hour, and a day, and a month, and a year," was assumed, in some cabalistic way to mean a period of 391 years and two weeks. This was supposed to concur with the prediction of Constantine. As the Turks took Constantinople on the 29th of May, 1453, you must add to this the 391 years and two weeks, and you will have 1844 of our era, which is the year 1260 of the Turks, and 1260 is the number of years fixed for the duration of the Turkish rule in Europe. So that in 1844 the power of the Sultans should have ceased, but it did not. It will be many years yet before these splendid views, now made interesting by mosque and minaret, shall glow with the gilded cathedrals of the Græco-Russian Church, as Peter the Great fondly wished and untruly foretold. When the colossus of the north becomes a little more assured of his personal health and life at St. Petersburg and Moscow, he may possibly help to cipher out the "revelations" which his ministers thus far have failed to make prophetic.

We take care before descending to note the haven which has been one of safety to navigators from the wintry and tempestuous Euxine. There, across the way, are the Cyanian isles, about which Greek narratives are horrific and garrulous. Upon one of them, which you may reach in calm weather on foot, is a white marble column. Its carving is not a little marred by time and flood. It was once an altar. What it may mean, the poets have sung who have located Jason, his myths, and company of fifty Argonauts along these points. Here, too, geology once agreed with tradition that the pressure of the waters of the Euxine broke a passage through to the Dardanelles; but science has proved that the fissure was made by fire, which created a passage that the waters followed. This passage has changed the political and social destinies of mankind. Upon one of these isles are still seen emblematic altars to agriculture and fertility. These are doubtless Roman, for they are dedicated to Cæsar Augustus.

Look down upon the promontory at the mouth of the sea on the Asiatic side! The tower of Medea shines in white, as a lighthouse, while the ruins of the temples to the gods and goddesses, protectors of the sailors, are everywhere to be seen. Our double summit of a mountain—sometimes called Mount Joshua, and sometimes the Back of Hercules—has its present name from a giant's tomb, which we visit. The tomb is forty feet in length. It is said to contain only the foot (*ex pede Herculem*) or toe of the giant, who was accustomed to sit on the top of this mountain while he bathed his feet in the Bosphorus. The tomb is covered with square blocks of stone, and is much reverenced. It has various legendary histories. From the minaret our military Minister discovers a neat fort and battery at our feet, near the shore. Its guns are covered with white canvas, and all its appointments are in nice order. At every angle of the horizon, far and near, historic, classic, and mythic memories start into view, and make our afternoon quite a religio-classico-Anglo-American festivity.

We are called to the lunch. It is nicely spread on the grass, near an old well some three hundred feet deep, which has a marvelous echo. The lunch is prepared by our hostess and her graceful daughter. Twenty of us quaff the wine of Ismid, and drink to the health of our departed friends, Jason, Hercules, and the rest, not forgetting the sovereigns of our respective countries. Tearing off some fragments from our handkerchiefs, we place them, as the customary votive offerings, upon the tombs of the saints. Then mounting our araby and moving at dusk down the mountain, through the shadows of the trees of the Turkish camp, where many dusky figures are seen praying toward Mecca, and after some gentle and profane dalliance as to backsheesh with the natives who surround our boat, we rejoin the launch, and end our pleasure at the wharf, where our flag is supposed to fly for our protection.

Yesterday we were summoned by our friends for a last enjoyment of the hospitalities of the Legation. To these were added something unusual in this locality. It was a serenade by moonlight on the waters. It was a success as a scene, for there were no harsh Greek or Turkish voices in the serenade. The Austrian Minister, Baron Hirschfeld, was the projector of this Venetian entertainment, this carnival of the Bosphorus. The quay was lined with spectators by nine o'clock, and the stream and bay with caïques and illuminated barges. The names of the musicians sound so that one cannot mistake them for other than Italian, German, and Polish. The rockets and colored lights, and the thousand boats full of the beauty and chivalry of the upper Bosphorus, followed the steam tugs and larger caïques as they moved about from Buyukdereh to Therapia, giving to the waves the melodies the waves returned. Instrumental music thrilled on the clear air and moonlit stream, and aided the effect. Altogether it was unique. Was not this indulgence of occidental and Orphic luxury under oriental skies a fit ending of our rugged journey from the boreal North? These gay songs of the elegant embassies and their retainers—how much they contrast with the rough days of crusader and paynim, of sword and scimitar, of cross and crescent. How they contrast with the elder days of sea-fights of Genoese, Venetian, and Turk in these bays, now illuminated by American petroleum, and choral with soft voices on the stilly air.

CHAPTER V.

EXCURSION TO THE ANCIENT OTTOMAN CAPITAL—BROUSSA AND ITS ATTRACTIONS.

*As the thought of man
Flies rapidly, when, having traveled far,
He thinks, "Here would I be, I would be there,"
And flits from place to place, so swiftly flew
Imperial Juno to the Olympian mount,
And there she found the ever-living gods
Assembled in the halls of Jupiter.*
—Bryant's Iliad, *Book XV.*

OUR excursion to the Giant's Mountain stimulated to another. We resolved upon a visit to the ancient Ottoman capital—Broussa. It is south of Constantinople, and across the Sea of Marmora. Our experience there, with its silks and caravans, its fruits and fountains, its baths for health, and its sepulchres of the founders of the Ottoman empire, form a chapter of romance. This trip inducted us into the mysteries of Asian land-travel. In Constantinople we had met many peculiar types of men and many muffled forms of women. They are hard to understand. In vexation we exclaim:

"These are spirits, clad in veils,
Woman by man is never seen!
All our deep conniving fails
To remove this shadowy screen."

But when we conquered the reserve of the interior, and its mixed travel, by steamer on the way, the *yashmak* fell and the muffler dropped. In this trip we were associated with an Irish solicitor and his amiable daughter. You may well believe that in such society there was a richer indigo to the azure of the sea, a new sparkle to the lively waters of Broussa, and fresh glories to Mount Olympus, at morning and evening, as we talked and smoked beneath its roseate hues and cool shadows; rare fun when we stopped in our druidical groves of oak, half way, amidst camels and donkeys, turkeys and chickens; other wonders in the capacities and oddity of the animals which carried the cocoons and other burdens to the city from the sea; more attraction in the strange brown faces of the turbaned beggars, and more alluring beauties in the broad vales made fruitful by streams from Olympus which spread beneath us—from our hotel balcony—like the vega of Granada, as seen from the walls of the Alhambra.

This is our first really hot day. Its discomforts need the mitigation of society. Another addition to our hotel group were some Germans and French, including two young Austrian princes, "just as nice as two young girls," as the Celtic daughter remarked. Loving brothers indeed they were. We met them at every place of interest in our excursion. They left us at Broussa, having concluded to ride over Olympus and its lonely range to Ismid on the sea, where they take the boat. As it is a risk, I remonstrate. The brigand would like such a prize, for the elder of the young men is very rich, and there are always in these hostelries some confederate rogues to give notice. However, they send for their Austrian consul, and engage the police—two stalwarts with rifles ; and after examining their revolvers, set off.

"Brave boys ! and polite as brave ; good luck to ye !" the Irish solicitor exclaims, as they bid us adieu. They were the Prince and Count Deidrichstein.

There was along our Greek guide, Dionysius. He was our companion to the rocky castle on the mountain, and to the tombs of Othman and his conquering son, Orchan—the earliest heroes of the race. From the 14th century these Mussulmans—Sultans and soldiers—have lain, in honored retiracy, under their cashmere shawls which cover the mother-of-pearl tombs of the oriental marabouts here, undisturbed even by the earthquakes which have waked up many dead cities, and which stirred Broussa in a lively way in 1801–2. The jewels, stars, and crescents remain guarded by careful keepers, and in honor of the precious bones of the leaders of a race not yet extinct in European diplomacy and fighting.

Minarets and mosques, neat buildings and active industries, give to this old capital a fresh, cheerful look. It is no idle or dirty city. Its streets are clean, and in this it is unlike other Turkish cities. From early morning till late at night the men are moving on their beasts of burden or working in their factories. The women seem to be the only folks of leisure. Morning and evening we see them pass our hotel, along the mountain side. Most of them ride astride on donkeys. Their children are in the creels, and peep out funnily. It takes two to balance the pannier. You want twins or quartettes, triplets are unhandy. Whether these women are happy or not, we could not always see, as their veils were down; but they had the right of locomotion, and used it. They go a mile or more to the hot baths. These are ancient and celebrated. They gush from the mountain side in the south of the city. There is no newspaper in Broussa, though it has 80,000 population. Are they happy? There is no sewing society—though much embroidery; so that if there be any news stirring, it is to be got as of old in Rome when the gossips met at the baths of Caracalla and "swapped" their information.

Dionysius jokes the dragomans of the prices. Dionysius is a tender-hearted Greek, and amenable to fun. When the other dragoman was looking at a fountain in the great mosque he espied a cup, and tried in vain to reach the fountain for a drink.

"Aha!" says Dionysius, "your heart is tainted! Only those who are pure, according to the old custom, can drink of these waters," and he makes a successful leap for it himself, quite perilous to his person. His *amour propre* is satisfied.

"The donkeys of Broussa," says our Sancho Panza, "are its clocks. They tell the hours. One of them got wrong and brayed out twelve yesterday when it was only one. He needs correction!"

We visit the most sacred mosques and kiosks, where the bones of the many-wived Sultans repose. We found ourselves surrounded by little Abdallahs and Mohammeds. They ask for alms. These mosques have outbuildings and grounds. The trees and their shades attract many women and children, as if it were a health resort. About are old tombs. Fig-trees and fountains abound, and red pomegranates peep over the walls. There are no Roman ruins in Broussa. It is more French than Arab. It is also Turkish and Greek. Old Greek churches are here, as usual, turned into elegant mosques. In the best mosque, Donad Monaster, on the west side of the town, lies the tomb of the Sultan Orchan. It had once a dome of silver. An earthquake or something changed the silver into marble. There is a green mosque here. It is the sacred color of Mohammed. Enamels and carvings of most delicate beauty by native art, vie with the many-colored marbles, to make this a peculiar temple of this religion. In some of the mosques are stained glass. Diamonds and other precious stones decorate the tombs.

However dirty and dusty the Moslem appears upon his travels or in his home, he has the virtue of cleanliness in his worship. This city of mosques and fountains is adapted to this devotion. The Moslems about us are indulging in ablutions and prayers. They wash the arms to the elbows, and feet to the knees before they pray. Their prayers are chiefly recitations of the attributes of God; when they speak of his power they kneel and touch the forehead twice to the ground. They seem— they are devout. Better have this faith than none. When they can repeat the Koran by heart, they are considered perfect.

After my wife had made her promenade of the silk bazaars, with much cost and instruction, we called on a merchant, at his house, to see some "portieres." He, with his wife and mother, received us. The latter sat at her embroidery frame; and when my wife expressed a desire to see how the work was accomplished, she smilingly resumed her labor. A fine steel crochet needle is held in the right hand, close to the face of the velvet, while the bobbin of silk or gold thread is held in the left hand under the frame on which the velvet is stretched. The needle is pushed through the material and catches up the thread underneath with great regularity and rapidity. This is the way the rare Damascus fabrics are adorned. She laughed heartily to see our look of pleasure and wonder; and tapping madam heartily on the shoulder, said, "You see it is easy." Before we left, refreshing syrups were served us.

Half the population are engaged either in raising mulberries or weaving silk. The *flora* of the Olympian slope are exceedingly abundant, especially as compared with the denuded and parched isles of Greece. Geraniums, primroses, anemones, crocuses, laurel and juniper, evergreens, oaks, and ferns, not to repeat a long Latin nomenclature, are as abundant as the botanist or the lover could wish. Woodcock and partridge, with now and then a vulture and an eagle, fly around over the haunts of the wild boar and wolf, deer and jackal, in the mountains. I saw one noble bird of freedom swoop around Olympus—the bird of Jove. This happened, by the clock three P. M., just at the time a jackass gave three dissonant melodies. I hoped that the bird would do a little carnivorous business.

We visited a silk factory, where some eighty pretty girls, both Moslem and Christian, work the silken fibre off the cocoon in the heated water, and reel it into convenient compass and shape for weaving. The proprietor kindly shows us his establishment, and out of our visit grows much economic comment on tariff. The cheap labor is a franc a day for the girls. Let the protectionists put that down! The proprietor is a Frenchman, and has been here for twenty odd years. There are forty silk factories in Broussa, and their product is cheap. So is their labor. We are not to buy it, however. It is too cheap; our women must go to New Jersey and pay two prices, to enhance private wealth.

On the Olympian slopes are the finest mulberries for the silkworm to be found anywhere this side of China and Japan. Most of the silk here is peculiarly striped with red, and brings to mind our ensign of beauty.

It is quite a delight to sit beneath Mount Olympus knowing that from its eminence there is a sight of old Troy. Looking off from the highest of its heights, 5,500 feet, with its snowy crest, how small the donkeys appear on the plains, even when loaded! The Lombardy poplars and cypresses are not as big as thistle needles. The flat dark roofs of the city are leveled with the green in which they are embowered; and the domes of the mosques—and they count here by hundreds—look like little bulbous toys. The old palm-trees, some of which measure twenty-four feet round—ever honored in the East, as well for their shade as for some genius of the past—look like little shrubs even under a magnifying glass. From the height of the classic mount, the Sea of Marmora, and the Euxine, the minarets of Constantinople, the Bosphorus and the Dardanelles, and the tall grandeur of Mount Ida and its range, and the rivers, lakes, green belts, and broad savannahs of the valleys, appear in splendid array. It is a grand observatory for a superb panorama! Whether Dr. Schliemann has or has not excavated the real old Troy and fixed aright its situation upon the fortress hill of Hissarlik; whether or not the Scamander and Mount Ida have found their proper locality—are we not under the shadow of that mount which made Ilios sacred? No archæological debate disturbs our serenity about Olympus. Above us Jove held council upon the golden pavement. The range of the great poem was commensurate with the action of the deities. The clouds and storms from Tenedos to the peak of Samothrace, furnished the dread scenery at the fall of the "burnt city of gold." It is not difficult to realize that from these sublime heights the messengers of the gods came and went in such beauteous forms as that of Iris, and that even goddesses armed in the cloud-compeller's panoply went forth in chariots drawn by golden-bitted steeds, to fight in human affairs, under the ægis of—Destiny. After the every-day sights and sounds of the great city, it is an exaltation to be surrounded by such epic associations.

Our trip to Broussa is a relief after our long stay on the Bosphorus. One drawback to our return is early rising. At three A. M. we are in our carriage. We pass market people coming to the city, with their beasts laden with melons and grapes and other products of this happy valley. Long lines of camels, dressed in red ornaments, pass us in the gloaming. They seem like monsters of the prehistoric epoch. We find them at daylight, under the oak trees of the half-way grove, resting after their nightly journey from the sea-side. Did you ever notice how strangely the camel is built, and how oddly he moves? Like a pompous antediluvian, he treads over the roughest stones and in the softest sands. The legs on one side move at and with the same Time, and then with a gawky swing of the shoulder and haunch of the other side, so as to keep up the odd locomotion. The beast seems to be put together on loose hinges; but, as with the elephant, you may get accustomed to its ungainly gait. We find resting with us at the oak grove many buffalo, which are also used for draught. Police, too, mounted and armed with rifles, come and go as if the brigands were not all gone out of this valley. Our driver finding one of our own horses blowing, gathers handfuls of dust, and throws them up the nostrils of the animal. I asked, "Why?" Would you believe it? He responds: "To stop its trouble, and refresh its lungs." We have some merriment with our small carriage boy, who has a fight with an old and big gobbler. It is young Turkey *versus* old Turkey; and old Turkey succumbs, and turns tail with a protest.

As we start afresh, the clouds which hung half way over Olympus and its range float down into the valley, but no goddesses came down to our aid, as in Trojan times. From the coast hills we look back upon a roseate lake. It is no mirage, but an illumination of the clouds below, out of which the brown mountain tops rise like enchanted isles. It was upon such a morn, "dressed in saffron robes, that Jupiter would have summoned the Gods in Council, on many-peaked Olympus." We are aroused from reveries of blue-eyed Pallas and white-armed Juno, by the supernal physical beauty of the scene.

Our driver and his aid talk no French and English; and we have good practice in making sense out of the unintelligible.

At noon we reach our seaport, Mondania; whence we sail five hours over the blue Marmora; and have a richly colored picture, never to be seen too frequently, of the beauteous mosques and minarets, the walls and towers of Stamboul.

CHAPTER VI.

CONSTANTINOPLE AND ITS PEOPLE—WALLS, GATES, AND TOWERS.

> *The European with the Asian shore—*
> *Sophia's cupola with golden gleam—*
> *The cypress groves—Olympus high and hoar—*
> *The twelve isles, and the more than I could dream.*
> —DON JUAN.

THE unaccustomed is always attractive. In Constantinople even familiar objects do not cease to attract. In our visit to our friends at Therapia, at the head of the Bosphorus, the iteration of the scene, like the refrain of sweet melody, ever pleases. So, too, in gazing out of our window of the hotel, the prospect never tires in pleasing. Whether, as now, under the noon radiance, the blue waters of the Bosphorus and Golden Horn mingle under a shimmering haze with each other, and a fleecy veil hides but does not wholly conceal the mountains, which curve gracefully on the Asiatic side; or whether, as we saw the scene the other night, when the Ramazan season was closing, and the minarets were all afire with illuminations, mingling the double lights of water and sky with those of the mosques and their surroundings, there is no more exquisite scene! On the south-west roof of our hotel, and from a height of two hundred feet above all the neighboring houses, there is a view, with no unpleasant scenes of the front streets to

THE SULTAN'S PALACE.

detract from its beauty. Scutari likewise is a picture in this vision. It rises gradually from the opposite shore of the Bosphorus, skirted in its rear by graves of green—the burial homes of the Turks, who are sceptical about their permanency in Europe. Scutari looks doubly beautiful by night, as the closing of the fast adds its illuminations. As we gaze upon the nocturnal splendors, new lights, as changeful as the hieroglyphics of the Turkish letters, appear. Indeed, they are texts and names, in fire, from the Koran. They are strung from minaret to minaret.

When we were here many years ago, it was Ramazan season; but no effort of memory has reproduced such brilliant visions as these from our window. Everything depends on your point of view. We are now domiciled in Pera, where the Franks live. We are near the great tower, Galata, from which views are often taken of this city of seven hills and many hundred minarets and domes. From it may be seen the course of the Bosphorus, with the kiosks and palaces along its banks. Below us, overlooking a few mosques on the margin of the river, are the steamers of the nations, and the tugs and ferries hurrying about; while within the Golden Horn are massed indiscriminately, between the old and new bridges, the shipping which makes up the body of the commerce of the port.

This beautiful scene is merely external. It gives you no idea of the narrow streets and miserable degradation across the bridges in Stamboul. This we have seen in all its dirt and degradation, by night and day, as we visited St. Sophia twice to see its closing services of the Ramazan. As I write, the guns of the forts thunder out the exultation that the fast is over, its month of abstinence by day ended, and the feast of Bairam begun. One fort echoes another; the flash of its gun, before its report, signals the flash of another gun across the waters, until each one of the seven hills is rejoicing in the festival season.

If it be supposed that this religion is losing its hold upon this people, and is waxing old as a garment, it is a mistake. The same devotion which we saw thirty years ago, exists without so much intolerance. The Ottoman empire may be crumbling like the walls about this city; it may and does require props and guarantees; the intercourse between foreigners and natives is easier than it was; there is more education, general and technical, among the Turkish and other youth; there have been conclaves and parties and liberties, indicating progress; the faith in the prophet may be ready to vanish away—into Asia or Africa, where it is growing; but as a faith it yet holds in thrall one hundred and seventy-five millions. Among them are but few infidels and sceptics compared with other religions. Mohammedanism has its education in the harem and in childhood. It is tenacious, and would, if it could, be just as belligerent as ever. One picture of the prophet, as I saw it in a history dedicated to one of the Swedish kings of a hundred years ago, is that of a zealot drawing his light from above, with a sword in one hand and the Koran in the other; and another graphic scene is that of the prophet riding as a white flame upon a horse, with a peacock tail and a woman's head—covered with a fez—completely concealed by the flames in and about him, which issue from the checkered and gorgeous throne of Allah!

Professor Grosvenor, upon our visit, dilated on the interest attaching to the walls, gates, and towers about the city. They have a history coeval with the Eastern Empire and its Greek masters. We saw the best part of them in a seven-hours' jaunt, under the guidance of our Greek guide, who makes the Greek relics a specialty.

An engineer would not be at a loss *à priori* to locate most of these walls, as there are certain natural fortifications which flank the city. Two continents and two seas justified the founder, Byzas, in the selection of the site for a grand emporium and capital. The city dates 658 years before the Saviour.

These walls had many an attack of the Persians under Xerxes. Pausanius recovered the city and rebuilt them. Internal wars for democracy and its rights made these walls memorable before Philip of Macedon attempted their reduction. Variously allied in the days of Roman conquests, the Byzantines made their city " free," and it was so regarded by Rome, until other conquerors arose, and fell, and arose again; until Constantine the Great became its genius and gave to it a new baptism of blood.

It became the centre of the empire of the greatest of the Roman emperors. Its story has been grandly told, as if it were an epic. It is worthy of the historic muse. How many have visited it, if only to view the city to which Gibbon has given his imperial style and illustrious dignity. By nature its position is strong, but in history its name is immortal. Its climate is temperate, being of the latitude of New York. Its surface is that of a triangle, whose obtuse angle is toward Asia, and made beautiful by the Bosphorus; while its northern side has the Golden Horn, and its south the Sea of Marmora. It is attached to Europe on the west. The three points of the triangle are—at Seraglio Point, which I see from my window; at Eyoob, a gate on the north, and on the south at the famous "Seven Towers," almost due south. These sides of the triangle are the old walls. They extend thirteen miles, but there is a city of the living and the dead, outside still! There is not enough interest felt, even by engineers, now in walled places, that I should be more particular.

But for the fact that these walls are coincident with the main boundaries of the old and new city, I would not be thus particular. The walls extend as well on the land as on the water side. Sometimes they reach the water, and are submerged. What ups and downs have they not had! Destroyed by earthquake and war, and as often repaired and elevated, "countermured" or fortified, sometimes threefold, and with moat and water protection, outer walls enfolding the inner, and with gorgeous towers numbering two thousand and more, and with twenty-eight gates, all having a special beauty and character, like those of oriental cities, there is not, in history, anything comparable with them! If there be, it is Babylon! In circuit and enceinte, in its crowning towers and grandeur of height and decoration, in stairways and massiveness, as well in the counter-walls as in the innermost walls, in depth and width of moat and water which surrounded them, Babylon cannot be named with the city of Byzas, Theodosius, Tiberius, Theophilus, Constantine, Palæologus, and Mohammed II. For the splendor and size of the city within them, few cities can compare, even to-day. If we should take its census now, there would be revealed over a million of population, most heterogeneous and motley, of divers religions and races, of strange employments and customs. It was to survey a portion of these immense walls that we gave up one day.

When we were here thirty years ago it was difficult to get a carriage, and when got, what good was it over such streets? The donkeys could then hardly navigate. A pasha on horseback had then a footman to clear his way. But now the city has many good streets, though our course, after we crossed from Pera over the new bridge of the Golden Horn, did not take them in. Winding around through the narrow lanes and crowded thoroughfares of Stamboul, amidst the quarters of the old Turks, we did find, at length, some quiet though narrow ways, where the cries of the street sellers were only occasional, and where the population were fezzed and turbaned. The jalousies of the overhanging gables were not as strictly drawn as we expected. At length we are in a wide street, with a tramway. Between it and the Sea of Marmora is the Adrianople railway; so that out of our unprogressive quarter we discover civilization, as it meanders with the shore of the sea.

At every step we are reminded of the "Arabian Nights." What do we see? Cobblers in the street mending the "shoon" of the pilgrims in waiting; shoemakers indoors, and sometimes in the gala costume of the Bairam season, pegging away; blacksmiths and brass-smiths working at the forge, and with less grime on hand and brow, for it is festive time to all Mussulmans; slaves of ebony hue, in gaudy striped dresses, hooded as if they were the houri, leading along black-eyed white children to their mosques or cemetery for the holiday; old red and yellow houses, with knockers as antique as those of the Palæologus days; stone fountains at every corner, with inscriptions over them from the Koran; women in gay silken attire, some from cleanly Broussa, dressed in red and white stripes, which made me feel like embracing the—star-spangled banner, flag of my native land, etc.; fig-trees in gardens, and fountains in streets. Our two hours of jolting and observation, not unobserved by the curious population, is relieved by the glimpses of the open Sea of Marmora. We peep at it through cafés and gardens of inviting beauty, where narghiles and chibouques fill the air with smoke, and fruits of all kinds, melons and grapes predominant, are sold. These make the jaunt and scenes attractive, until we reach our destination. It is the "Seven Towers!"

Dionysius, our guide, summons the warder of the main tower. He comes—smiling at a prospective fee. He is a good-natured Turk. Indeed, we have not found here one snappy custodian—as we used to in England—in charge of the public works. He ushers us within the fortress. Once there were here seven towers of immense solidity, crowning this fortress, which looks out upon the sea. Now but three are pre-eminent in size and roundness. They are notable for something else than size. The one we first enter is filled with old baskets and charcoal. It had once several stories of floors for dungeon purposes. It is very gloomy. From it the prisoners were allowed egress sometimes into the air. Upon the stones in the wall, in Greek, Latin, and French, we find old inscriptions, like those in the Tower of London, cut by doomed prisoners. Some we decipher as of the date of 1699. One prisoner scratches : " It is a sad place—no law here for man, and none from God!" We go up some hundred steps or more to the battlemented walls. On looking down, we see within quite a garden. Gourds, cucumbers, figs, English walnuts, and maize are grown. A little mosque with a minaret is in the centre. Around the court are small cloisters, used for a silk factory, where girls work. On the walls themselves are almond, fig, and locust trees, and snails by the thousand, hanging to the shrubbery. We go higher, and with some difficulty clamber to the topmost lookout. Through the turrets we survey the panorama. My compass tells me the points. To the west are bare, dry hills, earthworks, and plains. Dionysius points out a solitary white house, a mile or more distant, and observes:

"There is where the Russian army, three years ago, were encamped."

"All of them?" we ask.

"No; only those under the Grand Duke Michael. The rest extended to Varna—to the Danube! He was ready to take the city. The Sultan had not answered the summons to surrender. The last trumpet sounded the attack!—when lo! a mounted pasha with a scroll and a white flag rushes upon the scene, crying, 'Ah! ah-h! ah-h-h!' He is followed by the priests of the mosques and churches. They are ushered into the presence of the Grand Duke. Down they go on their knees, and cry, 'Great is the Czar!' The pasha, to illustrate the fidelity of the Sultan and the desire for peace, snatches a red fez-cap from the head of a soldier, and, tearing it to pieces, exclaims, 'Let us be forever friends! Long live the Czar!'"

Thus, with gesture and animation, Dionysius gives dramatically his account of the nearness of the Russian to the taking of Constantinople, and of the meditated attack whose success the great powers prevented by prodding, at the last agony, the dilatory Sultan out of his fatalism, into some action upon the terms tendered.

I ask Dionysius to inquire of our Turkish guide if he ever heard of America. He asks the question, but gets no reply save a blank look.

"Does he know that the earth is round, and that America is on the other side?" Another failure.

"Bah!" says the Greek; "what know they but their pilaf (rice) and smoke-pipe!"

They are hopelessly ignorant; and yet is not this race connate with that which gave arithmetic, algebra, chemistry, and astronomy to the world?

As we talk, that enormous white bird with the black tail, which has been following us around since we left Odessa, flew out of the tower, and made a sensation among the chickens in the court. That bird is an evil genius, like the cormorant of North Cape. Our guide grows garrulous, and gossips much about these walls. One of his stories is romantic: An Englishman, Leander Jarndyce, fresh from India, and burdened with rupees, falls in love with an American girl at the hotel. Her name is Mehitable Twitchell, and she is as sharp and as beautiful as New England can furnish. She has a sister and her papa along; and her Leander has a friend. Leander became almost as much engrossed by the "Seven Towers" as with Mehitable; and Dionysius, as their guide, was required twice a week, for forty days, to have a landau ready for the party, which came out here to breakfast on the ramparts, and to study history. They brought their déjeûner along, and with high style, overlooking the splendid country, and amidst belligerent battlements, ate their mutton cold, while warming to each other over Medoc and champagne.

"Ah!" says Dionysius, "many a bottle have I hurled from these towers of Grecian glory!"

Said I to the guide: "How did it all end?"

They got married, and are on the Burrampooter, where, between hunting tigers and fighting the bile, Leander is happy with Mehitable. This is an "o'er-true tale," as it was set down to me; except the names, which are my own felicitous selection.

CHAPTER VII.

AMONG THE CHURCHES AND CEMETERIES, AND AROUND THE WALLS OF CONSTANTINOPLE.

The little I have seen of the world, and know of the history of mankind, teaches me to look upon the errors of others in sorrow, not in anger! I would fain leave the erring soul of my fellow-man with Him, from whose hands it came.
—LONGFELLOW.

LEAVING the "Seven Towers," which are at the angle farthest down the Sea of Marmora, we go outside the walls, following their land side, across the city, and through the road lined with cemeteries, to the Golden Horn. The road is dusty and the day hot. The walls, where scarred and split, are a reservoir of old lime, pulverizing with the motion of the railroad and with every breeze. We notice that some of the triple walls have been torn down. The Sultan Abdul Aziz, about whose death there is much controversy, gave to his mother the privilege to sell the stones of the walls for building purposes. Their immense width and height rendered this gift a fortune; but England, through her ambassador, protested against the profanation, and it stopped. One point—tally! for John Bull. Spirits of Theodosius and Constantine, take notice from your sapphire walls, if indeed you look down from them, upon this degradation of your once proud city! The moat has been filled up. Vegetable gardens are fenced in by its walls.

We entered one of the towers. Another is used for a cartridge factory and powder magazine; and I had just lighted a cigar! We found the famous gate of gold, somewhat diminished. It was once a triumphal arch, and bore an inscription, with a gilded statue of Victory. It was set up when Theodosius conquered Maximus, and was used by the emperors on their victorious return to the city. It was by this gate, six hundred and twenty years ago this summer, that Michael Palæologus entered after driving the Latins out! A Greek patriarch, whose book I have read, pays a great compliment to Michael for his grace to the Bishop, who met him here on his return, and to whom the King piously bent the knee. There were here once marble towers of columnar grandeur and of rare art, besides statues of the chained Prometheus and of the labors of Hercules; so that, take it altogether, this must have been one of the finest of the twenty-eight gates of this mural triangle of thirteen miles.

Outside, we begin our drive from this gate of so many golden memories. Over pavements where triumphant armies marched, and where shouting thousands assembled, and where passed captive men, slaves, and symbols from India to Italy, and from Gothland to Persia, we march; but our march is not triumphant; for the air is dust. The air is as hot as the dust is historic. We drive past the graveyards and hospitals of the Greeks and Armenians. These are outside the walls.

"What a world of people must have died here!" we exclaim. "The graveyards are more populous than the city."

The city is itself encircled by these cemeteries,

and their medley of tombs are so confused that it would render the resurrection futile, but for a miracle! These, let it be known, are but a portion of the immense cemeteries of this vicinity. Scutari, on the Asiatic side, is more populous with the dead than upon this side; but upon every hill, and far along up the Bosphorus, the same unperpendicular tombstones appear, under the high and dry cypresses. The romance of the cemeteries disappears when you are within close sight of them. If there be two millions of people in and around these cities, there are as many tombstones also—if not more.

We enter a Greek church. It is known for its sacred waters. As there are so many of these sacred water sources around the walls, it may be worth while to refer to this, the most celebrated one, and from one learn all. It is at the Pighi church, and has great celebrity. On Fridays and Sundays the environs and church are jammed with the thousands who come here to wash and drink and carry off the water in bottles. Our Greek guide, Dionysius, drew out a bottle from his pocket; he said it was for the porter at the hotel, a Greek of pious inclination. This church has had its fires and earthquakes, and also its rebuildings. It was once the seat as well of wealth as of palaces, of royal marriages and poetic frenzy. Its grounds were in the earlier centuries carpeted with flowers, and there was a cypress forest of great extent. We went below to the spring and the crypt of the church, where there are pictures of miraculous cure. As all were permitted to use the water, whether a Greek religionist or not, we took a drink and a wash. It was refreshing. There are fish in the fountain. They, too, are called holy. There is a story about them. It concerns the taking of the city by Mohammed II., and the remark of a Greek priest that he would as soon expect to see the fish he was then cooking leap out of the frying-pan into the fire, as the Turks take Constantinople from the Greeks. Just then a half-done fish leaped out, and Constantinople fell! Out of this story—which is, like other oriental stories, to be considered as a parable rather than a fact—it is alleged that the custom of regarding the fish as sacred grew apace. May be, it was for some reason more interesting, viz., to honor the apostolic fishermen of Galilee.

Here, too, the sick are brought and bathed, and, if they need further care, by an excellent provision, the hospital of the Greeks is near by for their reception. We saw garments left by some of the sick in the stone well where they are bathed. The water may have medicinal properties. Certainly there is much evidence to show this; and we perceive, as is customary in all such places where folk are cured, especially in the East, that there are many votive offerings. No doubt there is healing in the waters, or in any water properly applied. Our guide relates many instances of cure, even of Turkish children. He believes in them, and I would not distrust him or them; for did not a grateful Turkish mother leave a priceless ring as her offering to the church of the infidel, for the cure of her child?

While we are going about the church, a priest accosts us. He begins to write us down. We ask his meaning. He wants a list of our dead. Heavens! How did he know we kept a private graveyard, and if so what did he want of the list? Ah!

he would say some prayers, for some piastres, and for our dead! This was kind; but Dionysius, who is of the same communion, and chancellor of our exchequer, was not to be hoodwinked, and as a good Greek and guide, and from the island of Ithaca, too, where the wise Ulysses ruled and Penelope spun, he protests against the mercenary sacrilege.

"You see these people are strangers, from far-off America, not Greeks, nor of the Greek Church. Why do you follow them about? I will report you to the patriarch, and into jail you go."

The priest retired in a hurry, and kept clear of our guide. We saw the prison afterwards, at the patriarch's palace, where the unruly and bad priests are kept. This a curious sort of *imperium in imperio*. Yet the Greek Church has an ecclesiastical tribunal within the body of the Turkish polity, which is itself so closely attached to its own faith that all outside are *supposed* to be regarded as dogs, only worthy of spurning.

"Suppose," I say, for there is some doubt about the Turks, after all, being so bigoted. They have had, like other people, their frenzied zealotry; but the history of the early Turkish Sultans, while rulers of Asia Minor, and before they conquered Constantinople, shows that they ruled with moderation. They treated other sects with a toleration unknown to other religions at that time. Although the Turks are but seven millions, they are at the head of nearly two hundred millions, whose religion is that of Islam. Their early power was built and cemented by education and charity; and the corrupt Byzantine empire easily fell before their stalwart prowess. To-day, Armenians, Greeks,

Bulgarians, Syrians, and Maronites live in Turkey and enjoy their faith in comparative freedom. For myself, let me say, that it has only been by some misadventure of our own, that we have been treated by them, in and outside of mosque or cemetery, with other than absolute courtesy. Once to-day we were ordered away from the tombs of the Sultans with a gentle and silent wave of the hand. We learned that it was because a great Turk was about to be buried. There is an expression they use, "*Haide git!*" It sounds American, but it simply means, "Off with you!" It is only used toward beggars. We had none of it. At no time have we met such a reckless disregard of their own faith from them as was shown by the Greek priest of the sacred waters. The Mohammedans will not allow an unbeliever to be other than an observer of their service. This Greek priest was ready to pray for us or our dead, for a consideration; and irrespective of our relations to this or the other world! Whether he will go to the prison or not, depends on the magnanimity of Dionysius. The descendants of the old Greek colonies along these shores are not regarded by such patriots as our Dionysius as of the blue blood. They are called rayahs, and speak Turkish. They have their own laws within the Turkish empire, and the patriarch here and his bishops are ex-officio magistrates. They also have a part in local civil affairs; so that when our guide threatened, he meant what might be done.

Within this Greek church of the Sacred Waters is represented "the cosmogony." It is a series of pictures, beginning with Adam and Eve and the serpent, and running through Biblical lore to the three wise men, on white camels, who, star-led, came to worship the Babe of Bethlehem. It included the altar of sacrifice, with Abraham and Isaac. St. George and the Dragon, as in Russia, so here, is a favorite saint, and is susceptible of graphic representation. He is here in gilded breastplate and red plume, and upon his steed of white, charging upon the hideous dragon. The altar is very expressive in its simplicity. Generally these Greek churches have not regarded the precept of the poet, but have had—

> "Too much of ornament; in outward show
> Elaborate; of inward less exact."

At least this was our impression of them in Russia, and this church is hardly exceptional in some respects. One of its simplest features is the picture before the altar—of the One All-Seeing Eye! It illustrates the intense love of symbolism, peculiarly Oriental. It is found even in the whirling of the dervishes, who, in closing their eyes, see the Invisible, and in whirling see him at every quarter to which they turn. There is a tinseled appearance in and around some of the shrines, which reminds us of Moscow, and the pictures seem of the middle ages. There is a picture of "Abraam" entertaining the angels, with a Greek inscription, *Philoxenia*, which Dionysius interprets, " Friendly travelers ;" and a shrine from the isle of Tenos, to which, instead of going home, the natives of that isle resort for worship. I am thus particular in these points, because there are seventy millions of people who worship after these methods, and I am not of the little handful of Samaritans, who, looking down from Mount Gerizim, insist that where they are, is the only place where God is to be worshiped, and the rest of the world is in delusion.

Outside of this interesting church, and covered with Greek inscriptions and crosses, are the marble tombs of the patriarchs. We visit them as a farewell to this peculiar church, and take to the road again, along the historic walls. We pass many people of all nationalities; some on their horses and donkeys between big panniers; others, including the hooded Turkish females, walking toward their cemeteries in their best clothes and with their families, and all having a gravity and decency, in their Bairam feast, quite in contrast with the drunken jollity we saw in Russia on saints' days. We pass a Turkish cemetery, and gaze within. The gravestones are so thick that they have become common. They are used for fences, for we see the names and inscriptions of the dead, with scraps of the Koran upon them, in the walls along the road. A well had two turbaned headstones as uprights to support its wheel. Upon the great city walls we perceive hundreds of trees, mostly fig-trees. They are as large as our apple-trees. They grow on and out of the top of the wall, their roots wrapping around the huge stones with a vigorous vitality. Even from the gaps made by the earthquake the vegetation springs, repairing the catastrophes of nature with gentlest garniture.

After a rest at a café, outside the Greek cemetery, and a cup of coffee and some *rehatilicum* (or fig-paste), we go within. Some of the tombs show the old love of the Greek for the beautiful. Upon them are cut emblems to represent the avocations of the deceased—a compass and axe for a carpenter, scissors and an embroidery frame for a seamstress, and so on. These grounds of refreshment outside have old plane-trees, and crowds of men, women, and children are sitting under them. They have been within the church to partake of and bear away the sacred waters. Men are playing checkers, as they sip from neat little Viennese cups the black, milkless, and highly-sugared coffee; and all about is a gravity which knows no laughter, and indulges in no frivolity. We take up our march for the Armenian burying-grounds, near by. There are two Armenian sects. One is Catholic, but it is not theirs we visit. No crowd seems to be within their inclosure, nor any ostentation, like that of the others.

The head of the Catholic Armenians is one of the ripest scholars in the world. As religion seems to be the salient object in the Orient; as its ceremonies are everywhere presented to the attention; as the Orient is the select home of devotion to the Great Unseen and Supreme Being, from whence all forms and faiths have had their source, it would be impossible to give a sketch of the outdoor life of these mixed peoples here without some distinctions as to their creed.

Mount Ararat stands nearly 18,000 feet above the sea. It stands on an elevated plateau. We know its history and tradition. This plateau is Armenia, and from it came a remarkable race, a race which has had more periods of vassalage and freedom, of war and peace, under Assyrian, Persian, and Roman empires, and under Latin, Turkish, Mogul, and Russian rule, than any other race. They have been scattered abroad, like the children of Israel. They are now surely advancing; for they trade and study, as well as travel and worship. They have a rich literature. Their church is not unlike the Greek Church. The costume of their priests is a black robe and a high black hat. It is said that they are less superstitious and bigoted than the Greeks. They, too, like the Greeks, have a chief patriarch here, and civil relations similar to those of the Greek hierarchy. They constitute a sort of nation inside of this Government; having a limited self-rule. One branch, I have said, is Catholic. We recognize their priests by the long black veil flowing from their black hats. They are men of singularly handsome and benign faces. They have had the protection of Western Catholic nations, and have schools in Europe. The members of this communion are superior scholars. There is also a small "nation" of Protestant Armenians, mostly the result of American missionary labors. They number about 25,000, and form an important colony in the Orient. But it is curious that the only proselytes worth mentioning as Protestant, have been among the Armenians. This is ascribed to their zeal for education and their serious character.

CHAPTER VIII.

AROUND CONSTANTINOPLE—AMONG THE DEAD—FORTUNE-TELLING—SACRED WATERS.

The spider has woven its web in the palace of the Cæsars,
The owl shrieks its nightly song on the towers of Aphresiab.
—FROM THE PERSIAN.

WHAT troubles the mere superficial observer here is, to determine who is who, among these various races. The Greek is very like the Armenian, and both not unlike the Hebrew and Turk. Hence Government used to order the different races to wear different costumes, and separate "quarters" were assigned to them to live in. With large, dark, expressive, oriental eyes and black hair, it is impossible, when dressed alike, for a stranger to discriminate between these oriental classes of the Semitic family. The fez cap does not indicate the Turk always, but only a Turkish subject, for the Armenians and others sometimes wear it. The Armenian women wear the Turkish yashmak, to conceal all but their lustrous eyes; but even their gauze veils are becoming more transparent with the advancing time. Our American College here has many Armenian students. They are said to be exceedingly gifted and eloquent.

When we ventured within the Armenian cemetery, and found it was a fête day, and the grounds full of people, we carried our memories back to

Mount Ararat, and spread them over quite a large area, so as to enjoy the new relations between the dead and living—the ancient and modern epochs.

A curious gathering is that which we find in the Armenian inclosure. The stones are lying flat, and in as much disorder as in the Turkish grounds. There are trees, but no grass; dirt, but no decoration. All sorts of people are here, among them many priests in their long black robes and high black hats with a rim at the top. The priests are chanting prayers over the graves, in the presence of the bereaved, while dozens of men and boys, bearing jars from a well in the cemetery, pour water upon the grave. A few coins to the water-carriers, a few piastres to the priest, and kiss upon his hand, and the bereaved goes his or her way.

We perceive a crowd about a singularly-dressed man who flies two white pigeons from a stand, as a sign of his employment. He is a literary soothsayer. The pigeons are mere couriers, to announce, as they flutter about his box, his presence and business. We join the group. He has a box with several compartments. Within it is a reddish-golden bird resembling somewhat a canary. After paying your money, this ominous bird nips out a card, with your fortune on it! It is written in modern Greek in prose or rhyme. It is not inspired by any mystic moonstone, but drops from the bill of the little bird. Did we try our fortune? Of course. In an Armenian cemetery, near the walls of Constantine, and in the face of several thousand years of human activity and divine demonstration as to these children from Mount Ararat, what more suitable or magical place for divination! Here, if ever place was fit, is the oracle, truer far than oak or tripod. My ticket was translated by Dionysius, thus :

" The little bird says that you have plenty of friends, but some of them are betraying you. They will not succeed."

" Good," I say ; " go on ! "

" You are a man who has enjoyed many honors ; and more are in store for you. You have not reached the top !" Considering that my ambition has been well satisfied, this was interesting.

" Do not rely on ancestral help, but on yourself ! You have had much money, and have lost a good deal."

This was true; for was I not in politics, without "star" bids or "credit" of any kind, but such as came of honest service ?

" But your luck will turn, and you will become rich again, and live till ninety-two ! "

" Good ! " exclaims my guardian angel near, remembering that our salary and income are going in travel, and that the winning of the $20,000 at the Grand Prix in Paris, which was reported in the papers, was by another Mr. C.

Then came my wife's future. It said : " Never fail to recall the beautiful teachings of your beloved parents. Your fortune is being envied by your female friends. They cannot harm you ; and you will survive all jealousies, and be buried at the age of eighty-four, rich, honored, and respected ! " These were as satisfactory as foolish ; only we did not like the idea of surviving each other !

The patriarch Constantine, whose volume I had studied for to-day's excursion, gives twenty-two pages to the Sacred Springs around this city. There is a gush and rush of sacred waters from every hill and beneath every church and mosque, and even under the Bosphorus! These waters have had the reputation and the virtue of protecting the city, amidst plague and war, decadence and diabolism! The Bosphorus itself is most sacred in the eyes of this enthusiastic Greek writer, who exclaims: "In this corner of the earth, unique in its kind, in which all the charms of earth combine to astonish the human mind, soft and gentle breezes blow, and one may often hearken to the sweet songs of the nightingale and other melodious birds." What would the eloquent Father have said had he seen the springs of Colorado and California in our mountains, or the Yellow-stone, with its laboratory of wonders!

Nevertheless, under his inspiration we went to one more spring, the "Little Balourki." The church over it has long since been destroyed. We found its spring under ground forty feet, and in a cemetery! We descended the arched way, and found it dry, but outside, beneath a spreading tree, sat a family of Turkish women. They did not conceal their faces as they made their meal. The leading lady reclined on a rich rug, and had a blue-and-gold-colored yashmak drawn but lightly around her shoulders. A slave near, wore, as is the custom, colored gauze over eyes and all. The lady, when she saw me gazing at her, coyly drew over her pretty face the yashmak. She was eating grapes, which suggested our refreshment. In a twinkling we had ten cents' worth, or two and a half pounds, upon cool leaves freshly plucked. The little Turkish "Mary" of the family plays with a pet lamb, led by a ribbon, and wearing a bell and some beads. The lamb was sure to follow wherever she went.

We leave reluctantly our shady place, but the late afternoon admonishes us; and we resume our way along the triple walls, between piles on piles of tombs, until the very air seems freighted with the dead and their memorials.

A splendid ruin appears, which draws our attention. It is massive and interesting. It is the palace of Belisarius, so renowned in history. It shows signs of Byzantine arches and great skill. It is remarkable to us, because of its name. Singularly enough, there passed us, coming down the steep banks and led by a child, a blind old man; whereupon Dionysius relates the story of the old "White ctzar," and the "old man" gave it practical exemplification. It was to this palace, through one of these grand gates, that Mohammed II. resorted, amidst the hurrahs of his troops, after the taking of the city. He then repeated the Persian verse at the head of this chapter.

We heard no owl hoot here, though we did from the "towers of Europe," built by Mohammed himself to assist in the taking of the city. We have seen no spider at its work, amidst the dusty ruins of the Belisarius Palace; but we have seen the silk-weavers in the subterranean cisterns of the Greek Emperor Constantine, near the grounds of the Hippodrome. Persian poetry is pretty, but facts are stubborn prose. History tells us, that before Belisarius and his conquering army fell Hun, Persian, African, Vandal, and Goth. He was the glory of the Greeks. In the Hippodrome he received apotheosis for his exploits. Yet he was the same who, poor and blind, dragged himself along the highways asking alms at the base of the monuments his valor had preserved. It is a reproach to Justinian that such ignominy should have been allowed under his enlightened reign. Belisarius achieved a final victory over the Huns at these very gates, and for it was once more immortalized.

It may not interest American readers to dwell upon these remnants of old empire; but still, those who have read the history and romances of the elder day will take some interest in them. I met a young graduate of Yale traveling all alone here yesterday. He was from Pittsburg. I asked him the object of his coming away off here, amidst the dusty spoils of Time, leaving Paris and London, in their living luxuries, to study the decay and fall of empire. He said: "I read Gibbon, and I could not rest till I looked upon this capital of the Eastern Empire." I admired his perseverance, and saw through his eyes my own enthusiasm of thirty years ago, when I came here under similar impulses.

One more mosque, and we will move toward the Golden Horn. It is called Chora. It is a wonder, not merely because it is older by one hundred and fifty years than Sophia, but because the Moslem priests, who control it, have allowed the "infidel" pictures of the early Greek Church to drop their smear of paint and whitewash and come to the light. The mosaics of a thousand years ago, with the Greek crosses, are here in resplendent gold and hues, as plainly as they were when Comenus ruled, and his daughter directed their execution. It is not a large church, but it is interesting. A few Koran passages are inscribed in gold on green ground. I ask the priest to interpret them. He said:

"All who follow where I go reach Paradise!"

A few sacred pigeons fly about the dome; while

all about was written, as if because the air was shining with Christian illustrations, the word: "Allah! Allah!" A singular picture of Noah's ark hangs upon the walls; the meaning of which, just there, I could not decipher. My wife found, in an old bronze door, the "key pattern"—a labyrinthine institution with which she seemed familiar, and which has come down with the Greek civilization to make embroidery beautiful. This church, like those of the middle ages, had separate latticed apartments up-stairs, like those in the House of Commons, for the gentle sex. From its windows we look upon the Golden Horn and the tower of Galata in Pera, and toward the hill of Scutari beyond. Coming from this singularly mixed church-mosque, and following the walls, we are still pursued by the turbaned gravestones. Upon an eminence overlooking the Golden Horn, and to the end of it, where are green islands and the "sweet waters of Europe," we perceive rural kiosks and palaces, while around us we find ourselves again surrounded by the tombs of dead Ottomans! They are of a higher grade, however. This one is that of a Sultan's officer of rank, for there is a crown over it; another, with a large turban of peculiar size, is one of the Sultan's guard; two daughters of a rich man are without turban, and have gilt letters; a green and red turban indicates one of the large family of Mohammed; another, with bunches of grapes, shows the number of children the dead mother bore; and so on, in every variety.

Just as we are pondering over the infinity of tombs, a shrill, ringing voice comes forth from the minaret below, echoed by some one from a neighboring minaret. It is the cry to prayers. A stork, frightened by the cry, starts out of the cypress grove below. Proceeding down hill to the walls, we are still amidst the tombs, but they are of better quality. They are now shut in with sacred care. One is that of a hermit in a vault, into which we look. The coffin is of green, for he is of Mohammed's family. A tin cup hangs out, and a fountain near, so that the devotee may throw the water in upon his grave. Still going down the hill, we pass the temples for the tombs of the Sultans, into which we do not enter. We gaze in upon them. They seem arrayed in mother-of-pearl and Cashmere shawls. An extinguisher is over each of the large candles which stand around, an emblem of the light having gone out.

Our last adventure is to the patriarchal home and conclave of the Greek Church. To this we are admitted. We approach it, not without due respect; for in the convents of these religionists were preserved not merely the truths of our gospel, but the classics of the great Greeks! A whole chapter might be written about the libraries of these scholars, which time, ignorance, bigotry, and war have destroyed. It was with a pain at the heart that I read this translation of the words of the Greek patriarch, whose book has been my Mentor in this day's tour. How curiously it treats of the inductive and other philosophers: "With the precipitate fall of the empire the lights of Greek instruction were also extinguished. Some remains only (thanks to the clergy) found an asylum in the Patriarchal School of Constantinople, and were preserved down to our time. But in this school the works of Plato were committed to the flames by the Scholarius Gennodius, who became patriarch after the conquest of Constantinople. Then the works of Aristotle were destroyed by these eclectics, who would not tolerate the liberty of thought. Descartes was the first to show that one must judge freely philosophical systems, without regard to the authors, be they whom they may. The immortal Newton introduced in society the right to examine and freely to treat upon different subjects—a right abolished now some two thousand years!"

We look upon the portraits in this seat of power and scholarship; we see about, their emblems of authority. Their power over their church is assured by their loyalty to "the powers that be," which was tested in the troubles between Greece and the Porte. The portrait of the new patriarch was there. We saw him the other day, in a caïque, on his way to his summer home, above Therapia, and his clear, high forehead shone with the mental power he is said to possess. To be the head of any of these eastern churches, in a locality like this, where the literature is in many tongues, and where the ordinary trader must be master of several languages, requires that scholarship should go hand-in-hand with high qualities and lineage, and suavity and firmness be ever alert to assist and defend the ecclesiastical polity which has come down through the ages.

CHAPTER IX.

THE OLD SERAGLIO—ST. SOPHIA—THE OLD GREEK HIPPO-
DROME—THE MUSEUM OF ANCIENT COSTUMES—
AMONG THE HOWLING DERVISHES.

Be ye certain all seems love,
Viewed from Allah's throne above;
Be ye stout of heart, and come
Bravely onward to your home.
La Allah illa Allah! Yea,
Thou love divine. Thou love alway.
—FROM THE PERSIAN, BY EDWIN ARNOLD.

WE desired to see the old Seraglio Point within itself. It juts into the stream and forms the entrance of the Bosphorus, dividing the Sea of Marmora from the Golden Horn. When we were here before, the harem was there. We visited it then, went inside the palace where the Sultanas lived, and rambled in the luxuriant grounds which yet rise about it. The interior was then disappointing. The divan and drapery of the gorgeous East were not there. Tables, chairs, and poor French prints were the only decorations; but the baths and fountains we remember well. They were characteristic and Eastern. The marble halls were bright, and the honeycomb fountains within murmured a lullaby to the Sea of Marmora without. But the place then had the odor of blood, even upon its white pavements. There were more sighs lingering about the mysterious opening upon the Bosphorus than the sweet air could hold. The

Adrianople railroad now runs through the old palace ground, round the point, to the depot on the Golden Horn. The abode of the Sultan, which was regarded as a sacred spot in 1851, and into which we passed unsandaled, has given place to the goblin of steam, whose shrieks are more mellifluous to the ear than those of the wives who were sacked into the stream at this once convenient point of perpetual divorcement.

The day of our visit happened to be the anniversary of the Sultan's coronation; and we were allowed, without hindrance from the chief of the public grounds on the point, to go about without the customary firman. A fairy kiosk stands high on the point. There the Sultan sometimes stops, and, from the further side, reviews the troops, when war begins, and drops upon them his blessing! This kiosk rises above the gardens of the Theodosian column. It is shut in by a whitewashed wall. This beautiful antique column has been almost inclosed since we were here by trees. Thirty years in the life of a tree or a man makes much change. The beauty of the column is hardly seen for the foliage. On its iron fence, the dirty linen of officials hangs out to dry. This column is sometimes conjectured to be the column of Simeon the Stylite, but it is only conjecture. It is Corinthian and beautiful. It held the statue of Theodosius once, and was built in his honor, because the Goths came here then to offer submission to the Roman power. These Northmen asked to be permitted to colonize Thrace and Asia Minor. If they had been accepted as the colonists in these now barren lands, what would have been the state of mankind! Where, if their genius had been given to Asia, and not to

Europe, would have been the great Teutonic nation and the relation of the races?

From this point across to Scutari you perceive a yellow building. It is the Nightingale Hospital, of gentlest renown. It is now used in part for a barracks. Beyond it is the British cemetery, full of Crimean heroes, and with a fitting column. All this, out of the Crimean war, since we were last here. Those very rocks in the mist, which are near the Prince's Isles—little rocky isles—have themselves changed hands. They belong to Sir Henry Bulwer's heir; and he keeps them anchored safely, rocks as they are, by a Turkish guard. From this point you may see the windings of the Bosphorus. These turns—which make its bays and currents—are so awry that navigation is not always happy or safe.

Let us go up into the open court above the old Seraglio. It is most interesting ground, and has not been so much changed even by fifteen centuries of royal residence. It used to be three miles around, and had a wall on all sides. The most of the old palace was destroyed by fire, a dozen years after we went through it. The harem portion was rifled at the fire; but the old ceremonial inclosure, called the Seraglio, with its public buildings remains. To that we venture, not without trepidation. Our first look is at the enormous sycamore tree, which would make a fit counterpart in size, if not in height, to any tall sycamore of the Wabash; but, unlike it, alas! it is hollow. If it were solid—as our Mariposa trees are not—it would give them quite a race for size and celebrity. It is at least forty feet in girth. It used to be occupied by the chief janizary! In this court is the Sublime Porte, the old one, for there is now a new one, not so redolent of ancient associations. It is a grand arch, with Arabic texts over it, and towers about it. This old Porte, by which the Turkish government is known, does not look like a palatial entrance. It has rather a police look, and there are soldiers about it. It used to be kept by fifty porters, hence it was Sublime! As we could not go into the Mint, where the jewels are; as we had a clear recollection of our former visit to the armory, where the keys of loyal cities, flags, and arms are kept; as the kitchens were of no moment now, since the Sultan does not dine at this place, nor visit much at the new kiosk above, we gave our mind to the recital of the horrors of the place which Dionysius did not exaggerate, but illustrated with faithful detail and gesture. Pointing through the Porte to a window within, he said:

"That is the throne of the Sultan. He sat there. He could see, but none outside see him. Here ambassadors were presented, who could only feel the presence. Here, too, he sat to observe the beheading of his unfaithful subjects. Here, on this path, and right on this stone, was placed the platter with the bloody head!"

Sweet thought! reminding one of a Herodian picture which, I think, we have seen somewhere in some of the galleries of Europe. Then, as Dionysius saw our open-mouthed wonder, ready to take in whole hecatombs of slaughter, he dilated on sanguinary Sultans till the air grew red hot.

"Here where you sit"—how I leaped to my feet!—"on that very stone, the heads, when chopped off, were mashed into atoms, after being dried three days upon yonder crosses above the gate!"

Just then a eunuch (for they still hover about, though the dear ladies are gone up the river on the hill opposite) comes along, swinging his beads, and looking as black as ten devils, and as ugly as sin. We get out of his way.

"Who is he?" I ask.

"He is the head jailer of the female prison that we saw yonder outside the gate."

Although the sack may not be used now, the prison is handy and useful. I lean against a fountain to rest. I am satiated with headless cadavers. I try to read an inscription over the fountain, when I am startled to hear Dionysius exclaim in hoarse whispering to my wife:

"Lady, you are sitting on the very stone on which were these bloody executions!"

She turned her head calmly, though I saw she was pale. It was a stone nicely arranged for a seat.

"That fountain," he says, "used to run with——"

"Blood?" say I.

"No—water! There the executioner washed his gory hands after he used the axe."

I turned pale also. I shall never forget these three sanguinary stones and that polluted fountain, not as long as a deadhead haunts a theatre or rides upon a railroad.

Going out of this court we pass the porphyry tombs of the old church of St. Erin, where, in Greek and with Greek crosses, the early Greek rulers were celebrated. Some pumpkin vines innocently run about these tombs now. They bloom and bear, unconscious of the terrible scenes which this locality once witnessed.

Now to St. Sophia, Church of Divine Wisdom! Illustrious monument to Constantine! Built, rebuilt, rebuilt again by the great Emperors, beginning in the fourth and completed in the sixth century! Marbles, granite, porphyry of every color and from every quarry and temple from Ephesus to Athens, from Baalbec to Egypt! Fire and earthquake, and last, Moslem conquerors, have not destroyed but only added to its wondrous name. The story of its building, the number of its architects and workmen, the Emperor or angel who conceived it, the immense cost, the traditions of the seraphs who around it kept ward, the opulent altar, the immense cupola and dome, the doors of ivory, amber, and cedar, the veneered planks from Noah's ark, its courts, passages, vestibules, belfries, and galleries, its minarets outside and altars within; above all, its pillars above pillars, its majesty of artistic proportion, boldness of design, and splendor of execution, not to speak of the imperial seats and grand offices and dignities to which it was dedicated, make it the most wonderful edifice in the world, St. Peter's only excepted.

The spirit of the temple—ah! what is that? Seven different orders of priesthood, from the Imam to the Kasim, represent its genii now, where priests and deacons by the hundred served at its altar through the early centuries. Here once the most eloquent of divines, St. John Chrysostom, ministered and preached, and with silver tongue and golden lip made the Saviour and his Beatitudes most beautiful to the entranced Greek and enraptured Oriental; and here now minister muftis by the hundred, whose services we have seen on three occasions, and commentators interpret the Koranic law with a strictness worthy of a democratic canon applied to our constitutional charter.

The other night at ten, my wife and myself started for this temple of fame. She had not seen it upon our former visit, though we made a desperate effort. Our firman from the government of 1851 was complete. A Turkish soldier then accompanied us with a dragoman. There were four in our own party—a cousin of my wife, then a golden-haired Ohio girl, now a Chicago matron, and my wife's brother, of genial memory, now no more. We were fortified by two British officers, then stationed at Corfu, which was ruled by an English Lord High Commissioner. Well do I recall them. One, as I have read, was killed in the Crimean war, Colonel Fordyce; and the other, Captain O'Reilly, an Irishman, who made the life of our voyage most merry back to the isles where the Hesperides were fabled to be situated, and who furnished us golden fruit from its gardens. What has become of him? Has he given his life as well as sword to England in her wars in India and Africa? *Quantum mutatus!*—all how changed; and we here! I shall never forget the solid and gleeful company, made up of German and French, as well as Irish, English, and American visitors, as we marched and exulted that bright morning in July at the prospect of seeing this cathedral of the Divine Wisdom, so hallowed by time, history, and vicissitudes! It was also, as now, in the Ramazan season. We stood at the door, presented our passes, and each nationality had its cavass and dragoman. Word came out for us to leave. Our guides persisted. We held our places. A second word came, "We must go off!" It was accompanied by a remark that we were condemned infidel giaours, dogs of Christians, and some other tender epithets. Our guides persisted. Had they not the Turkish as well as other governments behind them? They counted foolishly. They should not have urged. We were not then fully advised of the power of the mosque above all other powers. Still we held our ground until some four or five hundred Moslems collected about us. With angry threats and suspicious movements, much like a mob, they rushed about the door, at which appeared—hideous object!—a black slave, a Nubian of most unpleasant aspect and grating voice. He held a rattan, and laid it cleverly over the shoulders of our dragoman. The soldier retreated. Our English officers, including the German and French, worked out of the crowd. My wife, brother, and cousin receded. I hardly knew how, but I was left solitary and alone, and covered my retreat with a Vesuvius stick which I had used on the volcano against insurgent lazzaroni, and still carried for protection against the dogs of this city, then more numerous than now.

The meaning of the performance, as we learned, was our ill-starred attempt, in Ramazan time, when the Turks were fasting and ill-disposed, and while prayers were going on, to enter this sanctuary of Islam.

However, next morning at daybreak, while the devout Turks were asleep after the excesses of the nocturnal feasting, some of us ascended to the gallery by a back door and through a long, dark passage, with the aid of a paid Moslem servitor, and there looked down and around upon the splendid temple. But it was a surreptitious and anxious gaze or peep from behind the porphyry and granite columns. How we sped in those few minutes from post to pillar, looking at the big letters of gold upon green canvas, twenty feet long to the letter, announcing that "God is the light of the heavens and the earth!" How we wondered at the nondescript six-winged seraphims—Gabriel, Michael, Raphael, and Israfael—companions of Mohammed, once orthodox angels of the Greek Church, whose faces are now purposely obscured! How quickly flew through our vision the 107 columns, each one a grand larceny from other temples, with the fancy capitals, and how swam in the mystical light the great void below the dome, which was lifted on four grand arches! Such were the hasty, but entrancing glances, or our recollection of them now, as the scene recurs to our memory.

In this my wife did not partake, so that when, the other night, we approached the dark rear gate to the same gallery we had not a little apprehension. It was soon relieved by a slippered and slippery Moslem, bearing a lighted taper, and under Dionysian guidance we reached the upper gallery, where the old time came back with its rush of associations.

It is Ramazan again, and on the 24th day. It is the night of Predestination, the night for special illumination by 6,000 lamps. Oh, for Edison, Brush, and Jablochkoff with their electric glories! But the Moslem lamps did very well without their aid. Perhaps the semi-gloom added to the weird scene. When we entered, the service from the upper and nether platforms, where the priests sit or kneel, was going on. The responses were made by the immense congregation, formed in lines upon the matting, all shoeless, or rather with shoes upon troughs of wood in front of the lines. These lines front toward the holy house of the Kaaba at Mecca, and therefore the faces of the faithful are not turned toward the old Greek altar, but to the south-east. This looks odd and breaks the harmony, but it does not change the lyrical cadences of the service, as with one accord, at a given signal, these devout people, in various costumes and of various tribes, but in unison, bow with foreheads to the floor thrice, and to Mecca always. Then a Quaker quiet comes—the hush as if for the Great Day. Then again, resting a minute thus, another chant or wail ascends from the priestly seats, and the crowd arises and stands in silence till a further chant rings through the vast arches and dome. It was the very quintescence of awfulness, and could not fail to impress the oriental soul. It was not for us to make light of this ceremony, though we saw some English visitors laughing at it as if it were a farce.

A second visit, along with the families of our Minister and Consul, whom we felt qualified to induct into this gallery and ceremony, did not weaken this impression. Nor was it strengthened on our visit yesterday to the floor and body of the temple. Without aid of firman or soldier, and without fear, we found ourselves within the gates. We put on slippers, according to the custom, and glided awkwardly over the matting, to see the altar, the lace-like carved marble capitals, the many-colored marble columns, and the gilded dome. We desired a nearer view. Whether because my slippers were modeled for Cinderella and would not stay on my tiny feet, or whether because my sense of noting was not keen, I have turned to my wife's journal. Here is her description:

As we enter the vestibule the guide calls attention to a side column with a hole in it, shaped much like an eye. Here those diseased in that organ dip their fingers, and, rubbing their eyes, with a murmured prayer, are supposed to find a cure. Our two visits have been made at night. Now, by day the mosque looks quite differently. Neat matting covers the floor, and we were given the usual slippers for entrance. We found them rather large and difficult to use, but by dint of slipping along, without lifting the foot from the floor, we managed it. S. S. happened to sneeze, and, as one does often by habit, expectorated after it, and immediately our Turk was enraged. He sharply reproved "the infidel," and, taking his handkerchief, commenced vigorously wiping out the supposed stain. We looked at our guide, but he only smiled disdainfully and sadly. It was a Greek smile which a Spartan might have envied. The matting was not laid straight across, but on the slant, that the devout might, in kneeling, turn toward Mecca. It was arranged in rows, and low wooden troughs were placed between each to hold the shoes, I suppose—possibly outer garments—thus preserving intact the neatness of the floor. After all, were it not for this sacred reverence in taking off shoes and using slippers, I do not see how these mosques would be fit for entrance, much less worship and prayer, for as these Turks bring in on their persons such a filthy lot of rags it would be unendurable. Then, as there are no chairs or benches, the floors are used for sitting, kneeling, and bowing, and to them many touch their foreheads.

The mosque is vast and airy; the marble columns of Ephesus are seen to better advantage, and those of porphyry are immense in diameter and height. At one-fourth the height of one of the columns is a break, like the cut of a sabre, were it of a material that a sword could cleave.

"This is its history," says our guide: "Mohammed II., the conqueror, rode into this church on horseback over the dead bodies of the slain Greeks, packed like sardines in this their last refuge from the victorious Turk, and it was he who struck this column with his scimiter, and afterward reaching across to the wall, he left the impress of his blood-stained hands."

This huge and bloody hand, with fingers wide spread, is there in outline; but it looks more like the thoughtless impress of the barbarous Turkish artist, on his undried paint, when, in his unartistic vengeance, he tried to obliterate all signs of the former possessors, the Greeks, by painting out every Greek cross and defacing every figure of the Greek archangels! But the mosaic outlines and forms of cross and angel remain beneath the Moslem's superficial paint; and these were pointed out with zealous pride by our Greek guide!

"Do you see those cannon over the door entry?" the guide asks.

"Yes; but they are stone, are they not?"

"There is a story about them, quite childish, but like others of this strange people. It is this: That there was a saying among the Greeks that this church and city would never be conquered by the Turks till these cannon of brass turned to stone; and see, stone they are!"

The faithful are assembling for prayers. It is a fête day, the fifth anniversary of the present Sultan's accession. A burly Turk asks:

"Why do you linger? We are going to prayers."

Our guide answers: "We have paid for the entrance, and do not intend to be hurried."

Three seven-year-old children, having long skirts on—we know not if they are boys or girls—are playing horse in a lively manner, and in imitation of Mohammed II., the Conqueror, who rode into this church. They ran at large over the mosque, to our astonishment; but they are soon called to order, and fall upon their knees and begin their devotions *à la* Turk. Last week we observed the same performance of five small children playing " ring-around," but between times keeping up a faint semblance of prayer by tumbling over each other, helter-skelter, upon their knees in proper though temporary devotional attitude. It would seem that children are a law unto themselves in a Mohammedan mosque! At times, with the recitative of the priest and the responses, the service was very impressive; and by night, in the dim light, it is a weird and striking scene.

Thus endeth the journal and our united impressions of this wonderful building and the spirit which it enshrines. It is an immense minster and mosque, for it is both, even yet. We leave it and go into the warmer air, haunted, as we were years ago, by those six-winged monsters, who seem like Sphinxes in the desert of human doubt and experience, and horrified at the stories of carnage forever connected with this temple of peace, into which the proud Moslem rode to defy and degrade its old Christian masters.

Dionysius, who is not very gossipy, makes a curious comment on this double relation and quality, by a story of some Russian ladies whom he gallanted a few weeks before the late Russian war. One of the ladies caught sight of her own cross half hidden by the Moslem gilding. Her eye pierced beneath the lacquer to find the forms of angel, saint, and Saviour, familiar to the church of her childhood. Bursting into tears, she was about to drop upon her knees and pray to the God—not of Mohammed, but of Jesus—when arrested by a gesture from the frightened guide, who turned pale at the consequences, in the then state of the Turkish mind.

"Is this not," she cried, "our church, ours? Oh! my God, ours?"

In a frenzy she was led from the church of the fathers of her religion.

Do you wonder that the Czars, who are the head of her religion, have yearned to take this city, where the traditions, history, and glories of their faith still repose, though suppressed by force and veiled by another faith?

Another mosque, that of Sulieman the Magnificent, which we visited, had no Greek glamour or tradition. It was built by the Turks. It has a beauty, cleanliness, and freshness that reminds us of St. Isaac's in St. Petersburg. But having seen one mosque, you have an idea of all. In this mosque are carpets and flags, representing Mecca and Medina.

There is a third mosque, called that of the Pigeons, into whose court we went. A few piastres for a handful of millet, and the pigeons fly down into the court in rustling multitudes from minaret and dome and every nook in the vast place. These birds are sacred to Mohammed, and receive hospitality, as do the dogs, according to some divine lesson in the Koran.

On our way to the Hippodrome we pass another large plane or sycamore tree, hollow and tenanted. A hermit, with sore eyes, lives in it, but he is not very astute. I asked him to write me his name on a card. He put his head out of his hole, and, to my discomfort, bawled for one of the cross-legged scribes, who, as in old Jerusalem, sit at the corners of the streets, and act as notary publics or scriveners for the people.

We are upon classic ground again at the famous Hippodrome. It was an old Greek circus, with seats and ring. It is now a square, filled with objects of ancient renown, which could not well be ruined by janizary and war, or eaten by fire and time. Here the actors, riders, and charioteers of the imperial days assembled. The gates are gone, the porticoes demolished, the columns dust. The Veneti, who were Greek prætorians, like the janizaries of the Turkish empire, here met and menaced the existence of society and order. From these factions and crimes came the final ruin of this Greek empire. Its obelisk remains, as fresh as when it came from Heliopolis. The machines by which it was reared are cut in stone upon its pediment. Commander Gorringe has improved upon the plan, with which, doubtless, he became familiar. It was erected as the goal of the races of the Hippodrome. The brass column of the three serpents, heads off, is greened by exposure. It has a mystical and sacred meaning and inscription, which Rawlinson in his Herodotus has explained. The burnt column is a singular wreck of upright matter, and yet it stands one hundred feet high, surviving fire and sword, priest and conqueror. The emperor or god, whose effigy once adorned its top, is not known. Other columns are around, and marked by inscriptions in old Greek and Latin, which marvelously survive much that had more seeming durability. One antiquity has been so buried that time could not touch it with a single tooth. It is the cistern of Constantine. It is under-ground. It had three under-ground compartments, held up by 1,000 pillars. The upper story remains. Into it we went. It has been filled with the rubbish of ages. It is a gloomy place, dimly lighted, and used by artisans. We found their wheels whizzing in the damp and murky air, and boys running about the pillars as if at play, reeling up the silken and golden thread so much used in the fabrics of the Orient.

"Why not," we asked of the foreman, "use machines?"

He caught at it at once. "Your English and American machines are too expensive. They get out of repair. We cannot make by them, as we cannot repair them. We prefer the old method. It costs little for our labor."

It is the old story of labor-saving machines, which have changed the employment of four-fifths of the world, and always under protest.

Then we visited a strange exhibition. It is the Museum of Ancient Costumes. As we went into the alley where it is, one thousand young Turks were rushing out of the Polytechnic School, where they are taught all the manual trades, such as carpenter, blacksmith, and others. Threading our way through their noisy unstinted glee—for boys are boys, whether under fez or hat—we enter a wax-work exhibition which Mme. Tussaud might envy. It represents the old Turks of different trades and professions, white and black eunuchs, as well as the other officers of the old régime, when the janizary was paramount, and the Sultan had his cook and dwarf, headsman and vizier, surgeon and eunuch, and each had a habit as well as habitude peculiarily his own. Such turbans and garments; such an arsenal of yataghans and pistols, and such bundles of sash and other tawdry toggery never was gotten together in a French opera bouffé to burlesque human power and weakness, or make extravagant its excesses and vanities.

Near our hotel are the dancing dervishes. I suppose there are ample descriptions of these dervishes and their mummeries, but I have not read them. I give what I saw. The dancing sect whirl around gently on their toes. Their arms are extended and eyes sleepy or dreamy. They keep their places, like stars in their orbits, as they move around, while a solemn brother, with arms folded and in prayer, moves between the revolving orbs! Their robes fly out as though they would make a cheese, as the children used to say. They have a sweet chant. Their closed eyes and whirl indicate that they see the invisible Allah wherever they turn!

These do not howl. For that we went to Scutari. There is a convent of them there. We passed behind the curtain and went up into the gallery, looking down into a court. There was an altar and a group of variously dressed dervishes. Some were soldiers, some boys, some little girls in tinseled dresses. Some were black as ebony, some tall, some small, some thin, some handsome, some hideous, and all joined in the prayers and chants. A few kneeled on sheepskin, while others formed a hollow square and began swaying and singing, while the tum-tum of the tambourine and clash of cymbals gave out the pleasing concord of a threshing-machine. When the agony was sufficient, and the steam was on with a full head, the swaying and howling and barking and snapping and jerking of head and body, and the frothing and hard breathing and general diabolism began. The song was repetitious, and not unmusical at intervals, where a flutelike melody, instrumental, came in as a prelude to additional howling. We stood this for an hour.

One man, of excellent appearance, with long, glossy auburn hair and a rich voice, as it sounded out "Allah!" and "Mahmoud!" seemed to be the chief, and ruled them with a look. He gave a glance, and off would go a coat, or a turban, or their high, white, sugar-loaf hat, and on would go a white nightcap. One African, of the worst aspect ever seen on a human face, if, indeed, it was not a visor hiding the human face, seemed to be as lithe and loathsome as a snake. He was six feet and more, and in his bare feet. His tongue would loll out, and his body would contort till you could hardly see what form it had. The negro minstrels, when they mimic the excesses of the negroes South at their revivals, are but faint copies of the wildness of this Nubian beast, as he twisted, snapped, clucked, barked, and howled.

We went out for fresh air, to return to see this strangest of ceremonies. The chief and some of his subordinates were sitting cross-legged and making sacred knots in white napkins when we re-entered. Then prone on their faces were arranged a dozen of children, from two months old up to twelve; and this dervish walked over and on their bodies. Yes, on them, each and all. I would not have believed it, had I not seen it. Not once, but four times, these prostrate lines of children were formed, and he trod on them each and all. Whereupon they arose sanctified and cleared of disease; for that is the theory. In came a soldier and lay flat. He had the rheumatism. Along with him a line was formed, some of the same little ones going flat again. Over the lot the chief traveled. The soldier got up and kissed the dervish's hand. The dervish placed his foot on the upper part of the thigh, behind. Any surgeon may tell you whether this is a vulnerable spot. Not a child whimpered, not a soul smiled. I could neither enjoy nor cease to wonder.

What is the solution of this seeming physical paradox? That question I asked of a gentleman learned in the customs here. He said: "Did you observe two priests in loose robes on each side of the line, holding the chief's arms?"

"Yes, but I did not see that they could have carried him safely over, allowing only a slight touch to the children with the priestly foot."

"That," said he, "is my solution, and the only one I have. Two strong men might do it after much practice."

From this puzzling and unique ceremony we rough it over some hard roads to the top of the cemetery in Scutari, saw the famed grave which the Sultan built over the horse which fell dead when the captain rode him to that spot with the news of the fall of Constantinople; and then, turning down many lanes and streets over Asiatic ground, we entered the English cemetery. It is a beautiful spot, and well cared for. It is in great contrast with the Turkish and other graveyards hereabouts. A magnificent granite column, supported by colossal figures, rises here to the memory of the Crimean soldiers. It overlooks the city and the sea, the Bosphorus and the Seraglio Point. In vain my wife sought in this sacred spot for the grave of her old friend, Mrs. Edward Joy Morris, who died here while her accomplished husband was minister. We left with many sad memories, which were soon obliterated by the cheerful breeze upon the waters, and after a day of days found our rest at Pera.

CHAPTER X.

THE CHANGES IN THE TURKISH CAPITAL WITHIN THIRTY YEARS—DYNASTY AND DYNAMITE—THE TOMBS OF THE SULTANS.

*With my own power, my majesty they wound,
In the King's name, the King himself's uncrowned,
So doth the dust destroy the diamond.*
—MAJESTY IN MISERY, CHARLES I.

WE find but few changes here, such as we find in other cities of Europe. The Asiatic still encamps upon both sides of the Bosphorus. Even the tombs of the Sultans are, notwithstanding the Koran, which intimates that Europe is no lasting home for the faithful, here upon this side of the river. Hotels, kiosks, terraces, palaces, villas, embassies, and conveyances have changed. Iron ferries fly the red flag with its crescent and star up and down the stream; large ironclads anchor near the home of departed houris; but the same gilded kiosk and gaudy caïque, the same veiled women, miserable cemeteries, and melancholy mosques; the same fountains, bazaars, and barracks remain, with the same dirt, dogs, and dervishes. Photographs appear in Pera at the shops, and French is more universally spoken. The ladies have more diaphanous veils, and the men less ostentatious turbans; but the old element remains, notwithstanding the Crimean war. The slave behind her dark veil, hiding every feature, still trudges behind her mistress. The mistress has exchanged her yellow, gawky slippers for high-heeled and gorgeous gaiters. The minaret tops all, and the mosques, with their mortgages upon property and soul, have not be encanceled. The age of archery and Greek fire, which foiled the Bulgarian, Goth, and Persian in their attempts upon the now dismantled walls, gave way to an age of personal chivalry in the crusaders' day and in the age of Mohammedan empire; and that empire is giving way, inch by inch, it may be, to the spirit which commerce "calls from its vasty deep." What a wonderful city! What changes in two thousand years, if not in a third of a century! As I reckon them by history, and not by my own experiences, there have been six changes of masters, and twenty from unsuccessful sieges. Rome had the city. After centuries she made it the capital of the East. Then its emperors besieged it, and then the Persians and the Arabs again and again; then the Russians four times; then the Latin crusaders, who temporarily succeeded, and the Counts of Flanders furnished the emperors under Venetian patronage and enterprise; and finally, when the western nations were preparing for adventure in a new world, and the Moors were fighting to hold Spain, Mohammed II. swooped down upon the city, and by the aid of the towers of Asia and Europe gave to it a new faith.

Since his day, from 1481 to 1882, twenty-eight Sultans have held their revels and their rule; exactly four hundred years, at the rate of seven Sultans per century, or an average of a little over fourteen and two-sevenths of a year per Sultan. If the present Sultan, Abdul Hamid II., holds on a few years more, the average since the conquest will be made good since the accession of the Sultan of 1851, Abdul Mejid.

Studying the mortality of these rulers, and in the light of recent dynastic dangers from dynamite and daggers on the Neva and Bosphorus, led me to think of the present Sultan and the situation. As I write, the guns of the forts are thundering out the fifth anniversary of his reign. It is well known how he obtained power. There is a party of progressists who do not look kindly on him. He is supposed to belong to the party which disfavors advancement. My judgment is that he is more opposed to the aggressions upon his rights and dignities by western powers than to reform. He may yet lead a Jehàd to save his empire.

He lives in great seclusion in his yellow palace, somewhat aloof and apart, on the hills of the European side of the Bosphorus. He comes forth but rarely and cautiously, as Czars do nowadays. He is bound to go to certain mosques on certain days, and on Fridays always.

We saw him the other day at the mosque below the palace; but we waited for him in a miscellaneous and unenthusiastic crowd for two hours. The soldiery were there on guard. They surrounded the entrance and lined the streets between the high walls. The people were not near. Bands came and played music; officers of state arrived and were ushered through the ranks. At length there was a blast of trumpets—a good deal like a circus summons for the grand cavalcade. The gates of the palace opened! We peeped into the secret and beauteous grounds. Lo! led by servants in gala attire, some riderless horses appeared. It is a custom which follows the Sultan. Then came a man in a plain fez and on a white horse. It was the Sultan! He seemed sallow; but he is not ill-looking. He is like all Turks, for they all look alike. The hush of expectancy was over. A rush and a crush was made after him as he dismounted and entered the mosque. A shrill cry went up from the priests, which reminded the Sultan that he also is mortal and God is great. The crowd dispersed, and the Sultan stayed and prayed.

He is in perpetual prayer, or is expected to be, in these fasting days of Ramazan and festive days of Bairam. At the close of the former he was married—again. It was his annual marriage at a mosque. It was public in one sense, but "no cards" to us. Every year the Turkish empire is winnowed for the handsomest young lady to adorn the palace as a new wife. The mother of the Sultan selects from the bevy of beauties gathered from "silken Samarcand to cedared Lebanon." One of the singular laws of royal marriage here is, that the wife becomes the slave, when married, to his Majesty. Why? Because the Crown Prince, or future Sultan, must be a born slave himself, and thus less in rank than the free people of the realm he governs! This is odd, but it is oriental.

Again, this week the Sultan appeared in Scutari, where he met all the military pashas, beys, and Ulemas, riding on white horses and wearing ribboned turbans. The latter are the priestly interpreters of the Law and the Prophet. They display great pomp in the procession when the Sultan enters the Church of the Six Minarets.

The present Sultan is not a large man. He is regarded as able, and manages his own matters with adroitness. When Abdul Aziz was deposed in 1876, Murad V. succeeded to the throne. He also was deposed after only two months' rule, because of an alleged weak intellect, thus making two weaklings who have given way under ministerial or priestly dictation. There is much unrest among the Turks because of these untoward and suspicious changes, which has been promoted by the recent extraordinary trial and exile of Midhat Pasha for the alleged assassination of Aziz.

Therefore, we were not a little curious to see the present Sultan, who seems to master the situation, which is surrounded by so much doubt and danger. We had once seen the Sultan Abdul Mejid, amid 40,000 troops, on a grand day for the reception of the chief of the Mohammedan religion from Mecca. No special guard was needed then. But dynamite and assassination have made necessary these precautions. When the anniversary of his coronation came the other day, it was said that the Sultan became nervous and uncertain. First, he was to give a grand dinner at his palatial seat, at which he himself was to preside—a rare concession and ceremony. He was to show himself very happy generally. The dinner was to be given to the ambassadors and chief men. It was discarded, however, on the plea of poverty. After spending several thousand pounds, it was ascertained that it would be indelicate to have a roystering jamboree when the pay of all the soldiers and officers was so far in arrear—a year or more. Making a virtue of this fact, the Sultan postponed his feast. A week or so ago, some Italian subjects of sinister motions and conduct were arrested for conspiracy to kill the Sultan. Their explanation was that their dynamite explosives were only intended for killing fish in the

Sea of Marmora. But something still less serious made a greater outcry. The custom-house officials stopped some balls having in them explosive materials. They consisted of four globes and three ivory pipes. The globes were sent to experts. The Master of Artillery, Ali Saib, was at the head of a commission to report. Chemists were called in. Three little suspicious perforations in the upper hemisphere of the ball were found, and found covered, but the cover was removed by a key! Sodium was found in them. It burns vividly when thrown in water. The commission decided that the balls were pyrotechnics, and so they were, but useful ones. They were intended to be thrown into the water in case of a person overboard at night, when the illumination would help to save. An instrument for life-saving was thus the means of affright. The consignees are out in a card in French, which I have just seen, saying: "It is not our fault if the *employés intelligents de la douane* cannot distinguish between salvation and destruction!"

I am half inclined to wonder whether some ghost of the dead past has not reappeared upon or within these walls, with the ancient Greek fire, at which the timid besiegers of Constantinople were wont to be baffled and astounded. In an old record of one of the sieges of this city, which lasted seven years, it is said that the Engineer Callinicus of Baalbec, a city of Syria, discovered the famous Greek fire, which being composed of several combustible substances, such as naphtha, sulphur, nitre, and turpentine, had the property of burning under water. Its flame, instead of rising upward, presented the opposite phenomenon, and its heat was so intense as to destroy stones and iron. It could not be extinguished except with vinegar, sand, and urine. When they threw it on a vessel or a building, these were consumed with a terrifying noise. Some pretend that the secret of this fire was discovered in 1756, but that it was suppressed through the wisdom of a philanthropic monarch!

Whatever the new discovery was, it doubtless led to the postponement of the Sultan's festivity. Still, the Bosphorus shores burned with innocent lamps, lit in crescents and stars by loyal subjects, and the embassies and pashas had their palaces similarly beautified. The shop opposite our hotel was illuminated—just as in London on the Queen's birthday the humble protégés of royalty make the largest displays. It was that of the Tailor to the Sultan.

It is not for me, after slight observation here, to make prognostics as to this government. It has survived so many left-handed omens that prophecy ought to be dumb. There is, notwithstanding the bad feeling as to Midhat Pasha, a feeling also of insecurity. Since the exile of Midhat there is said to be much suppressed indignation ready to flame. However, so far as it seems to me, the old order of thirty years ago, such as then I saw it, remains. There is no great or open violence, and certainly no drunkenness, visible in the city. Outside there is not so much certainty of protection and life. One of our friends, a Swede—Mr. Roos, a contractor—whom we meet at the Legation, has, within a fortnight, been attacked with knives by robbers outside of Therapia, on the hills beyond the Bosphorus, and again shot at, the ball going through his hat. A man was killed night before last, near our Legation, and there is not much or any sure punishment for the crime of murder. Considering the mixed quality of the population, these incidents are not more remarkable, perhaps, than similar ones in or near New York; and when we think of the masses of contrary-minded men of different races and religions, and of the Ramazan, when every Turk is cross, because hungry, the wonder is that nothing worse has happened. The wonder is that strangers, like ourselves, could pass, as we did, at night with a carriage, through the narrow and packed streets without a murmur of hindrance or trouble. No soldiers or police were visible when we made two of these ventures through the motley groups in Stamboul, on our way from the Mosque of St. Sophia.

In all these changes of city and dynasty, there is not, to our knowledge, one person whom we knew here thirty years ago now living here. This was my own private reflection. It had one exception, as I soon learned, and the incident which led to the knowledge of it is interesting enough to relate. I know that it is of more general importance to recount matters of public concern; but, after all, there is much truth in what "Eothen" says in his book, as to the interest which makes egotism the nucleus of travel and observation.

Observing this law of perspective, and recognizing myself as the centre of this interesting and restless capital, and reserving all statistics and history as the mere circumstances about my own personality, I will give my revisit to the tomb of Mahmoud II. He was the father of Mejid and Aziz, and is celebrated for his extermination of the janizaries.

These *turbehs*, as the imperial tombs are called, are generally in or around the mosques. Some of the Sultans have a mausoleum of their own, where the body is coffined in the ground; and in the sacred kiosk of rarest architecture above, is the tomb. It is generally covered with inscribed marble slabs, or invested with rich vestments.

I believe that after thirty years I could have gone alone to the tomb of Mahmoud II. Fifteen years after our visit to it, I had occasion to recall this splendid architectural tribute to the dead Sultan. When Mount Vernon was rescued from decay in 1857, by the women of America, many of the Congressmen were invited to visit the sacred spot and celebrate the event. On our return, upon the Potomac, after night, a splendid moon, in crescent, came forth to gladden and gild our passage to Washington. The Hon. John Cochrane, my predecessor from New York City, improvised some speaking on the boat; and out of my treasury of traveled experience came the memory of the circular and domed splendor, by the side of the burnt column at old Stamboul! Its white marble, its Corinthian pilasters, its gilded gratings, its mother-of-pearl biers laden with gold-embroidered velvet and cashmere shawls; the massive silver candlesticks and the tall candles holding the emblematic extinguishers of the light of life—all came to me then and there, to furnish a little rhetoric, and to point the moral as to our shameful neglect of the tombs of our great men! The moral has not yet lost its point.

When, therefore, we returned after thirty years to this tomb of the great Ottoman, not as a pilgrim gray like Honor in Collins' ode, nor as a weeping hermit like another abstraction, but as a real entity, did we find that time had effaced its beauty or relaxed the vigilance of its keepers? Had the velvets and shawls become the prey of the moth? Had rapine seized the diamond aigrette and plume upon the sultanic fez at the head of the tomb? Were the mother-of-pearl railings gone, the massive silver stolen, or the manuscript Koran burned? Let us take off our shoes, and with unsandaled feet enter. Ah! here still remain all these suits and trappings of external reverence. To them is added the tomb of Abdul Aziz, the son, and with it the massive silver candlestick and box holding another Koran, the gift of the mother, who melted down her own plate for the offering. The same beautiful illuminated Arabic Koran on the same stand was there by the great Sultan's tomb; and a boy is reading a Turkish edition near by, swaying as he reads, and smiling kindly on us as he sways. There seems to be no harsh or unfriendly feeling here. The warder of the tomb is a man whom I seem to have known. I ask him:

"Will you read me a passage of the Koran? Open it at a venture."

He opens it. He says: "I can read, but do not know what it means. It is Arabic. The letters are familiar, but I cannot translate."

"Well, then, I request you to read from the wall—the motto in gold."

He reads, and Dionysius, our guide, interprets: "Allah is the light of the world!"

I say to him: "This is not the thought of Mohammed alone. It is ours, as well as yours. In that all-seeing orb there gleams the light of the world for all His creatures. It shines on us, in a distant land, a far-beaming blaze of majesty! It brings me here from a land where there is a setless sun! Under that light men come and go, and come again! I went from this mosque thirty years ago, and have come again! Were you not here then?"

"Yes," he responded, "I was here thirty-eight years ago, and have been here ever since, as custodian. It is strange, most strange!"

"Do you recall the American party who were driven from the Mosque of St. Sophia, and who came here soon after, four in number, one a golden-haired girl—"

He pondered awhile, and at length he seemed to remember, or to believe that he recalled, us.

"Your name is— ?"

"Hafis Mehmet," said Dionysius. How good of him to remined us!

"The same," I said. "It is in my book and memory. It will be there again! May I live thirty years more, to come to you again, and may you be here to welcome me!"

"Isallah! If the Father God preserve us we will see each other again after thirty years."

"Then farewell, Hafis, my old friend."

"Adieu," he said in good French, as I proffered to him an unexpected hand, which he grasped.

"You are the only human being of this city whom I met here then, and recall now! Allah preserve and comfort you."

"*Allah! razi olah! Allah bereket versin!*"

"Praise to God! May God receive you!"

I would not have disturbed that man's creed for all the largesses of oriental empire. He may be a devotee of a "creed outworn," but he was the honest keeper of dead regalities, and faithful to his trust.

> "They do not wisely that with hurried hand
> Would pluck these salutary fancies forth
> As worthless weeds. Oh! little do we know
> When they have soothed—when saved!"

And so, resuming my shoes and the heat and dust of the pilgrimage of life, I leave Hafis to the "sessions of sweet silent thought to summon up remembrance" of the past two generations, which we have survived!

As I pass out I see a chamber full of all sorts of tombs, big and little, very well accoutred and cared for, but not regally as those of Aziz and his father Mahmoud.

"What and whose are they?" I asked of Dionysius.

Our guide is dazed at my tenderness toward the Ottoman with whom I just parted, or else his English and French are confused. He endeavors to explain, in a patois made up of Greek, Turkish, Armenian, French, and English, the latter predominating and utterly unintelligible.

"You know the Sultans have nusses—'vet you call them," he said.

"'Vet I call them? Why nurses, women with babies," I responded.

"Oh! yes, 'vet nusses. These 'vet nusses, vich give milk to the little Sultans, vich vill be big Sultans; they have little babies also, vich ven they nuss little Sultans, have no life more, and so they are buried here with their mothers."

This was not clear; I asked him to try it again.

"You understand," he resumed, "that when 'vet nusses suckle little Sultans, and have husbands and make new babies, the little babies have life no more, but in seven years they get killed because their mother nussed little baby Sultan, and must not nuss no more baby."

Ah, it dawns! These are the tombs provided by the lords of the land out of reverence to themselves, who alone should drink of the breasts of the nurse, to be followed by no vulgar little child at the same maternal source; for after seven years all such babies are killed, as there must not be two living offspring fed from the same lacteal fountain! I am to blame for not at once understanding better this now perspicuous statement; but I had filled my fancy full of the fate of little dead Sultans and Sultanas, with tiny turbans and veils over their tombs, who, under certain policies of state, were strangled after birth in order to limit the line of succession to the throne.

CHAPTER XI.

THE OTTOMAN EMPIRE AS SEEN BENEATH THE SURFACE—ITS DEGENERACY—ITS CORRUPTION AND VENALITY—THE DEAD TURKISH PARLIAMENT—THE UNITED STATES AND TURKEY.

> *A feeble government, eluded laws,*
> *A factious populace, luxurious nobles,*
> *And all the maladies of sinking states*
> *When public villainy, too strong for justice,*
> *Shows his bold front, the harbinger of ruin.*
> —IRENE, *Act 1.*

ON the fifth anniversary of the present Sultan's reign, some of the journals here eulogized his rule for the progress made since his accession. The facts do not fully bear out the praise. What the external signs of Turkish wealth and progress are, I have shown in dealing only with historic events and social incidents, and as compared with my former visit here in 1851. It is of more moment to those who would study the empire for its lessons in economic and social science to know the real results of this peculiar civilization, and the present condition of Turkish industries, trade, and finance. This study I found partly done to my hand in a report made last month by our able Consul-General, Mr. Heap, which I am kindly permitted to peruse in advance of its publication. I select from it not the details, but some of the leading facts, leaving deductions to be drawn by others of a philosophical turn of mind.

That Turkey has partaken a little of the general advancement of mankind since 1851 is easily observed. Three new Sultans and divers Ministers have come and gone since then, but that is of less moment than the coming and going of the steamships and rail trains, which make of this harbor and city a picture as unlike that of 1851, as that of the New York of 1850 is unlike that of to-day.

We perceive in our hotel and from the papers that financial men are here holding séances with the financial minister, Said Pasha, as to the non-interest-paying bonds. We know, too, how strangely mixed are the revenues under the peculiar system of their farming and collection. All these are signs not unlike that of a coroner's presence, that a dead body is about or about to be about. But for the miraculous resurrection of Turkey so often, we might regard her as moribund, if not deceased. Add the distrust occasioned by the singular death of the late Sultan, and the banishment, under a form of trial, of one of the progressive statesmen of this country, Midhat Pasha, and you may understand why Turkey is not exempt from domestic apprehensions as well as from external troubles.

These external troubles grow out of the unrest of the autonomous provinces of Europe, and the urgency of the treaty powers for promised reforms, as well as of the incipient impatience of Greece and Albania, where the chronic foe of the Turk lurks and lives. It is impossible to make a proper photograph of these serious aspects of Turkey without some simple statements as to its polity.

Turkey is a monarchy, with a Constitution, said to be limited. What the limits are, has been with the Turks and others quite as grave a discussion as the limitations of our American Constitution. The Ulemas have a chief, who is, like our own Chief Justice, the head of the judicature; but, unlike him, he is chief judge of spiritual matters. When he interprets the law, or the Koran, or the Constitution, he does it under the favor of the Sultan. If the Sultan be truly grand, like the second Mahmoud, who obtained a decision that enabled him legally to slaughter the janizaries, he will have his own interpretation of the organic statutes. Graciously permitting the chief and court of the Ulemas to interpret, he will pound them to death in a mortar if they do not interpret as he desires. This is no joke, and in the aforetime was a serious matter to the Ulemas. But when a Sultan like the present one is on the throne, there is no great fear that he will override the decision of the Ulemas, even if it be outside the record or opposite to his own view or will. The present chief of Islam and head of the Ulemas is, therefore, more potent than the Prime Minister of a Sultan.

There is a responsible Ministry here, which has charge, as in other countries, of departments; but the Legislature is an absent body. Did this nation ever have a Parliament or Congress? Yes; and have yet—on paper. In their stress, during the Russian war, a Congress was called. Its members were selected by the Governors of the provinces, and in some form of election. Still, it began to crystallize and talk, and make rules and inquiries of the Ministers. Questions quite inconvenient were put as to taxes and trials, revenues and rogues, and some bold young men from the remote districts began to grow eloquent, and bard-headed old sheiks began to show how sensible they were. All at once a proclamation dissolved, as a proclamation had made, them. A young and eloquent member from Antioch, who was quite anxious about certain corruptions, was sent home under Government convoy, and the honorable gentleman from Jerusalem found his city of refuge in London. The city of Solomon was utterly inconsequential in the affairs of war, peace, and taxation. This Congress was interesting as an experiment. It showed how out of mere gaseous elements there were gathering stars for an oriental heaven of oratory; Websters, Clays, and Calhouns of solid logic and eloquence, and Damascus blades and jeweled yataghans of wit and rhetoric. Sultans, as Presidents sometimes, do not like Legislatures to be near them; and the simplest souls of republics are those who bemoan the sessions of Legislatures as if they were more harmful than unrestricted and corrupt power.

Turkey has connected with her certain provinces in Europe which have some autonomy and some local legislative faculties. There is a pressure to increase this home rule. England has urged the Sultan to this end, and her urgency would have immense emphasis, if the Turk did not point to Ireland and smile!

Her provinces are ruled by Governors. They are divided into departments; and these again, à la mode Française, into arrondissements, with corresponding grades of officers. There are no titles of nobility, but there are affixes, like Pasha, Effendi, Bey, Aga, and others, which betoken official or family station. There is but one restraint upon these officials, that of the Sultan's will, if he chooses to use it, and that of the chief of Islam and his College of Ulemas. There is, therefore, not much responsibility among the officials. Like all satrapies, the provinces in Asia are governed by the will of one man, distant from the source of power.

There is an affluence of wealth in this realm, if it could only have the magic wand to strike the rock and bid it flow. But there is a fear of Christian or western control that stops enterprise.

The population is composite. Even at the start of the empire by Othman, a Greek woman became the wife of the founder, and the descendants of this woman still rule, to exemplify the mixed condition of affairs and people. There is no sentiment of nationality, such as Cicero describes, and as we and other nations have it. The Moslem faith is the common sentiment. Bagdad and Bosnia have a common Koran, and Broussa and Morocco a common Mohammed. Morocco may have her own local government, and so may Roumelia, but the faith, which is one, makes a mutual citizenship in all this vast theocracy of Islam. The theory is that the Koran being dictated by the Angel Gabriel, Mohammed received it passively, and all his descendants, including the Sultan, are under the law, not above it. When, therefore, a great thing like the killing off of the janizaries is to be done, the Ulema's decision is called for. One of the Sultans desires to drink champagne. The chief Ulema decides that it is not a drink to be prohibited, as it did not exist when Gabriel blew his horn and gave the law. In a word, citizenship is creed. *Dar-ul-Islam*, from Afghanistan to Bulgaria, is the world, and that is the country of Islam. All outside goes for nothing in theory. When, therefore, people speak of reforming Turkey they must reform Mohammedanism. This is no easy task, if we are to believe in the recent reports of its devotees. What a world it is—Africans, Malays, Tartars, Arabs, Chinese, not to speak of the people of Turkey. It is not bounded by Turkey in Europe or Turkey in Asia. The Turk is a chief sign and figure-head, but he does not rule the forty millions of Mussulman East Indians, or the thirty millions of Mussulman Malays, or the fifteen millions of Mussulman Chinese, or the ten millions of Mussulman Africans, or the five millions of Egyptian Mussulmans, and the other Barbary eighteen millions, or the eleven and a half millions of Mohammedan Arabs, or the six millions of Circassian Tartars, and five million others.

A careful writer in the *Fortnightly Review* gives a tabular statement of Islamism and its nationalities. They are computed from the arrivals at Mecca, and are astonishing, if true. It is an odd way of census-taking; but it is the best mode to be had, as no registrar or census bureau exists in Turkey or in the Mohammedan countries. He makes 175,000,000 as the total of Islam. There are among them many sects, but with these ideas as their bond, viz., one God, a future life of reward or punishment, and revelation to the forerunners of, as well as to Mohammed himself. There are some wine-drinking, polytheistic, and other heterodox opinions and creeds; but at least 175,000,000 are genuine orthodox Mohammedans, and the question often comes up when aggressions are made, as in India or Tunis: What if there were a Jehád, or religious war?

There was a sect called Wahhabites, numbering 8,000,000. They did not accept the faith as finished, but believed that inquiry and revision might ever be made. They were guilty of excesses. They destroyed tombstones and minarets, and the sect fell. Then reform halted. Heresy failed, and the Moslem of Arabia, where the reform started, relapsed into acquiescence about the shrines of Medina and Mecca as holy—alone holy!

It is, therefore, urged by some recent observers that reform in Turkey is impossible so long as it is impossible in the religion of the land, and that all attempts to make life and property safe, and the rights of conscience sacred, will be delayed, if not fail altogether. All analogies as to the refinement and progress made by this race, as in Spain by the Moors, is otherwise accounted for. All hopes growing out of the employment of skilled officers from other nations are disregarded, so long as the Koran is the fundamental law, the Ulemas its interpreters, and a compliant Sultan defers to these laggard hindrances. Hence it is prophesied that either these reforms must be made, even if gradually, with time for political discipline, or a catastrophe will end all hopes, and a grand rush be made for the loot and spoils, where in some retreat across the Bosphorus they may be enjoyed without the harassing intervention of European powers.

When that catastrophe comes, and the Turk recrosses into Asia, whose will Constantinople be? Who will have the provinces in Europe? Will it be Emperor, Kaiser, Czar, or Queen? When you answer these questions you may see one of the difficulties of rescuing these ancient empires, where so many millions once lived in prosperity. Before another year these questions will be answered by the strength and skill of armaments and armies.

The area of Turkey is 339,211 square kilometres, or twenty-six people to the square kilometre. A kilometre is about three-fifths of a mile. The population is 9,897,400, of which half are in the immediate possessions in Asia, and the rest in Bulgaria, Austria-Hungary, Bosnia, Herzegovina, and Roumania. These figures seem to be well digested from some six authentic sources. The largest province is Constantinople. It has about 2,000,000 souls, including 121,267 Christians and 22,943 Israelites. This is not the city (which has but 600,000), but the vilayet or province. It extends from the head of the Bosphorus to the Dardanelles. When you add to the population of Turkey in Europe and Asia that of the protectorates of Tripoli, Egypt, and Tunis, there is said to be 45,578,000, averaging seven to the square kilometre. Jerusalem has but 30,000, but it is increasing.

The foreign commerce from 1873 to 1877 shows a constant loss in exports and imports. In 1877 the exports are given as " ?," and imports as about $65,000,000. The exports of 1876 were about $50,000,000. The merchant marine is 34,500 tons, and steamers 3,350 tons. As to Bulgaria, we know how it is governed by the Prince Alexander. It has two millions of people, and is prosperous, though discontented. Samos, whose wine Byron sung, is a principality, and has a population of 37,701. It is decorated with a Greek Senate. Egypt, with its 18,000,000 people, is the most interesting of all the provinces of Turkey, if indeed it be one in any substantial sense. Complications are racking this land of renown. This cradle of civilization is being rocked by the military, who, copying the janizary tactics, are endeavoring to control the new Khedive. As other powers have interests there, commercial and financial, the Government has become more anomalous than that of Turkey itself. It has an army, navy, and a debt. Another canal is projected, so well does Suez pay. In 1879 there passed through it 3,236,942 of tonnage. As to Tunis, the hold of Turkey has slipped completely into the grasp of France. In time Tripoli may go to Italy, and perhaps Egypt to England—who knows?

The finances of Turkey are given in piastres (5 cents), and in that currency make a grand show of totalities. In 1879 the expenses are returned at 1,424,582,000, exceeding the revenues by 120,245,-559. But there is such a confusion of the currency that I am not able to make out just what the deficit, debt, or anything else absolutely is, without risking some errors. The debt is 1,590,887,433 piastres. Of this sum the foreign portion is about one-half, and a little of this is guaranteed by England and France, and more by the Egyptian revenues. On the other portion of the foreign debt the interest is suspended, and on the railroad obligations and Ottoman Bank debts no interest is being paid. This is the case with the paper money, which is put down at 75,000,000. Make this budget as pretty on paper as you may, it is still an exhibit of bankruptcy, and the commission of foreign bondholders now here have treated it accordingly. The army consists of 75,200 men. It has been reorganized since the Russian war, when it fell to 12,000. It is not paid any more than the debtholders. There is a small navy, but I am told that there are some first-class guns.

The currency of this country is mixed, both in quality and quantity. Its values are first based on gold, then silver, like the piastres—which are 107½ to the 100. Another kind, the "metallic," is mixed, alloyed. It is 205¼ to the 100; then the veshlik, a kind of copper alloy, is worth 209¼; then a silver issue, altelik, is 127 to the 100; then a copper, adulterated, is 650 to the 100. It is taken in the interior; then caïme paper (greenback), 1,450 to the 100. There are six kinds of currency. The greatest liberties have been taken in paying it out, such liberties as only such a government may take.

It has been impossible to obtain any trustworthy statistics of the trade of this empire. Where and when sought, the facts are given reluctantly, or not at all. I have given the latest which the *Almanach Gotha* gives. I now resort for more details to our consul. Very incomplete returns after the war with Russia show, that for two years—1878-9—the exports were $36,493,499.34, and the imports $86,996,629.82. This is not flattering to Turkey; but it is to be remembered that prior to these years there was a great war, which absorbed the labor of agriculture, and that the laborers were in arms. England received the greatest amount of the exports, and France next. Russia, Greece, and Egypt came next, and the United States about $400,000 worth. As to imports, England furnished half, France, Austria, Hungary, Russia, Italy, Persia, and Greece the most of the residue, while the United States imported here only $1,809,970.

Before the Crimean and Russian wars Turkey furnished raw silk to France and Switzerland, and rice, olive-oil, and cereals to Europe. In the absence of authentic returns our consul cannot give other than *disjecta membra;* but it is seen that in the European provinces, since the Russian war ended, over ten millions of dollars' worth of grains were sent to England, mostly *via* this port; while Asia Minor gave maize and wheat amounting to two millions. Out of this abandoned land, however, the "sesame" has a significance hardly up to the returns of Aladdin; but a quarter of a million of this seed came to the world from the Asiatic provinces. Wool, when not used by Government, has had an export; but the fine silky mohair has been taxed out of existence. I saw some few of these goats going out to the Cape of Good Hope; for where they have not been sold and sent abroad, they have been killed by their owners for food. Such is the blind cupidity of this miserably managed Government. Carpets, rugs, sponges, rhubarb, dye-stuffs, oil of roses from the one hundred-leafed roses of Roumania, hemp, tobacco, opium, emery, copper, and chrome, as well as dry fruits like the fig, and fresh ones like the orange, might under a decent system here thrive, with a trade, more abundantly. Coal, too, has been found on the Black Sea shore, one hundred and fifty miles from the mouth of the Bosphorus; but since the finding in 1854, and some practical mining during the Crimean war by the British, there has been no enterprise. These four hundred and fifty square miles of coal, holding sixty millions of tons, may yet figure in some Turkish census, if ever the Government can get rid of its bribery, and give honest concessions to work the mines, and for railroad companies to transport the coal when mined. It is so with iron, copper, and silver. No one can get a firman to work these mines of wealth without giving backsheesh to the lazy Turks who hold the interior power. True, Turkey has in Europe nine hundred and eighty-eight miles of railway running west to Adrianople, and from Adrianople southward to Makito, on the Ægean; but the shares which sold at one hundred and eighty francs are now quoted at fifty-nine. In Asia, there are eight hundred and fifty miles, running out from Smyrna, under English control and capital. There is also a road from Scutari to Ismid, following the north shore of Marmora. There are some street railroads here, one of five miles and another of eight and one half. These once trebled in value; now they are trebly less. There is a little underground affair I have traveled on from the port to the top of the hill here in Pera—five hundred and thirty-six yards—in three minutes, drawn by a stationary engine, first-class ticket, a piastre or five cents. I should say it is doing well. It is in the European quarter. The ferry of the thirty-five steamers up and down the Bosphorus is held by Turks, and makes money.

The great need here, however, is communication. In Asia Minor this is indispensable. It is mountainous. It has no river transportation except the Euphrates. The exactions upon that river and elsewhere by tribes and local sheiks require an armed escort. He who trades or travels risks goods and life. No one has any desire to produce more than enough for a bare living. In these lands, where millions once lived—where cities of wonderful size and opulence on seashore and inland existed—where now the archæologists are delving, under safe conduct, for the relics of ancient power, glory, and prosperity—there is nothing of *transport* to or from, except the enthusiasm of genius. The local wants and the taxes take all. If you should stay here for years, and pay out your fortune in bribing the underlings and eunuchs of these offices you would go away moneyless, and with no concession to employ either your capital, skill, or labor to develop these rich possibilities in these ancient empires. Therefore the best advice to be given to those whom I see here, adventuring into these ancient haunts of history, is from the Psalm of David:

"Gather not thy soul with sinners, nor thy life with bloody men, in whose hands is mischief, and their right hand is full of bribes."

Armenia is the worst sample of the condition of this country. There the Mohammedan raids the Christian Armenian, and adds to the destitution of absolute famine all that the locusts will leave in their march of destruction. An earthquake at Scio, a fire at Treboli, a pestilence on the Euphrates, added to agitation among the Syrian tribes and general imminency of war, are but feeble plagues compared with the affliction with which this Government is menaced. The body of this people are "wasting their strength in strenuous idleness." Agents are here from other Governments, urging reform. They are asking for opportunities to employ capital and skill. I have talked with some of these agents. They despond. They are not paid themselves. The revenues of two Asiatic provinces were promised to pay the Government employés engaged in bringing order out of chaos, and honesty out of corruption, when it was found that these very revenues were already pledged. If frugality is ever practiced here, it is that thrift may feed success. Not long since, the Prime Minister, who spoke for the Sultan, deplored this condition. In speaking to the bankers here, who were urging concessions for improvements, he said: "When ignorant eunuchs obtain a voice in the State councils, Ministers cannot govern. I find hindrances to every attempt at reform."

Col. Baker (not the Pasha, but an officer here, and a thorough cosmopolitan, if not an American in heart) told me that he had just read Walter Scott's fiction, "Robert of Paris." It is descriptive of the old Greek policy. He says it is an exact picture of the present Turkish rule in its employment of foreigners, its disingenuous expedients, its bad faith, its corruption of officials, and, I suppose, in its supple rascalities and pious frauds generally. He is supervising the constabulary force in process of organization for all Turkey. He lives in Northwest Iowa, or his family does. He has his property there. He has fought Russians and has trophies of East Indian conflict. He is exceedingly American, and has a romantic experience. He gave me much insight into this Turkish laggardness, which arouses the spleen of all Europe, England not excepted. For eleven months he has not had his pay, and for thirty-one months no Turkish soldier or officer has had pay.

All the exhortations of the European powers here fail. This Government is not tractable to their peculiar reason, or to anything but force. Day by day its resources fail and the exactions increase; the production diminishes, and the mortgages are renewed and redoubled. Yet with all this inefficiency, impoverishment, and corruption, the Turkish soldiers continue their patriotic devotion without pay, hoping that the future may be better. Mr. Consul Heap gives the disease and the remedy in a few words. "Turkey," he says, "cannot remain stationary. Her entire policy must be changed. Her present danger is the entire want of confidence in her, which prevents the influx of capital. The bonds of society are loosened, and the laws are becoming powerless. Brigandage, anarchy, and poverty are spreading. The outlook is gloomy. Many believe that this is a season of trial and probation, and that if they are true to their creed and traditions, a sun of glory and power will arise and shed its beneficent rays over Islam. Others, and these the most numerous, look with utter despondency on the future, and bow submissively to that which is written in the book of fate." In one word, Kismet sentences Islam, and writes her doom in the book of time.

All this I record. It has been recorded of other nations. But which is the nation to cast the first stone at the frailties of Turkey? What will Utah say? What the conqueror of India and Algiers?

The difficulties of resurrecting European Turkey are not altogether from the Moslem religion. In these provinces, where various religions are found, the Christians are now getting along very well. Greece has acquired territory and comparative quiet, and it is likely that there will be an exodus of European Mohammedans to Asia. I am pointed out beggars and pilgrims—men, women, and children—at the mosque doors, who are Mohammedan refugees from Europe. Eastward the star of Mohammed takes its way, never to go west again, except through Africa, whose tribes are suited to that faith, and, as it is held, improved by it.

Of course in all this the American nation has but a remote concern. The greatest interest we have here is in our missionary enterprises, our Bible House, and Robert College. There may be in reserve for our petroleum and cotton fabrics a future market of some consequence. But as yet it is in embryo. Turkey knows that we are of little moment to her, as she is to us. The United States Minister has been here, as his predecessor was, for forty days without reception or recognition. He has presented his credentials and had his speech examined, but Ramazan and Bairam—fast and feast—are the pretexts made to defer his reception.

I am anxious to be here when the reception comes off. I am promised to be one of General Wallace's suite, and having a taste for the theatrical, I am practicing the proper salaams. I am told that it is quite a good school for histrionic essay. When General Longstreet was about to be received, he invited the officers of one of our vessels to be of his suite. A fat officer, who had been posted on the subject from the traditions and gossip, was drilling his brother officers. He was holding up his abdominal muscles with exemplary courtesy, his elbows akimbo, and his upper half at right angles to the other half, and was backing out of the presence of a supposititious Sultan, to whom his bows were fancied to be as grateful myrrh and frankincense, when, alas! he sat down on a brazier of red-hot coals! He arose. The drill was quickly suspended with peals of laughter. I recalled a similar incident of my boyish days, when, in bowing out of my aunt's presence, I suddenly sat down in a tub of melted tallow which was prepared for dipping candles! It is needless to say that I also arose with alacrity. This incident has made me cautious all my life of overdoing politeness. Besides, I have heard of a large-footed Sultan who booted a Grand Vizier out of the audience chamber for being too obsequious. I believe that I can strike the golden mean. If the Sultan only knew that I was to be of the party he would hurry up the entertainment. General Wallace has suggested only one embarrassment to my presentation. It is that I am a Democrat, a leveler, a hater of royalty, and that the suspicion of dynamite may attach to me as a member of an explosive body.

"What may you not carry into the august presence? Will you promise to empty your pockets and boots? Is there anything dangerous about you?"

I replied that I had one thing which I had seen ruin many a man. I had used it with success. It was terrific.

"What is it?" he exclaimed in agitated tones. "In the name of those amicable relations which bind together two nations with a twin relic in Turkey and Utah, I demand to know."

"The previous question! The clôture!"

"Great Allah! will you dare to——"

Here I am stopped by a perspiring courier from General Wallace, at Therapia, to inform me that Tuesday, at 3 P. M., Frank time, is fixed for our reception. I am requested to get up a crushed hat and a swallow-tail. I am all tremulous with excitement. I feel exalted in advance. The honors I have had in the past all fade. I grow visibly in altitude. I feel like the giant of the Scottish song:

> "He wad upon his taes upstand,
> And tak the stars down with his hand,
> And set them in a gold garland
> To deck his wifie's hair!"

My wife also shares this intense excitement. Our trunks are being eagerly ransacked for the palest of ties and the reddest of stockings. It is too much.

CHAPTER XII.

RECEPTION BY THE SULTAN.

*This hidden Paradise, this mine of fanes,
Gardens, and palaces, where Pleasure reigns
In a rich, sunless empire of her own,
With all earth's luxuries, lighting up her throne.*
— Tom Moore's Epicurean.

WHEN word came to be ready for presentation to the Sultan, there was an unusual flutter around our trunks and in our wardrobe. It was no ordinary occasion. As one of the "best men," in the bridal of the Bosphorus and the— Wabash, I determined to be *en règle*. I had heard of one of our Secretaries of Legation being received by Louis Napoleon with marked distinction because he had donned his Odd-Fellow regalia. I knew, from reading Sartor Resartus, the value of toilet. I knew that the successor of Suleiman the Magnificent was a man of choice tastes, and I resolved to adorn for the ceremony, so that Indiana might not blush for its *suite*. Nor did I fail to remember that the Sublime Ruler who was about to open his Porte to us represented something more than the present Turkish power and Mohammedan Caliphate. Was he not the successor of leaders of armies against whom the hosts of Europe had struggled often and in vain? Had not his predecessors lifted the crescent above the cross? Did not the blood of the "Thunderbolt" run, though sluggishly, in his veins? Was he not now the pacificator between Christians contending for the holy places? His fiat, once so potential, might it not again arouse a conflict—a Jehád—at which the world might tremble? Was he not the titular, if not the actual, head of nearly 200,000,000 of one faith?

Having hastily written a wish that Prof. Grosvenor might be added to the party, so as to give the flavor of the ancient classics to the presentation in this old Greek imperial capital, I was proceeding to lay out the proper clothing, when it occurred to me that my shoes were disreputably immense, and that my Texas slouched hat was only fitted for the boreal North, and unfit for the precincts of princes. I needed a crushed hat and distingué pumps. The swallows had furnished me a dapper model for the cut of my coat, and the thrice bolted snows of Sweden could not vie in whiteness with my cravat. I knew that I could borrow diplomatic shoes at the Legation, but the lack of a crushed hat gave me trouble. Summoning the guide, Dionysius, I appointed him ambassador to a shopman who sold and let out fashionable attire, as tailor to the Porte. He responded. After much negotiation, I hired a crusher for ten francs. It came. It was tried. It had a spring like a catamount, and a report like a Krupp gun. Its size was almost that of the Moscow bell, and it was fully as metallic. It would serve two purposes, for it could be both fashionable and salutatory.

Thus prepared, we steamed up the Bosphorus, and arrived at the Legation a day in advance. The excitement there was enhanced by my crushed hat. General Wallace stood its fire, and

the consul was ecstatic over its magnitude. The
ladies were at first timid when I fired it off, but
they got used to it by the iteration. The waves
of the Bosphorus seemed to be more agitated
than usual that evening. We retired to rest in
feverish anxiety. At six in the morning, when
the golden light from the Orient flushed our windows, we heard loud talking outside on the quay.
The voice of Mehmet, the cavass, was dominant.
What was the matter? Hastily leaping from my
couch, I saw a ten-oared barge and its ten rowers,
rising and pulling in their rhythmical movement
and sweeping toward us under the gesture and
command of our excited cavass. Mehmet was
dressed in his gala costume, with a loose jacket of
blue, embroidered in black. He had on his fez
cap, and wore an immense red sash. The sash was
loaded with yataghans and pistols, and the corpu-
lent official looked a very *Falstaff* in rotundity and
bravery.

Looking out toward the Euxine, the first object
that caught my eye was a fleet of steamers and
ships awaiting entrance at the mouth of the Euxine. I had forgotten the custom of the empire,
which allows no entrance within the Bosphorus
until after daylight and under *pratique*. Could
they be waiting to convoy us? Or was it only a
calm which had collected them? Was that calm
the ominous prelude of a tempest? The Giant
Mountain opposite, which we had ascended the
other day, where Jason looked upon his promised
voyage toward Colchis, seems covered not with
clouds of golden fleece, but with lowering canopies,
betokening flurry and storm. There is an insensi-
bility to our situation at Buyukdereh—unworthy the

"great powers" whose Ambassadors there repose —for the villas and vessels of the embassies and the palaces of the Princes, Pashas, and Sultanas rest in soporific indifference to the forthcoming event. A heavy ironclad is moored at the base of the cliff on the opposite shore. Its stack has a dark pennon of smoke, but at the fore it flies the crescent, and we are reassured. Perhaps it will be our convoy.

If ever there was a thing of beauty, it is that long, trim, golden pinnace coming to convey us to the enchanted chambers of oriental power. This barge is the more interesting, for it bears the flag of my country. My heart leaps up, as though it beheld a rainbow in the sky—for is not our ensign born of the select and triple-hued splendor of the prism?

After breakfast a rehearsal was suggested. It was deemed impracticable, as my hat invaded its solemnity by going off at the wrong time. The shoes were obtained. They were too long at the toes, and left a great vacancy in the heels. I do not wish to depreciate the other personages, much less the Minister, but truth compels me to say that Mehmet looked the Turkish janizary of the most truculent kind, and was the most picturesque of the group. Besides, he shared my anxiety more than the others, for had he not been out upon the quay since daylight—seven hours in advance of our time—watching for this golden caïque? The ten stalwart Turks in white dress, red jackets and caps, and bare breasts and legs, were his obsequious servitors. It was a long morning from breakfast to lunch. It was a sad lunch. There was too much anxiety at the board. It was increased by an explosion in the hall.

"Allah il Allah!" cried out our soldier Minister. "Your previous question has gone off spontaneously. I forbid that hat. It is only next to dynamite!"

Having quieted the Minister with a glass of Medoc, and set my hat anew, the lunch proceeded.

At one we are seated in the boat. We are a picture for an illustrated magazine. The Minister is in a Major-General's uniform, with twin stars upon his shoulders. He holds a rich sword upon his knees. His lips are set, his will firm, his eye collected, his form erect, his spectacles trim, and his nerves placid. He sits in the post of honor at the stern. Beneath him are crimson cushions and robes. He glances proudly at the gilded eagle at our prow, supporting a flagstaff with our American banner. The consul, Mr. Heap, and his son and myself, drop in by his side, under the awning, which flaps its scarlet scallops in the breezes of the Euxine. Mehmet is in the front, and all is arranged. The order to move is given. The ladies in the balcony, smiling but anxious, wave their adieux with handkerchief and hand. In the midst of the flurry my hat goes off with a report. This disconcerts the rhythmic stroke of the rowers. They look surprised simply, for the Turk never smiles. The ladies did. Then the Minister calls for cigarettes, and we compose ourselves for their enjoyment. I had taken the precaution to provide a sufficient quantity, knowing their importance in Turkey and in diplomacy. We are out in the stream. The waves of this classic stream carry ripples of pleasure to kiss the shore, where the handkerchiefs still flutter, and the shore or the ladies rippled and kissed their hands in return!

St. George flies his flag from the English Legation, but there is no dragon about its portals—only a sleepy dragoman. The princely villas of the Greeks who make Therapia their home are in summer repose, and seem to care little for our western hemisphere, embodied in ourselves. The waters are as lucent as though they had never been incarnadined by naval combat. Passing the quiet Kalender and the vine-clad Yeni Keni, we find our prospect enlarged by the best harbor of the Bosphorus, Stenia. Cypress groves follow us to the Bay of the Battle Axe, where a villa built by Reschid Pasha, and presented by him to his daughter Fatmeh, makes this prominent promontory regal in beauty. Then we run under the grand, gloomy, and fantastic towers of Hissar, where, beneath the shadow of the American College, we take on board the Professor. He gives to our discussion of the etiquette, that classic fullness without which these receptions are tame. We pass Italian vessels, tugged up the stream, bearing American petroleum. That leads us to discuss our own meagre commerce. Our national pride is at low ebb as we remember that we bear the only American flag in this grand harbor. Here earth has lent her waters and the air has lent her breezes in vain for us, and sail and steam glide in ceaseless interchange for all nations but our own. Our enterprise at home is enslaved with a burden under which we bend—we, the progressive, inventive nation among nations!

We row by the ferry steamers of the Shirket-i-Havrie Company. Their mixed crowds open their amazed eyes at our richly caparisoned boat, with its strange flag, its gayly-attired canvas, and its Major-

General and suite. "Crack!" goes my hat, and the amazement becomes consternation. Only for a moment, and we renew our cigarettes. We pass vessels full of melons, hay, and fruits, floating down with the "devil's current." Their sailors stop their swaying motion to gaze at us. The hat settles them, and in dazed confusion they wonder what it all means. Not a smile irradiates their faces; they seem, after the oriental style, awed at our imposing state.

We reach Arnaut Keni, the Albanian village where the stream narrows. Crowds of Greeks of both sexes are on the banks. They seem, like the fool in the fable, to be watching for the river to run out. Then appears the village of the "Dried-up Fountain"—I forget its Turkish designation. It is full of the poetry of history, in which Medea and Justinian, Michael the Archangel, and Simeon Stylite of the column, figure. What are these dead memories to our living present? Around the bend above Ortakeni, past the palace of a sultanic sister, and about whom we gossip as we glance at the cemeteries and their cypresses, the umbrella pines on the hills, the curious costumes on the quay, the pomegranates and oleanders peeping over the walls, the latticed windows, and the ragged beggars beneath, and then at the palace of Cheragan, where Abdul Aziz died. We listen to the Professor rehearse the story of his death. The time does not pass slowly, for as we move downward amid the river craft we have leisure for much discourse on our surroundings, and about home and the sad events there transpiring. Soon St. Sophia looms up in majesty at the Seraglio Point. Stamboul looks gorgeous in dome and minaret, appareled in celestial light. The Professor gives us of his lore and store appropriate associations for each object, to which the Minister adds his experience in New Mexico. I am curious about the early Greek empire, and its marvels of architecture and august rites of religion. We talk of Chrysostom, the golden-mouthed preacher of St. Sophia.

"Tell us of him who outdid Plato in his larceny from the Hybla bees, and left them honeyless. What was the secret of his power? Whence the spell of his oratory?"

"From my reading of his works," responds the Professor, "his charm is in the grand sweep of his thoughts as to the shortness, insignificance, and meagreness of our mortal life compared with the endless beatific glory of our immortal destiny. This was his favorite theme, and although his language is not as opulent as the classic Greek, it has a richness and splendor of diction of its own worthy of the muse of Sophocles and the eloquence of Demosthenes."

We pass palace after palace below the Towers of Europe. Then we perceive a crowd on the marble steps of the Dolma-Batchke palace. It is a splendid picture. The palace is Corinthian. The eye is caught by the towering mosque. This is our landing-place. Near it is the old Kiosk of the Melons. It was once a favorite resort of Selim III. In earlier times it was the port of the Rhodians. It was formerly called Jasonian, as it was here that Jason went on shore with the Argonauts. Our first step, therefore, is on historic and classic ground. Here was once heard the jubilant song of the victors after many a naval strife; and here, when the Sultan Aziz was dethroned, fifty odd boat-loads of his women were emptied out of the harem, but happily housed at the Seraglio. We are received in a style worthy of the spot. We are expected. Amid a bizarre crowd of turbaned and fezzed citizens, all agape with grave curiosity, and surrounded by some handsome young men, who are United States Consular and commercial agents, we discern the tall form of our Greek friend, Mr. Gadjoula. His black eyes are radiant with welcome, though his brow is corrugated with anxiety. He is the United States interpreter. On him we depend. He, too, has his "crushed hat." It is safely moored under his arm. I lift my hat from over my ears, and shut it up with noiseless solicitude, for there are soldiers and officials around. They are all smoking cigarettes. We are presented to an affable young Turk, Ibrahim Bey. He is *L'Introducteur des Ambassadeurs.* By his side is Galib Bey. He is also *l'Introducteur des Ambassadeurs.* They were too courteous to observe the shuffling gait of my immense shoes, but the latter looked curiously at my hat. They were elegant in carriage, men of mild manners, and wore new fez caps. They greet us with suavity as we land. Being only a secondary personage, I linger with the canaille, firing a subdued *feu de joie* at a small Arab vending fraudulent matches. Not a smile, only a curious, dazed expression radiates from the juvenile delinquent.

We pass through this grand gateway of the quay, and out upon the street. There our cavass, not without difficulty, mounts a spirited horse. His burly form looks well upon a charger. We enter gilded coaches, driven by gold-laced coachmen, who light cigarettes. We settle down to our own cigarettes. Driving through the long lanes and streets we pass under salutation of the brown-faced Turkish soldiers at the barracks. This the General returns with easy, accustomed grace. We pass eating-houses, where Turks are sipping Mocha and smoking narghiles. They lazily drop the amber from their lips, and languidly regard the unwonted pageant. Venders stop their cries of grapes and melons, silks and cigarettes, to gaze. The rags under which beggars sleep are stirred to liveliness, as though the fleas were on a fresh raid. Odalisques drop their mufflers coyly to peep, and mounted soldiers and officers in French uniforms, plus the fez, salute us at various points, where floats the crescent. We drive between hot yellow walls, within which are foliage, mosques, minarets, and dome, until we are within the palace grounds on the hill. These precincts are not romantic, nor is the palace Oriental. It is marble and modern. No gazelles are ambushed under roses; no fountains send their spray to the sun. Some parterres, between graveled winding walks and drives, some shrubs and trees, not comparable with Windsor or Peterhof, and we are in front of the gateway of the Sultan's palace of reception. Here we are received by the officers of the day. We are introduced separately. My hat is held quietly under my arm, and, after some cigarettes and bad French, we are conducted over Turkish carpeted marble pavements to a hall leading to an oblong chamber of audience, lighted by windows of ground glass, where a company of dignitaries await us in decorous reserve.

The Minister is presented by our interpreter to *Le Grand Maître de Ceremonie.* His name is Munir Bey. He is handsome, large, and well-proportioned, and his manner is pleasing. He inquires after Aristarchi Bey, the Turkish Minister at Washington. When I say that I know him well, he is pleased to pay me special attention. I take the opportunity to say that no Minister is such a favorite socially, and none so sagacious and reserved diplomatically. The Bey is pleased to hear this of his friend at our capital. He graciously presents me to *Le Premier Chambellan*, Hamdi Pasha, who presents me to *Le General du Palais Imperial*, Nedjit Pasha, who presents me, not merely as *l'homme d'état*, but, by the clever suggestion of our consul, I am presented, with the sounding title of President of the Foreign Affairs Committee of the American Chamber of Deputies, to *Le Ministre des Affaires Étrangeres*, Assim Pasha! Thus ascending, I approximate the apex of this pyramid of greatness. Then I take breath and a cigarette. Rousing all my pet French phrases, I study a few compliments, for everything seemed French.

Assim Pasha is an elderly man. He stoops a little. He has silver hair, and not much of that. Mr. Heap, the consul, ever watchful over my inadequacies and inexperience at court, points out, sitting on a red divan, the hero of Plevna, Osman Pasha. He is Minister of War. He is built like General McClellan. His face is unmistakably Oriental. His eye is large, black, and lustrous. He is an equable, handsome man. I caught his eye upon me, and held my hat with a tighter grip and fumbled for a cigarette.

"Would you like to be introduced?" said the consul.

"Surely, it would be a supreme delight," I replied, for I was becoming superlative and Oriental. I was presented to the hero.

"You have been long here?" he asks.

"A month ago, waiting for this honor and the end of the Ramazan."

"You came by way of England and France from America?"

"No, General; from the North Cape, in the Arctic Ocean, via St. Petersburg and Moscow."

"Ah! *est ce que c'est possible?* You like Russia?"

"I was relieved and happy when I reached the Sultan's dominion. The Czar's assassination casts a gloom over that country. Strangers are feared."

This reply inspired some animation. "Were you interested in Russia?" he asks significantly, for he is no lover of the Sclav whom he fought.

"After seeing the midnight sun, other objects were not so interesting until I came here."

Thereupon Mr. Heap came to my help, and to the wondering Pashas and Beys he made me the hero of the unsetting phenomena of the Nord Cap.

"Have you been in Constantinople before?" asked Munir Bey.

"Oh, yes, before you were born, I think; for you look youthful. Thirty years ago, when Abdul Mejid was Sultan, I was here, and I longed to renew my memories."

There was a little chorus of surprise, sedately expressed as only Turks can express it, and another fusillade of questions. "Have you found any changes?" "Are we progressing?" "What do you see different?" "Do we move with the age?" "How do Americans regard us?" To which I gave reply that I found now convenient steamers, an underground railway, tramways and railroads, newspapers in a half dozen tongues, steam and light, better streets, and sumptuous villas. "True, the Seraglio palace is no longer here, but your palace crowns the hill. You have had a great war, and we find more courtesy and tolerance of strangers. We visit St. Sophia and other mosques with comparative freedom. No, you are not behind many other nations in the race of improvement." All which seems to give pleasure to the listeners. I begin to feel that I am an old and familiar friend of the family. I describe the former Sultan, as I saw him in a grand parade on the fourth of July, 1851, and Munir Bey promises to show me his portrait on horseback in the palace. Then we take cigarettes. Before they are ashes, liveried Nubian servants — in red coats, gold-laced, blue plush trousers and gold stripes down the sides—appear. They bear the daintiest porcelain cups ever fairy conceived or Dresden fabricated.

They are truly æsthetic, and crusted with diamonds. We long to carry one home, not for the gems—oh, no! but for the artistic beauty. No sooner does the surreptitious thought enter the mind than the servants gather them up. We then form in line, behind the Minister, and under escort proceed up the staircase to the audience chamber. We pass up between soldiers, fine large Circassians, in their native array, who look at us impassively. African eunuchs, in strange contrast with the Circassians, in rich attire, stand like statues upon the steps. Officers with side-arms and soldiers with rifles are in waiting. We halt a moment at the head of the stairs, and, looking within through a large chamber, perceive in the grand salon before us, a well-made man of medium size, and of serene, almost melancholy, aspect. He stands alone. He wears a blue uniform, or frock-coat, with the inevitable fez. He holds a sword—hardly a scimiter, though it curves—of golden sheath and jeweled hilt. It rests upon his patent leather shoes. A rich sash is over his shoulder. It is green, for green is the Mohammedan color. It is the symbol, I suppose, of the growing, fadeless 'Caliphate. We approach in due order, gallanted by the Ministers, and make a formal bow. Our suite form a crescent around the Sultan, with Major-General Wallace with his two stars in the concave. Next to him on the left is Assim Pasha, and on the right the interpreter, his hat still secure. After several rather elaborate bows from the Sultan's officers, we await events. The Sultan raises his dreamy, languid, thoughtful eyes, and his sallow face lights up a little. Then the confabulation begins.

There is an austerity of dread, a painful hush, as the Foreign Affairs Minister, in low, husky tones, announces the function and purpose of the visit. General Wallace catches the solemn spirit of the scene, and, subdued to the oriental quality, makes, in low tones, proper reference to his predecessor, and in the name of the people of the United States, with an emphasis prepense on "the people" which made me grasp my hat, expressed their desire for the good relations that had always existed between the two nations, and which he would endeavor to strengthen. The Sultan drops his impassive eye, with now and then a sidelong glance at us in turn. I take this opportunity, without discourteous curiosity, to look about the large chamber. A dim light enters it from the east. The Sultan has his back towards Asia. The group is interesting. The atmosphere is one of funereal quietude. The gods are shod with wool; so are sultanic servitors. Neither the dresses nor the movements and speeches are loud; quite and painfully otherwise. It is pomp, but pomp in unassuming display. The scene is not ornate nor Oriental. There are no trellis nor lattice casements, no tapestry nor ottomans, and no exuberant nor vulgar signs of luxury. No crystal jets shake their "lessening silver in the sun," and there are no arabesques nor fantastic imagery. The surroundings are as simple as the audience is decorous. No groveling obeisance is demonstrated. A few pictures decorate the walls. They represent Bedouin chiefs in the desert, pictures of local color, all but one, which rivets my eye. Unless I am in error, this picture on my left is that of the midnight sun, with its languishing light, hanging over the hazy horizon at Nord Cap! Then I thought of the verse of the American moralist:

> " The bark of tempest, vainly tossed,
> May founder in the calm,
> And he who braves the polar frost
> Faints by the isles of palm."

Although a polar navigator, I felt the calm influence; and, comparing the situation with the bleak and desolate scenery which we had so recently viewed as thus pictured on the wall, I felt the contrasts of our summer voyaging.

I am recalled from my reverie by reflecting upon the power of the Sultan. He is a man of calm dignity and superior intelligence. Mohammed II., the grand progenitor of this line, who took the city from the effete Greeks, may have had more *élan*, as he had a larger army, but he had no more reserve in his eye than his descendant before us. Was he not administering, amid troubles for which he is not responsible, a great empire of various nationalities and religion, and under manifold embarrassments? By his illustrious descent and inborn dignity, by his position as the heir of the Othmans, Amoraths, and Suleimans, he receives, as the oriental chief should, that Occident which has never encroached upon his prerogative or domain, and has no inclination nor object in doing so.

I confess to an enthusiasm for this monarch. He is a king, every inch, and without any dramatic ostentation ; for I learn from our consul that he deserves great regard for his rare ability. He is his own adviser. Amid the troubles and care growing out of the equivocal death of his predecessor, and with the populations of divers religions and races which he must reconcile to rule, he is not unworthy of the fame of Abdul Mejid, whose memory is to me a part of my earliest association in this city, whose praises then were on every tongue.

After the translation into the vernacular of the Minister's speech, and when it was expected the ceremony was done, General Wallace broke through the formal etiquette, and, stating that it was a custom of his country, and a sign of cordiality, tendered his hand. The Sultan timidly, but blandly, breaks his reserve, and cordially replies. This reply is translated, when, in the same subdued whisper, and with much emotion, he asks the Minister the latest news of President Garfield's condition. The Minister remarks that the news is better, but not encouraging. This episode engenders a human sympathy, and then we are in turn presented. I am denominated, in French phrase, a "statesman," and my face assumes the color of the Sultan's fez. We have no elaborate, theatrical bowing. The only one who seems to be specially Oriental in his salaam is Murid Bey. He bows quite low, and with singular grace, his hand to his head, breast, and lip, signifying that his mind, heart, and speech were complaisant; but even he is not obsequious. Securing my hat and guarding my shoes, and without special trouble, I back out of the presence with the rest, and return to the salon below. There sherbet is served, with cigarettes.

Then we are conducted back to one of the rooms above, where the pictures on the walls are shown and described. Three portraits are eminent in their attraction. One is that of Abdul Mejid. He was the son of Mahmoud II. He died in 1861, and much virtue was entombed with him. Another is that of his brother, the unfortunate Abdul Aziz, who was deposed in 1876, and lived in utter retiracy. The other is that of the present Sultan, Abdul Hamid II., whose presence we have just left, the successor of a thousand years of domination, illustrated by more moderation and tolerance than the outside world is apt to believe.

The picture of Abdul Mejid represents him on an Arab steed, whereat we are entranced. We indulge in equestrian talk. Murid Bey asks after American horses.

"You are fond of horses in America?" he asks.

"Our finest horses are proud of their pedigree from the famous steeds of the desert, and we are endeavoring, by the aid of their high lineage and blood, to make our horses win the prizes of the world."

"You have won in France and England," he replied.

I never felt any special pride in the American racers. The human race, not the horse race, is my study; but a glow comes over my face as the Occident and Orient here again meet in mutual gratulation. Then Murid Bey asks after the Arab horses presented by the Sultan to General Grant, as to which I was nonplussed, not having had the run of the General's paddock.

Then we turn to the likeness of the unfortunate Aziz, the late Sultan. The white horse which bears him is a superb animal, worthy of Wouverman's pencil.

Murid Bey says: "He is alive still."

"Who?" said I, in surprise; "the Sultan?" That was my first lapse from the courtesies, for not a word had been uttered about the Sultan Aziz or his woful fate.

"The horse," replied Murid Bey; "he is still alive. He is the pride of the stables."

I look again at the steed. It was from life. It was portrayed with thin nostril, eyes like embers, and mane flowing like the ethereal hair of a Murillo Madonna. The Sultan sits upon him like a centaur, proud of his mastery of the noble animal. The steed curvets under a shaking bit with sidelong pace. I think of Job's war-horse, and then we are called to cigarettes again. Now we saunter around, and, after lingering a few minutes longer, descend to the open air. Here, bidding farewell to our polite hosts, we return to our carriages and to the quay.

The windows of the villas on the Asiatic shore are blazing like burnished gold under the sunset. The Bosphorus is alive on bank and stream with the throngs, who seem to revel in the serenest of evenings. Our ladies have promenaded down the shore to meet us on our return. The hat does its final duty in salutation, and we receive them in our caïque. Returning to the Legation, we dine in sumptuous glee, and live over again our gala day.

Was there a surcease of these delightful and novel experiences in sleep? No. Such spells, we are told, haunt eye and ear, mix with our dreams, and form our atmosphere. Such pleasures are not like poppies spread, for when you see the flower the fragrance is not shed.

Under the influence of an anodyne it is said that Coleridge fell asleep, after reading "Purchas's Pilgrimage" about the palace of Kublai-Khan, and dreamed out as a phantom architect his pleasure dome. I, too, had my dream. It was more harmonious and congruous than that of the drugged poet. In my semi-slumbers, half dozing till morning, half listening to the lapse and relapse of the waters below our balcony, and with the strange scenes, where eunuchs and Circassians, Ministers and Sultans, in chambers of arched beauty, sipped Mocha from tiny cups of jeweled beauty, I had the psychological experience of the dreamful poet, constructing out of my own consciousness a pleasure dome where sacred rivers ran through caverns measureless to man down by a sunless sea. Each gale wafted Idumean fragrance of incense-bearing trees in sunny spots of greenery, and damsels with dulcimers sung of Mount Abora and other heavenly heights, until I awoke to break my fast on something more substantial than honey dew, and to drink something more stimulating than the milk of paradise.

CHAPTER XIII.

CONSTANTINOPLE—OTHER CHANGES IN THIRTY YEARS.

Magic casements opening on the foam
Of perilous seas in fairy lands forlorn.—KEATS.

BEFORE we sail hence, let me record some of the salient points, changes, and customs which, after a lapse of thirty years, have struck me as worthy of written observation. One may tire of these costumes and streets, dogs and dirt, cries and mosques; but one can never tire of the cool midsummer breezes of these waters, nor of the salubrious delights of these hilly and historic shores. A month's sojourn here during the hot season, and awaiting the fall months for our Judean travel, has not made stale the supreme delight which we have enjoyed in these scenes. The excursion up and down the Bosphorus, from the bridge of the Golden Horn to the opening of the Black Sea, is some fifteen miles. It never fails to give solace and delight. Certainly, it is a benison in answer to the prayerful and heated mind and body. Besides, with its landings—some seventeen up and as many down—it affords the stranger a chance to observe the influx and outgo of the many-raced people who use it for recreation and business. Priest and soldier, dervish and officer, Frank and Greek—Greek in native costume and in the French style—Armenians in plenty, and Circassians, some in black and white sheepskins, and some in both, and every other nation here, meet and move on this river, and with them the women, and then the large-eyed children, innocent of veil and happy to breathe the fresh air of the running water. After you pass the old warehouse, where a sign can just be deciphered—"Jason Coal Wharf"—the ladies of the palaces and villas, accompanied by their eunuchs and children, begin to deck the dock with their "Turkey red" silk; and the fashionable Broussa women, in motley as their only wear, appear now and then accompanied with slaves, whose faces are hid by dark-figured gauze veils, and others whose dark faces need no veil. This ferry company has its thirty-five boats, which make seventeen trips a day. They charge twenty-two cents a trip up, and as much down the river. If they make six hundred double trips, at that rate, there is a gross receipt of $2,400 per day.

There is a fine margin for dividends, and these dividends, as it is said, go to the palace, where the stock is owned, if not by the Sultan, by his pet pashas and their eunuchs.

It is wonderful how the prejudices of race here are worn off and out. The eunuchs are all black as night, and as cunning as Satan. The other blacks which we see on the street and river mix in perfect equality with the white and brown of every kind and station. They compose the merchants and servants, soldiers and citizens; and seem to be perfectly content thus to mix with their brown-faced brothers and fair-faced sisters. Where do so many Africans come from? The slave market, they say, is no more, either for black or white slaves. They say so, but I do not believe it, as I know of a Turkish editor who recently lost his wife, and who said that he knew how and where he could go to market for another. This secrecy of the slave-trade is one sign of progress.

Speaking of the Turkish ladies, a lady friend gave a curious experience of her own. She was on the boat going up the Bosphorus, and was seated near the curtain which always divides a certain portion of the boat in the rear from the other and more public part. This division is for the Turkish ladies more particularly. An English lady came in, and carefully placed her basket by her side. Soon an old Turkish woman entered, and, as the boat was crowded, she took a seat on the basket. As my friend knew some Turkish, she tried to aid the stranger in protecting her property from being crushed. This enraged the Turkish woman. She turned upon the lady with great venom, and, seizing the arm with her teeth, bit it most painfully, scolding loudly between times. As all this was going on behind the curtain, no one could see what was the matter. It created a scene. And then, greatly to their amusement, the old virago reached out under the curtain for a renewed attack, but the lady had drawn her feet up on the seat out of reach of the prowling fingers. A Turkish lady mildly protested against the proceeding; but, as she said afterward to my friend, "I saw it was of no use;—the truth is, our days of fasting in Ramazan makes Turkish people cross and inflammable; but I sympathize with you, and you were quite right in all you did." Indeed, we were told that Ramazan was not a good time to visit the bazaars—Turkish merchants were not so affable then.

In Spain they put wine in pigskins. Here the water is carried about in them, and the ugly porker sweats outside as he lies on the pack-saddle of the porter. He looks, as some one well describes him —like a hog that had been drowned and bloated. Here water is a general beverage, and liquors the exception. As there are no carts or drays, all articles about town, including bricks and stone, are carried over the slim backs of donkeys and horses. Donkeys and men do most of the hard work, and do it well, considering the uphill work, narrow thoroughfares, and impeding dogs. The dogs are not so much of a nuisance by day as by night. A strange dog out of his bailiwick gives rise, at night or day, to a mob of other dogs, and a concerted howl, which is most hideous by night. Yet these dogs are not very troublesome to those who leave them alone. True, they have no owners, except the public, and lie in your path, asleep, but gentle. It is a pity to arouse them. I always walk around them with reverential awe. They have a wolfish look when aroused, but they are not any worse than the human race when undisturbed. This congregation of sacred dogs has not been much lessened with time. One of the consequences of their number and scavenger trade is that they generate what Mark Twain, when writing of Switzerland, calls chamois! Some one has said that the chamois is a good illustration of ratiocination, while the eagle is of "imagination all compact." The chamois climbs step by step to the height of some great Alpine argument; while the eagle, with a grand swoop, pounces downward from his eyrie. The Eastern flea combines ratiocination with imagination.

The dogs of Turkey generate both. When they are in active exercise they give abnormal activity to those in pursuit. Oriental experience is dead and dull without fleas. No locality is free from them. They sit on the pillar of Theodosius in the Seraglio gardens, and, like Simeon the Stylite, have a penitential pillar of their own elsewhere; they prowl about the Ambapadus at the Seven Towers; they penetrate the palaces of the Sultan and the hollow tree of the hermit at the Hippodrome. You perceive a beautiful odalisque at her lattice, looking down at the Bosphorus through her yashmak. She suddenly disappears. Ah! why? You see a devout dervish whirling, and with eyes shut and clothes making a periphery. All at once his whirl is accelerated. Ah! why? You dine at *table d'hote*, with a select company. like that at our hotel, where we have princes, marquises, counts, admirals, bankers, and ministers; but there is a restlessness among them. Diners leave the table prematurely and suddenly. Ah! why?

"What good are fleas, anyhow?" I asked of a learned man.

"To make this Eastern folk, who are disposed to be lazy, industrious," he replied.

"You know," said a friend yesterday, "that nature has its compensations. How happy is that revelation of the microscope which shows us that the activity of the flea is partly caused by the parasites which live upon its body." Science is consoling.

The watchmen who go about the city are heard from in the night. They are dressed in light clothes, wear a turban, and have a heavy stick, with iron at the end. With this they strike the stone of the pave till it rings. Thus they go the rounds and make their presence known. Sometimes a series of metallic raps indicate trouble or fire. The watchmen of Dogberry are not yet obsolete. We saw them, with lantern and staff, crying the hours and the weather, in Southern Spain. In Norway they exist not to apprehend "vagrom men," but to watch for fires, and because of old custom. The *voegter* of Norway carries a morning star,—not literally, but that is the name of his long, knobbed, and spiked staff. They are pious. They chant rhymes in the night. If the night be many months, it is quite a drain upon inspiration. This is the way some of their verses sound: "Ho! Clock struck nine! Praise the Lord! The night is fine! Wife and maid! go to bed! Master and lad! Don't be bad! Wind is west; do your best! Say your prayer! Hallelujah! *Lovet vocre Gud vor Herre!*" The Turkish guardian is not so poetic, but he is just as noisy.

We heard a watchman last night not only cry out something alarming in loud Turkish, that rang in and through the narrow streets below our window, but he rapped until the night became hideous, for the dogs took it up, and made this ancient capital howl. It was a fire. The Sultan's stables burned up, and some of his splendid stud. The light shone into our window, and made, with the moon on the river, a pretty antagonism of firelight and moonlight, with shadows to match.

Fires here are of frequent occurrence, and very destructive. Watchmen are stationed day and night on Galata and Seraskier towers, in Pera and Stamboul; while a high hill below Kaudili, on the Asiatic side of the Bosphorus, serves the same purpose for that division. At this latter place cannon are fired to indicate the location of the fire, and a red balloon lighted within is raised to the flagstaff. At the towers of Galata and Stamboul colored flags are hoisted, while waiting firemen, fast runners, are despatched in all directions, informing the regular watch and crying the quarter in which it occurs. How easily a few clicks of the telegraph would obviate these devices. The engines are small boxes. Each one is carried on the shoulders of four men, who run, crying "Fire!" When they arrive at the place, they wait to be employed by people whose houses are in danger. Another set of firemen are soldiers. These are armed with axes and long poles with iron hooks. They tear down the wooden houses, and so isolate the fire. The fire engineers, who are paid, enjoy special privileges. The narrowness of the streets and the combustible material of the houses are the causes of these frequent fires; but it has become customary now to widen the street after every fire, and to rebuild with stone. After every fire there is a change of street. Thus we have found in Pera and Stamboul quite an improvement made by the aid of conflagration; but there is abundant room for more fires.

What an immense mausoleum of the past are these hills and mountains! What a museum could here be collected to illustrate these generations of moving millions along these shores. The Turks have an archæological museum at Constantinople, which we visited. It might well be thought that Turkey, having dominion over so many ancient lands, would have a splendid collection of antiquities; but richer and more curious nations have the best of the Assyrian and Greek disinterments. Just now Hormuzd Rassam—who has been thirty years digging about Assyria for the British Museum, and who has not limited himself to Babylon—has scoured the whole Tigro-Euphratean undercountry, with wonderful results. These are just being made known. Other wonders are coming to light. It is an era of archæology here and hereabouts, and although this museum is a poor specimen, it is a beginning in a good location. There is a big Assyrian god of hideous aspect upon its porch, and plenty of Grecian torsos and Roman emperors and broken things inside and about. Dionysius, our guide, takes us by the hand, with a solemn mien, and points to a tomb, within whose marble case are the bas-reliefs of two persons, and the inscription in Greek says that these are Dionysius and his wife. He has lines of anger upon his face, while I may say for her, after two thousand years, that, without fear of her deceased lord and master—

> "Ne'er did Grecian chisel trace
> A nymph, a naiad, or a grace
> Of fairer form or lovelier face."

We had some pleasantry at the passionate aspect of Dionysius, in which the attendant, who knew our guide's name, joined. We had our fun in time, as the Irishman said about getting in his playfulness at the bull in the pasture before he landed over the hedge; for I had no sooner proceeded to sketch a little mummy in a glass case, with its swelled head and cracked skull, old rags and funny eyes, plastered with white, before in rushed the outside warder, and without either dignity or sense ordered me to quit making images and to destroy what I had made! Well, as this was only an æsthetic exercise, and not in a holy place, and as I had violated no rule of Mohammed or the Koran, I held on to my sketch.

The horses here are small, but lively. They have not degenerated, but they are spirited, for a reason not necessary to write. There are fifty carriages here now, where there used to be one; but there is not a very great improvement in the streets. The ride over these pavements is worse than over our pioneer corduroy roads. Every street has its shops. Those in the bazaars are open, so that all a man has in his shop can be seen at a glance. In the bazaars the merchants sit cross-legged, and, when not too busy, smoke their narghïle, chibouque, or cigarette. The last is smoked by everybody, old and young, from the Sultan down. Every one is privileged to ask another to light his cigarette. I have illumined a dozen times those of boat-hands and pashas. The *hamals*, or porters, who bear burdens six hundred pounds or more, on their backs or on poles—or those who drive donkeys, loaded with wood, panniers, stone, brick, or vegetables—are always smoking. They will stop to wipe their sweat and light a cigarette. They will stop any one in the street for this comfort, which allays so much of their discomfort. The women also smoke, in and out of the harem. In the apartments on the steamers set apart for them, there arises a cloud of fragrant incense.

The street-criers are harsh and loud. These men bear candies, grapes, coffee, cakes, meats, goods, wares, etc., upon their heads, and with them they tread the narrow, uneven streets with light step. This custom makes the men straight and their walk handsome. No better walkers—"as-you-please" goers—have I ever seen, both in city and country, than the drivers of donkeys and camels, who pursue, or lead, with quick step and lofty mien their animals. The street cries are a torment. Was it not John Leech who said that his life was shortened by organ-grinders? Well, it will be one of the gains in leaving here, when we leave these horrid, barbaric yawps behind. There is an air of seclusion as to some of the higher dignitaries, just as with their tombs. The people and government seem to be very careful of the tombs of Pashas and Sultans, and guard them with more vestal vigilance than those of the dervishes and hermits. But the tombs of the general cemeteries are neglected. The cypress trees are as dirty, rusty, and ragged as the beggars of the streets. One charge against Aziz, the assassinated Sultan, to prove his insanity, was that he went about in a friendly way shaking hands with his humble subjects! But in death his tomb of mother-of-pearl is loaded with rich vestures, cashmere shawls, and silver ornaments. These Turks may kill off their Sultans; but certainly they honor them when dead. The cemeteries, even those in the heart of Pera, and where there are thousands of headstones, are being despoiled. Over the leading cemetery there is now a Greek garden, where people of all nations commingle to drink coffee and wines, have meals and ices, and listen to music. Wells are sunk into these grounds. The wife of our Minister confidentially told me that she had drank down the remains of a generation of Turks, carefully held in solution and drawn from these wells. One wonders if the spirits of the dead Turks below these pleasure-grounds do not grow restive under these diversions of the infidel dogs!

"Far-away-Moses," celebrated by Mark Twain, just called with some stuffs to show my wife. She found him in the Turkish bazaar here. He is now going over the purchases she made in Broussa this week. He commends her success. He sends his compliments to Mark Twain and Mrs. Clemens, whom he greatly regards. He said some kind words over the rumor which he had heard that Mark Twain had become insane. He seemed to credit it. He said that Mark imagined himself to be a pyramid, or some other Egyptian monument. This was painful, but it was a noble sort of insanity. Forty centuries hallow and look down on it! As such, Moses commended it. He intimated that when Mark Twain was "beside *himself*" he had good company.

The costumes worn are peculiar. The dress of the Turks is baggy, and made so as to enable them to sit cross-legged, and pray with facility. It is quite flowing, so that sometimes you cannot tell the sexes. Especially is that the case as to children. I lost a wager the other day with an Irish solicitor, as to the sex of a young child. It had long hair, and wore pantaloons and coat. It was difficult to ascertain, but our dragoman made it out. It was really a boy. Beggars are plentiful in the street. They have learned the art of personating misery by rare theatrical and facial expression. The other morning, while a lady friend was dilating behind her fan on the eccentricities of the female toilet, in her earnestness she dropped the fan, but her hand and fingers went on, outside the carriage, and with such gesture, that a dozen beggars began the race, over the bridge, after the backsheesh. Lame, halt, aged, deaf, and dumb, all except the blind, joined in the pursuit. It was suggestive and amusing.

As we go up and down the Bosphorus, we see the strangest contrasts. Palaces there are, walled in, where figs and pomegranates are in fruit, and oleanders and geraniums in flower and growing in profusion on wall and in garden; while beneath the gorgeous walls lies a bundle of rags with a body inside of it, asleep, but ready to wake and pounce upon any intruding stranger, for alms. One cannot but feel that the Turkish costume is very inconvenient, except when they sit cross-legged, or when they only pretend to sit and do not, resting hands upon knees. This I have seen both sexes for long periods do without apparent fatigue. Yet with all this peculiarity of trousers, turban, sash, and coat, there is seldom one man or boy dressed exactly like another. That is the case especially in the country; for there the different villages or provinces have peculiar and distinctive colors and clothes for head and body. They are all, however, generally gay in color, red being most preferred. Some of the localities may be determined by the breadth and length of the rear of the breeches. Some of them carry a good deal beside their persons inside of their large, bulgy breeches. They are very useful to conceal contraband goods. The sash is sometimes two feet in width, and carries everything, from the tobacco-pouch, pipe, pistols, and knives, to the dry-goods and provender of a family.

The nursery maids here, especially for the better families, are—men! Fathers seem very fond of their little ones. The husbands of the lower orders of Turks are frequently seen caring for their babies, and seem to be quite maternal. The women are neither immodest nor forward. They have, without exception, beautiful eyes, though awkward in gait. Their skins are sallow. The children are all pets and beauties, and their eyes are radiant with kindness and simplicity. As an evidence of unprogressiveness, the bridges over the Golden Horn take toll from horse and foot, which is a great annoyance to the million and more of people in and about these cities. An old fashion, especially among the Greeks, obtains here yet, as we saw it a score and a half years ago. It is the use of beads, or *comboloio*, in conversation. Every time they drop a bead, they have or drop an idea. It assists in talk, just as the handling of a watch-chain or eye-glass aids the orator.

We had made trial trips above and around the city with a guide; but all at once, last week, we were for the first time left alone without our guide to meet us at the landing in the city. Can we find our way without him? We get off at the bridge and endeavor to pursue our way through the devious streets to the hole in the hill of Galata, that takes us, by tunnel, up to Pera. I resolved to inquire my way in good English, for I get weary sometimes of my bad French, and so I accost a natty man, Frank by nation and nature.

"Can you tell me the way to the tunnel, monsieur?" I ask with suavity. He says, "Pardonnez moi, m'sieu. Vich vay you come from the esteemiare, so you go." Not understanding that, I ask for the tunnel.

"Ah! you have leetle time to get ze billy. I vill run and get zare first, m'sieu."

"Don't," I replied, fearing a bill, and not a billet.

"I dont want you to go; tell me how—which street?"

"Ah! you will go down ze rue, voilà! and zen make turn of ze leetle street dere, voilà! Soon aftare you will have see a leetle dog—two, tree, four leetle dog—do not kickee ze dog—go ze detour round ze dog, and round more dog, and more dog, and more dog, and you will zee ze dark hole of ze tunnel."

As the dogs are the principal object of observation in the streets, we had no difficulty in seeing them, but more in going round them, and after much worry we got into the hole and the car, and ran up fourteen degrees elevation in three minutes without a glimpse of light. This is the latest evidence of progress in the East.

Thirty years ago we were here! It made me feel that I was a quasi-posterity to—myself. The echoes of the past—the shadows on the dial, which have numbered nearly two generations—have a peculiar influence at every aspect over my observations. On the day we landed, there was an exultation in the hope of making comparisons; and the four weeks since have exalted them into something out of the ordinary experiences of human life. Ah! if these shadows and echoes could only talk—not merely of things which have happened here, but at home, as to which I have been both actor and looker-on—the big war and its excesses, and the wondrous advancement of our beloved land, since, in all that makes one proud and patriotic. These years have broken many of the mystic seals of Moslemism, and restamped these Eastern elements of weakness and power with a new signet. New shibboleths of party and new phases of institutions have also come and gone in our own country ; and with them what great events ! Here, in spite of the lazy movement of affairs, and the habitude of the Oriental to say, "*Inshallah Bukera !* "—" Please God ! to-morrow "—still there are marks, deep and clear even in my own experience of these climes, showing that this Eastern world is not altogether moveless and stagnant.

CHAPTER XIV.

THROUGH THE DARDANELLES WITH AN IRISH CAPTAIN—SEA-COASTS OF ASIA AND ITS DEAD EMPIRES AND CITIES—DOMESTICITIES OF THE PEOPLE—ARABS AS CATTLE DROVERS—JEWS PERSECUTED—BEIRUT REACHED.

Sheep climb and nibble as they stroll,
Watched by some turbaned boy,
Upon the margin of the plain of Troy.—PIERPOINT.

THE peninsula between the thirty-sixth and forty-first degrees of north latitude is one of the most remarkable countries upon this planet. It has but one rival, and that is a similar block of land five degrees wide upon its south-east. The former is known as Asia Minor. It is fringed and tasseled by rocks and waves, and somewhat remotely by the Isles of Greece and the Ægean. On its north, from Constantinople to Trebizond, it has the Black Sea as its blue border; while on its east it includes and is limited by the Armenian plateau, with Mount Ararat, and the supposed Garden of Eden. This sounds not a little like the bombastic boundary of our native sunset border—by " a fellow-citizen." Out of this eastern boundary are the confluents which make the rivers Euphrates and Tigris. Their upper waters bend toward Aleppo, and give hints to English and other engineers of the Euphrates railway *en route* to India. Then turning to the south-west the Euphrates seeks the

Persian Gulf, through rich alluvial plains which once supported their millions, and were as blooming as the gardens of Babylon. Therein lies Bagdad. It once gloried in her caliphate, and had a sceptre reaching as far as Granada and Gibraltar.

Lying between the crooked windings of the Euphrates and the ranges of Lebanon is the uninhabited waste known dimly as the "desert." It is as well marked on the horizon—by its peculiar phases—seen from the hills of Jerusalem, upon the east, as it is from Damascus. One of its little offshoots is in the south. It is the desert of the Exodus and the Bible. But from the western line of this Syrian desert to the Mediterranean, there is a narrow, mountainous, sunburnt, calcined slip, hardly three hundred miles long, by one hundred in breadth, which is as bleak in look as it is bare of population, and as meagre in production as it is renowned in sacred history. This is known as Syria and Judea. Its mountains and plains, its caves and temples, its seas and rivers, from Hermon to Tabor, or rather from the Rhas El Ehanzir to Sinai, are the sources of rivers as well as of moralities, of streams for a thirsty soil as well as of religions for a thirsty soul.

When we concluded to sail along these apostolic coasts, we were lucky in having our former vessel, the *Nakhimoff*. We had crossed the Black Sea in her without fear of dynamite, explosion, or wreck. Besides, was not her captain a Corkonian? So that when Captain Thomas received us on his steamer, in the Golden Horn, we felt that not only was the starry flag about us, but the green ensign of Erin was " still there," behind the double-headed eagle on the Russian flag-staff. Under these protective surroundings, and with a load of Turkish humanity utterly indescribable, we passed the Dardanelles, the old scenes of Troy, the new city of Smyrna, the shaken isle of Chios, and found ourselves at last afloat for a week on this sometimes fractious sea.

Two generations have gone since last I passed this way; and an active life, filled with the strain of every sinew of such energy as I had, had not lessened one iota my early love for the FIRST FAIR and FIRST GOOD, which made my early study of Greek literature, mythology, and history an enchantment. I well remember how eagerly I looked out of our French steamer, in July, 1851, for the plains of Troy. Since then they have been made the object of much excavation, and almost of as much disputation as the kings of Greece indulged in around its walls, or scholars of polyglotical tongues since, as to their location. Then, as now, little was to be seen; not even if you land and go into the recent "diggings."

The reader will know that the plains of Troy, and Troy itself, have given rise to something more than mere logomachy. A rival city, or rather a city on a rival site, was built by Alexander the Great upon a spot upon the coast, which we viewed in a haze below the point where Dr. Schliemann and others locate old Troy. I have not time nor ability, in the absence of my books (for who can work magic without his books, not even in a "Tempest?"), to fight over again the battle of the Greeks and Trojans. My hero in that ten-years' fight was Thersites. He was never honored as he should have been. He was called democrat, critic, buffoon; but he ever used his logical *ad absurdum*, and his gifts of wit and principles of honesty, to expose "star bids" for Troy, and to push the dilatory toward conflict, and to punish the venal and debauched.

With a passing look at the plains of Troy as we went out of the Dardanelles; with a curious wonder at the contents of the *tumuli*, which, like those in my native Ohio, loom above the levels of the plain and shore, we retire to our cabin to discuss with a learned Greek, once a teacher in America, Mr. Constantine, and now an eloquent minister of the gospel in Smyrna, the meaning, situation, mythology, and scope of the Iliad. We had some disputation, as who does not when Homer and his home and epic are the topic? Whereat a lady at our table smiles with a "knowing satisfaction," which is not unnoticed. We call her out. She talks English handsomely. She is of Dutch descent. Her maiden name is known in New York, and her Polish name (for she is married) is known to the roster of Polish nobility. The one is Van Lennep, and the other—well, I must not risk its "spell." This lady is a descendant of one of the old Levantine company from Holland, who came to Smyrna for commerce a century or more ago.

As in New York, so in Smyrna, the Dutch have not given way exactly. They have been submerged somewhat by a new influx of commerce and enterprise. This lady settled our Trojan war over the site and authenticity of the ruins on the plains; for did not her aunt own a farm on the very site of Troy? Was she not herself a resident—*animus revertendi*—of Priam's old home? Had she not borne five children there? She surely ought to know. She was going to her relatives in Smyrna for a respite from the fever which was in her system; for Nature, rising above epics, will have her revenges, and the very route which Achilles took, as he dragged the dead Hector around, is cursed worse than the Potomac flats with malaria, and requires more quinine and whisky than the Maumee ever did in early Ohio.

One advantage of this travel is, that even the inconveniences of a motley crowd gave us an insight into habits only to be seen in the homes of men. These people travel much. When they leave home, they take up their bed literally and scripturally, and—steam to other lands, They bear their board along. Their families are on the deck. They cook, eat, and sleep, as if in their native huts on the bleak mountains of Syria. Separated from them, by being "first class," yet we observe, if not mingle with them. Their domestic distresses—even death,—their police regulations—even in guarding assassins, and their loving-kindnesses and religious devotions are under our eye. Besides, the vessel not only stops in the ports along the way, but stops all day, so that we can survey the cities and towns. Most of these isles of Greece and cities by the sea are seen, with their castles and mosques. They are seen from the ship, with a glass, without landing. Even when you cannot see the historic, sacred, or traditionary spot, it is pleasant, as the captain said, "to feel you are nigh unto it." When we pass the famed Greek isle, which is sheer five hundred feet of rock, from off which the Greek brothers, husbands, and fathers drove their women into the sea rather than that they should fall into the hands of the Turks, it was too misty—but it was pleasant to be "nigh."

Again we are in the open sea, but not out of sight of the Isle of Patmos, so weird in its "Revelations." Upon yonder rocky isle once stood the exiled seer. There he dreamed of the land he had left. The murmur of the wave upon the shore gave voice to his ideal. It kindled his rapturous eye, as he saw beyond the surges—beyond the horizon where the white sails gleamed in the sun—another sea, more smooth and crystalline, and a harbor of safety for our storm-tossed race of sin—the harbor of eternal joy! There shone the light, when the angel came to him, and pointed toward the pearly gates to which his soul mounted, and whence came the ecstatic song of the ransomed. Wondrous strange—the inspiration of these isles of Greece!

We are still in the open sea—to the right of Lero, Kalymno, and Kos, with their splendid mountain ranges, and between Nisyro and Telos—and ever in the sight of a constellation of terrene memories, each an enchanting gem set in the bluest of waters.

At length we leave the classics and the myths and their localities behind, for a vision of the isle of Rhodes, to the north of which we sail, and around whose extreme point, where the old city of the Knights of St. John is situated, we pass for a view of windmills on the lowlands. Its red palace is in the middle of the city, and its world-renowned Colossus—nowhere and no more! We saw the place—at the entrance of its harbor—the two points, rather, where the feet of the giant stood! It was no great thing, only a hundred feet high, though a "wonder of the world." It was not equal to the Brooklyn bridge in its span or—expense!

It was thrown down by an earthquake, and its bronze sold on speculation by an Ottoman officer. Rhodes has distinguishing features in history and politics. When I drew the first joint resolution for the exchange of prisoners at the beginning of our war, it was based on the prescript of Vattel, who found its element and precedent in the siege of Rhodes by Poliorcetes. This made Rhodes of special interest. Besides, its climate and scenery, its olden commerce and just codes, its elder day of fierce contests, and its new conflicts with the Turk make it only next to Cyprus in its interest to the tourist, statesman, and scholar.

Since we passed out of its sight we have had two days and two nights of serene sailing over these azure seas, and without a ripple to send us below. No Grecian god has thrust his trident into boiling seas. Only once or twice the southern and rocky coasts of Asia Minor have been sighted. Last night we crossed the Gulf of Adalia, and we were awakened this soft and sweet morning to see the little seaport of Mersina.

When we landed at Mersina we were only three hours from Tarsus, where St. Paul was born. We could have gone there, though under a hot sky, and with some protection, and still reached our boat before it sailed; but Tarsus now is not the magnificent city it once was. It boasts of Roman inscriptions; and it is quite a place for trade and Turks. Once it rejoiced in a splendid university. The Roman emperors selected tutors for their children from Tarsus. St. Paul was one of the students. He was also a tent-maker, as he called himself, and to this day there is a kind of cloth from the goats of Cilicia—of which Tarsus was the capital—which is used for tents. It is yet used there by the Turcomans. Here Antony fell in love, at first sight, with Cleopatra. Tarsus was a Roman city, and Paul a Roman citizen. He made good use of his rights as such, when his enemies harassed him. We did not visit this noted place, for we received at the port a telegram announcing the President's death, and felt in no mood for the excursion. In my wife's journal is this record. It is the ending of the long suspense, which was as much, if not more poignant to us abroad, than to others at home:

"Friday, Sept. 23d.—We are at Mersina for breakfast. A dispatch comes from Smyrna. Alas! our President is dead. I wait before giving it to S. S. I say to him: 'General Garfield is worse.' But the truth must have been felt, as he immediately inquires, 'Is he dead?' And the captain, not seeing my intent, says, 'Yes.' It was a shock. They had served together so long, and had been so cordial in their relations and sympathies. Our Muscovite Mohammedans, on the way to Mecca, who are in the cabin inquire, 'What is the matter?' They see our trouble. The steward explains, whereupon they express great sympathy."

We heard of the great calamity, in Norway, on the 6th of July. Since that time, two months have gone, during which we have not been without anxiety. Those at home can hardly understand it. For fourteen years I served with the dead President, representing, part of the time, the same State, and sometimes on the same committees. The loss is more than that of our Chief Magistrate. It is a personal affliction. God help and sustain the bereaved, and give wisdom to execute the established order.

These mercantile Russians are very kind. They are devoted to their religion. They speak Russian only, and read Arabic and study their tenets and Koran nearly all the time. They pray seven times a day, under the lead of a priest. I have learned to respect them greatly, although I can only talk to them by signs and through the steward. They dress in long, drab surtouts, and have a profusion of gold chains. One of them wrote me his name and address in Russian. His name is Ksamabden Castroff. He is wealthy, and lives on one of the remote streams which empty into the Volga. When on deck these pilgrims were not sure, owing to the turning of the vessel, which way Mecca lay. No wonder. We were amid the Archipelago; and after the mufti had called them to prayer, and their rich rugs were spread, I had the temerity to correct their direction. My engineering skill was in consequence of a compass—a charm on my watch chain. It has done duty twice in managing a Moslem prayer-meeting.

The captain likes these Cossacks, although they be Mussulmans. He does not like the Turks. "All the turf," he says, "in the bogs of Ireland, wouldn't warm me to them."

A description of our companions in voyaging would be of interest, as these Orientals take their domesticities along. We have a family on our steamer who are quite attractive, and with whom we regret to part. It is that of a Turk, Essad Bey. His photograph lies before me. He is Auditor of the "Six Contributions," as they are called in Constantinople—that is, certain reserve or farmed revenues. He is going to Aleppo, with his one wife. She is a daughter of Djemul Pasha, the Governor of the Aleppo District and a general of cavalry. Her name is Safvet Hanime, and her sign manual (not her picture, I regret to say) is upon the back of his photograph in dainty Turkish characters. She is the granddaughter of Nemik Pasha, the oldest living general in the Turkish service. She has several attendants, not the least attentive of whom is the husband. We thought at first that they were groom and bride; but she tells us she has a child at home. She is only seventeen, and has a winsome face and gentle manner. We have occasion to know, for she dropped her yashmak, after the first day or so, although still wearing it on her head. A voluminous silken ulster conceals her form. Her husband talks French, and we talk to her through him. The captain rallies her for hiding her beauty so often under the veil, as God intended all loveliness to be seen.

"There's so many ugly ones we see," he says; "ugh! the earth's heavy and the sea's groanin' wid 'em. So let your face shine!"

The captain is an æsthete, and believes that women are trustees of beauty.

They take our badinage good-naturedly, and with pleasant parting salutations we separate at the port of Aleppo, which is Alexandretta. She arose early in the morning and came to our cabin; but my wife did not know her, for she had put on the colored Arab veil, and was enveloped utterly. We waived them our adieus as we saw him mount his steed, and saw her mount a palanquin, fixed between two horses, for a three days' journey over the mountains to Aleppo, by way of Antioch. They gave us an earnest invitation to go along.

"How glad our mother would be, and father,

too." This was both hearty and courteous, and would have been a delight. It seems that her father has been to Paris, on the staff of the late Sultan, Abdul Aziz. He has advanced notions of government. When we rallied Essad Bey for his devotion to his wife, so unusual among the Turks, he said :

"Oh, my father and grandfather were the same."

The captain told me that Essad was the only Turk he had ever seen who had made a friend of his wife.

"Most of them," he says, "put their wives in a pen on the lower deck, and take a first-class for themselves!"

Alexandretta, where we leave them, is a hot place. It is in the extreme north-east corner of the Mediterranean, and unhealthy. The steward closes the windows of our cabin in his care for us. If ever the Euphrates railway is built, this port will be its entrepôt. Indeed, it is surmised that one reason for England acquiring Cyprus, west of this bay, is to consummate the route to India, by way of the rich valley of the Euphrates, and the Persian Gulf.

All day long we wait here, taking in cattle. We perceive caravans of camels loading and unloading on the shore. Much amusement is afforded in watching the chase of the frightened mountain bullocks that escape from the clutches of the Arabs as they endeavor to place them in the lighter.

"These cattle," says the captain, "go to Egypt, where, unless they arrive in season, there is a famine; but you see they are calves compared with those we fetched across from Russia."

We take on some sheep and hogs, which gives

the captain a chance to quote his favorite, Samuel Lover, one of whose characters says that "prices are so high in Ireland, by reason of the staymers, that makes gintlemen of the pigs, sending them on their thravels to furrin parts."

The native name for Alexandretta is Scanderoon. It is surrounded by a pestilential marsh. The village is a sample of a poor post town, built on land made by the débris of the winter streams from the mountain wash. Our vessel is two hundred yards from the shore. The water is very blue and smooth. There is a level plain to the right, and a line of low hills to the left. There are a few trees on the plain. The mountains above are wrinkled by streams. Evidently this head-quarter of caravans is subject to quakes or fires. There are few roofs on the buildings. There are twenty houses of stone—warehouses—in front of which are piles on piles of goods, mostly bales of cotton. The beach is neat. The noise on the shore is from a score of Arabs, in dirty clothes and dirtier turbans, howling at the cattle and jabbering with each other. Our baby engine is working the crane, lifting on boxes and bales. Consular flags are flying in the port—none American. Camels, laden, are moving out over the hills to Tarsus and Adana. Back of these mountains is the Antioch of the Christians and the Aleppo of the Moslems; and between them are churches of the early Christians yet standing, and, except the roofs, as perfect as when they were built. Up these defiles are the roads of the early conquerors of Asia Minor and Syria. Here, or hereabouts, is where Alexander marched and apostles and martyrs walked and talked.

The Russian consul and the steamer's agent

come aboard. Our steward again arranges the dinner on the deck, dividing us off by a sail from the noise and crowd.

As Simeon, the steward, brings upon the table the fish, he points out to us the precise point where the whale threw up Jonah. We get our glass and examine the spot. Sure enough, two pillars and a temple to "*Yonah*" (as Simeon calls him) appear. The "grand *poisson*" is discussed with much sauce. The captain says:

"The story is like that of the goose that diverted King O'Toole. It was a good goose for a while; but after a little it could divert him no longer without the aid of a saint. There's no whales in this sea, and never was." The Russian consul disputes this.* He had heard of one.

"Oh, it's a grampus," says the captain. "They can't swallow a herring."

"No! a real whale," says the consul.

"Baitheshin! it may be," says the captain; "but how could there be more than one Jonah? They have two other places down the coast, by Tyre and Sidon, where Jonah landed from the mouth of the whale."

This was a settler; but the Russian consul, whose mother was a Scotch Presbyterian, was not going to give up Jonah as easily as the whale did, and he returned to the fight.

"Sperm whales," he argued, "can swallow a man."

"But the whales you refer to as being here, were they sperm?" asked the captain.

---

* I have seen a whale since, in the Beirut Medical College, or its skeleton rather, found near where Jonah is supposed to have been disgorged. It was not sperm, however.

The consul is bothered. I closed the discussion by intimating that if any part of the story be true, it is all, very likely; and that if it be only a moral or an oriental parable, it may be just as wise, if a fiction; and if it be miraculous, the work of God, who shall dispute anything in the story, however seemingly miraculous?

> "In the darkness as in the daylight,
>   On the water as on land,
>   God's eye is looking on us
>   And beneath us is his hand.".

The captain then enlarges on the game in the mountains. He points to places, steeped in heat and glare, where he knew there were wild boars.

"I went there once," he said, "with a fowling-piece for birds. The bird I found gave a grunt, ugh! and ran across the road, as much afraid of me as I of him. We were both scared. I didn't waste any small shot on his tough hide; but shot myself—down hill!"

We laughed ironically. "The divil hang me wid ropes made out of the sands of the sae, if what I tell is not the thruth."

A delegation of Hebrews waited on the captain to ask a place by themselves, to welcome in their new year by their peculiar worship. There are one hundred and seven on board, flying from Russia and Germany to Judea.

"The Turks make game of us," they said, "and we want to be in the hold by ourselves." That is arranged; and the cattle, sheep, and pigs all stored, the water-casks loaded in, and we prepare to go on shore, after the sun sinks, to see the famous landing-place of Jonah. From this we are dissuaded by this story of the consul:

"It is all safe over on the right, where we live in the mountains. You are in no danger going there; but over to the left there are plenty of brigands. They are Circassians. They left the Russian Government after the conquest of their country, and were assigned these sterile mountains. They couldn't make anything, and so turned brigands." So we did not venture to the place where Jonah landed.

We have a hundred refugee Jews from Russia. They are going to Jerusalem. Most of them are of Poland, and poor. Some are from Germany, and have undergone great loss and trouble. Two correspondents of journals are aboard in the second class. They have been unfortunate. They had been walking the *via dolorosa*. They are going to Jerusalem, to write up for their journals the efforts at restoration and colonization in Judea. Efforts have been made, and are making, to this end. A Hebrew gentleman in Constantinople is striving to obtain the proper privileges; and money is assured for immigration, if the refugee be ready and assured of government protection.

The effort by the Union of the American Hebrew congregations is appreciated in its aid to the helpless victims of bigotry and persecution. The Alliance at Paris and its efforts are less known. It is to be hoped that the opprobrium of our nineteenth century, with its vaunted civilization, will be removed by the benevolence of mankind, led by the free spirit and abundant opulence of the Western Hebrew. No cause ever so appealed to human sympathy. When even the Spanish King reverses the record of ages in Spain, and begs pardon of the great race, which his predecessors despoiled and persecuted; when America opens a haven and refuge in the West, to beacon these hapless sons of Israel to its shores; when former disabilities disappear from England and France, and the civic and parliamentary offices, and tribunals of influence open to this gifted race in the lands where they were hounded unto death—it would not do for a country professing our liberalities of thought and constitutional guarantees to be backward in the race of sympathy and advancement.

But how much there is to be done to rescue the "despised and rejected of men?" Even in Turkey, where the Jew is much better treated than in Germany or Russia, I have seen, on the steamers of the Bosphorus, a Hebrew caned by an Ottoman soldier, for no other provocation than his being a Jew, and because the soldier had the sympathy of the crowd, and no one to interfere.

Upon our vessel, a Jew, who had made some mistake as to his fare, was not allowed explanation, but thrust out upon the gangway, tumbled down into a boat, headlong, in peril of life by breaking his neck or drowning. There he lay, stunned, in the bottom of the boat, to be sent ashore among strangers. At length he revived and sat up—to be buffeted by a Nubian rascal, as black in his face as in his heart. No one could interfere. This negro boatman pulled him about and struck him in diabolic glee. It made all the blood of my body boil. But this was done without the knowledge of the captain, who would not have allowed it. Quietly and unostentatiously the money for the fare demanded was raised among his co-religionists, almost as poor as himself, and he was permitted to ascend the gangway and resume his way to

Jerusalem. How kind these Jews are to each other; and so far as I know, charitable and hospitable to all. "They give and hide the giving hand," and in the end they too will "find that their smallest gift outweighs the burden of the sea or land." Certainly there will be compensation for this

> "Child of the wandering foot and weary breast,
> Seeking to flee away and be at rest,"

within the renowned city of his fathers. Still it is a sign of this bigotry, unmistakably despicable, and which requires heroic correction.

If we cannot do otherwise in its correction, in America, we can create a moral sentiment with some emphasis. Let us follow the splendid example of the head of a Polish diocese. How touching and beautiful is the pastoral letter of the Archbishop of the Catholic Church at Warsaw, in his protest against the wrongs committed upon the Jews, and his appeal for peace and harmony among all, however differing in creed!

What can exceed in bigoted baseness the Jewish persecutions of these latter days? It is not alone that at Kief, where we stopped. There some two and a half millions of dollars of damages was done to the innocent and unoffending Hebrews. The losses cannot be computed in rubles or dollars. The disquietude of families, the riots and the raids, are just as terrible in Prussia as in Russia.

And this is the race that gave us such patriots and scholars, soldiers and composers, philosophers, philanthropists, scientists, and statesmen as Soulé, Rotsher, Wecherly, the Herschels, Arago, Spinosa,

Mendelssohn, Rossini, Jacobson, Montefiore, Meyerbeer, Disraeli, Cremieux, and all the bright constellation which now irradiates our century.

As we rose next morning, the wail of the Hebrews and their sad ceremony began. Indeed it had begun the evening before. On Sunday morning we attended church, figuratively, at Laodicea, now known as Latakia. It was the seat of one of the ancient churches. It is a low, sandy beach, in a crescent shape, with a rise of greenery, which consists of olives and palm-trees. There are mosques and an old fort. From the amount of the freight, there must be an industrious people behind the huge, bare masses of mountains. Chickens are brought on board, and sell for three piastres, or twelve cents. At two in the afternoon we are at Tripolis. We have another dinner on deck with the local agents. There is a variety of spicy talk at the table, and plenty to be seen on the shore. The awnings are spread against the sun and the smirch of the smoke-stacks. The Moslem men are devoted to their prayers, while we are at our meal. As night comes on, the old crusader castle looks grim and grand amid its setting of orange, lemon, apricot, and apple trees. There is water here, as the groves testify. There is a penitentiary also, and the officers and soldiers prepare to land, amid great curiosity, the seven assassins we have brought with us from Constantinople. One of the murderers is an old man. He killed his son and daughter. There is a fierce, insane gleam in his eye, and he looks about for an escape by a swim; but, as they are chained together, that will not do. The soldiers stand over the group, with fingers on the triggers of their guns.

Our engine whistles for our departure. All the boats are off from our sides, when up rushes, pell-mell, a wild Arab. He has been left; he makes a howl on the gang-plank; no one does aught but laugh; I go to him and beckon him to "jump—jump big!" He saw a boat of ladies and gentlemen leaving the shore for a pleasure ride round us; and, feeling his way to be safe and clear, he doffed his pants, and, in his rather limited shirt, gave a "header" into the sea. He swam around with his bundle of clothes in his teeth, and amid the consternation of the females of the little boat, he crawled up and in. I sent a mejidia (dollar coin) after him, and received a hurrah!

The mountains here are the upheaval of terrific fires. The gulches and valleys, dressed in orange and palm, are the result of specific gravity and much winter rain. This city, and others of older fame, are but deltas of streams from these mountains. These deltas become fruitful under this sun of the East, where in abundance are the flowers, fruits, and plants which grow under glass with us. Upon the plateau, as we see them here at this ancient Tripolis, or triple city, is a half mile of olives. These furnish the indispensable oil for the human system. Commerce had here once her splendid ports, among which are Tyre and Sidon, and this city of Tripolis.

From these dry mountains and meagre ports, where the rocks, rifts, and runnels, marshes, meadows and mounds alternate, went out the swarms of men, for commerce, to Carthage, Cadiz, and London.

The performance, as we are about to depart from Tripolis, is a nocturnal tragedy and comedy of unusual excitement. It had a variety in its *personæ*, and the scene was the grand mountains of the Lebanon, Captain Thomas being manager, and ever so many costumed groups and races as supernumeraries. A Greek woman had lost an infant. The time had come to bury it in the sea, but with no persuasion would she give it up. She had suckled it upon a dry breast, and it had starved to death. Our Pasha's daughter had been in consultation for various remedies, in vain. The little Greek—Pericles it had been named—must find its final cradle in the blue depths. Looking down, along with Madame Essad, into the gloom of the after-deck, we saw the little white bundle wrested from the arms and breast of the mother. The lantern of the first officer lit up the sad picture like that of a Rembrandt. The sweet gray eyes of the young Turkish mother were dim with tears, and even so obdurate a person as myself could not refrain from weeping. With the murderers sent to their prison on shore, and the wail of the Hebrews —children of misery and double exile—there came upon the air the strange Arabic prayers of the Cossack Moslems. Slowly they move their heads around as they pray, their eyes looking upward for the Unseen, and placing their hands to their ears as if the all-audient One was listening to their praise of his name and that of his prophet. The Russian Consul-General at Beirut—decorated for a hundred benefactions—comes upon the scene. He has been up among the cedars of Lebanon, and has ridden all day down the mountains to meet this vessel. He says to us:

"Directly the lights will burst from the Lebanon! It is the anniversary of the finding of the

MOSLEM AT PRAYER.

Saviour's body! The Greek Christians of the Lebanon will thus hail each other by this 'fiery cross,' which will burn in every village for twenty miles around."

Soon, as if lit by an electric impulse, the Lebanon flung out its beacons, and the mountains put on their festal fiery garments for the splendid display! Before the curtain was dropped upon this scene, with the tumultuous hubbub on board and on the bay, there was much commotion among the many-costumed people on the lower decks. After a thousand boxes of oranges and lemons had been taken on board and the widow's cruse had been re-illustrated by more and more jars of olive-oil; after our ship had been packed above and below deck, with cattle, swung on from the lighters by their horns and a derrick; after five hundred sheep—ten at a time, tied by their forelegs—had been snugged away, a Babel of sounds—Turkish, Persian, Italian, French, Russian, and Arab—began! Roosters crowed and cattle lowed; sheep bahbahed and pigs squealed. The rattle of the crane and winch add to the hubbub.

"*Il Capitano! Il Capitano!*" cries a shrill voice. We are standing with the captain on the upper deck; the mate is in a fight. The captain, in a Russian brogue, responds—to put the man off. He is thrust down the gangway in a twinkling. It was sad to see him. The sun had crazed him. He had no real grievance. He is reconciled and retires, combing his long hair. He is a crazed Greek priest.

Arab airs are sung. A rush is made for our deck, to sleep there, as the night is hot. "Guarda! Guarda!" halloos a porter, his back bent under loads of chests and carpets. Soda-bottles pop! "Presto!" (which means "hurry!") cries the captain. Italian begins here, with an Arabic tinge to it. The mate hurries the tardy work. Germans come on board, and grasp each other for "faderland." Our mate is hoarse with announcing orders, and at length, by the skill and command of our Irish captain, we are under weigh. The lights along the Lebanon go out. The solitary palm-tree on a solitary rock of the harbor—an old landmark—is lost to view. Roars of fun and the hurling of melon rinds occupy the jocose Arab boys. The mountains of Lebanon fade into the night, Jupiter dominates the sky, the Dipper bends its graces over the arch, and we retire—to wake up in the harbor of Beirut!

We leave the steamer in the morning, and are ensconced in the hotel on the cliffs, surrounded by an amphitheatre of beauty.

The captain calls upon us in the afternoon.

"Ah! will you look at us as we go out this evening! I shall send up some rockets! You have been with us from Russia down, and our folks dislike to see you leave."

I reply: "We have not loved Russia, nor liked its government; but you have made its flag a comfort. It is because you are——"

"An Irishman!" he exclaimed.

"Yes! we have more Irishmen in New York than you have in Dublin; and whether it be the old capital, Moscow, or the other great capital, Constantinople, I feel like singing an Irish song, written by a reverend Irishman."

"I guess it," he exclaimed; "Father Prout?"

Yes; and this is the verse. It was in my mind

as I saw the Muscovite and Turkish capitals, with all their external signs, symbols, and beauties:

> "There's a bell in Moscow,
>   While on tower and kiosk, oh!
>   In St. Sophia
> The Turkman gets,
>   And loud in air
>   Calls men to prayer,
> From the tapering summit
> Of tall minarets—
>   I freely grant them;
>   But there's an anthem,
> More dear to me;—
>   'Tis the bells of Shandon
>   That sound so grand on
> The pleasant waters
>   Of the River Lee!"

"Good-by!" he exclaimed; "look out for the rockets," and he dashed down from the balcony. His boat was soon moving over the blue waves out of the harbor of Beirut.

Lifting our glasses—for we had been drinking from his own Crimean wines sent us in the morning—we gave him a stirrup cup. Night came, but no rockets. Celtic-like, in the absence of the rocket, he put a sailor in the mast to shake a lantern, as a signal of farewell, until the night closed over his vessel, bound to Egypt!

CHAPTER XV.

CITY OF SMYRNA—WATERS OF POESY AND MYTHOLOGY—ILL-FATED CHIOS.

*αυτό καθ' αυτό μεθ' αυτου,
μονοειδες 'αει ον.*—PLATO ON THE BEAUTIFUL.

FROM the Hôtel des Deux Auguste, situated upon the quay at Smyrna, we start on two expeditions, one to Ephesus and the other to Chios and the isles of Greece. There is much to see here which has association in ancient Greek literature, Roman history, and modern Greek heroism.

Each of these isles, including the peninsular points upon the Asiatic coast, has gems of memory—whole strings of pearls of thoughts. In fact, they are an *epos;* they make the epic of all time. It is difficult to believe, as I look out upon these waters of poesy and mythology, as dim and beauteous in their remote veil of fable as in their blue scarf of beauty, that so much of human belief was here concentrated into forms that never die. Poetry, sculpture, painting, architecture, every art and every artist from Homer to Apelles, whose birthplaces we see at every angle and under every sky, here had their impersonification and apotheosis.

What a civilization that of the Greeks must have been! It lacked only one thing. It was unsanctified in the highest sense. It may be that Egypt was but the dowager-widow of the antediluvian knowledge; but it must be confessed she was choice in her pupils, and Greece was her favorite. If Egypt reflects the Eastern and Hebraic thought, she was quick to cast that reflection upon Greece, and thence to the Scandinavian realm, where the poets of Iceland reproduced Eastern poetry, and to the Irish isle, whose bards bear a family resemblance to Persian poets. Moving along the Mediterranean, the children of Greece "entwined the myrtle of Gnidus with the mistletoe of Gaul. Provence echoed the Lesbian lute and Teian lyre, and the Druids hailed with the hand of fellowship the priests of Jove and Apollo."

I have spoken of our trip on the Russian vessel. We have had a perpetual feast on board; not grapes, melons, and Crimean wines, but the Cork captain. There are four hundred passengers, of all nations. We two and the captain speak English, barring its Irish; but the Turkish men and women have dropped their exclusiveness, and those of us in the cabin are at one, and at home, with each other, in spite of different languages, prayers, manners, and yashmaks!

How Smyrna has changed! Instead of the rough, open roadstead which we had for landing when here before, was a smooth bay and a nice mole. Along the front of the city, two miles or more, runs a stone quay. This is washed by wild waves. In the harbor, where even after the Crimean war an Englishman became bankrupt by trying the experiment of a steamboat, there are now eight ferry steamers—all making money, and not enough accommodation for the people. Smyrna has one hundred and eighty thousand. She is rich inside and outside—rich in a clever cosmopolitan and composite people. It is a varied people, and of great independence and energy. Although under Turkish rule, it is still a Greek city. Although full of the freedom of trade, the life of which is security, Smyrna has had feeble protection from brigands outside and robbers within. Not until the now banished Midhat Pasha became governor; not until he had arrested some one hundred and fifty rogues and took their photographs, and made them give leg bail or otherwise, did the Smyrniotes have any adequate security for purse or person. Now that Midhat has been exiled into Arabia, and a good-natured Pasha rules, it is said that the old insecurity returns. However, we only give rumors, for our experience was not disastrous.*

Thirty years ago, when we went on shore here, all damp with the waves, we were told not to venture far in the streets, and especially not upon the castellated mountain above; for then the brigands had accomplices even in the city, who whisked people away to their caves. Our former experience of Smyrna was therefore limited to the cafés on the shore. Now Smyrna has a railroad and tramway. We had a note of introduction to its president, Mr. Purser, from a London friend. We tried his railroad, the Smyrna and Aidin Railroad, on our way to Ephesus. What we saw there, and how unlike the experience of Paul and Timothy, Eunice and Priscilla, to say nothing of Diana and Alexander the coppersmith, may be hereafter written. It is a day not to be written *currente calamo*. On

---

* This remark must be qualified. Since it was written, Emir Pasha, the Vali of Smyrna, has effectually put down brigandage. The census of decapitated heads which he has sent to Stamboul has given him the name of the Iron Vali. Nor does he spare the official confederates of the brigands.

our return we found Mr. Purser at his beautiful home near the station, and after a tea in his garden, which overlooks the gulf, we took a tramway for the hotel. Our Irish captain came on shore to join us at dinner. After looking from the balconies at the people—many-hued and many-tongued—thronging up and down the quay, we retired to bed for the last land-rest this side of Beirut; that is, if the earthquake has not destroyed Chios, for on Chios we hope at least to place an uncertain foot!

The next morning we steamed out of Smyrna harbor. The city is almost inland. Its gulf is surrounded by rocky mountains, meagre of cultivation. They seem made of nebulous matter. On the south shore at the foot of the mountains are rich olive grounds, cemeteries, baths, villas, and ruins. Ruins all through here—earthquake ruins. On the north we perceive pyramids in piles like snow. They are salt. It is made by the sun from the low and lately-flooded lowlands. Fisheries are on either side, in the shallow waters, while golden plains of reaped wheat-fields are seen upon the rich delta of the ancient Hermes river. Our vessel pursues the channel out of the gulf which is limited. You cannot see the melon grounds, vineyards, olive orchards, and orange-trees from the vessel. The bleak mountains which bind the sea give no promise of the fruitful inland. We pass near Chustan Island, where the other day there was a shake-up that was both fearful and destructive. In fact, all these shores and isles, including Smyrna itself, and doubtless Ephesus, by its sorry look, have had their little turn at an earthquake or so. Then we boldly push for the Karabournon peninsula. We round its magnificent, dreamy mountain-heights, making for suffering Chios, the scene of the great earthquake of last spring, the *argumentum ad misericordiam* of all time.

"Do you see these two splendid peaks?" asks the captain, as he opens the chart and points to the "Two Sisters." "Their guardians near are the 'Three Brothers!' Notice how the pilot steers by them! That point yonder will be in line with the depression between the two!"

So it is. We pass fishermen in their boats, with painted sails. How queerly they seem, far off here—these Levantine fishers—with their churches and saints painted in red upon their sails, as if bent on a sainted gala day!

"We will soon see Chios," says the captain. "When I went there, just after the earthquake, it was rumored in Constantinople that our vessel was lost, as the fire had shoved up some of the dirty bottom, and my steamer had gone upon the newly-made volcanic rocks. Ah! didn't I feel my way neatly with the lead, when we sailed into the uncertain harbor. When I landed, ah! what a stench of dead bodies! Cologne and ammonia were of no use. One-third of the bodies remained under the ruins. But we will see! I will go on shore with you and your wife; for we will stay in the harbor for some hours. We have plenty of charitable lumber to land for the poor folks, who are rebuilding the waste places! God help them!"

At last, at two in the afternoon, Chios, the ill-starred, is in sight. As if she had not glory enough in giving birth to "the blind old man of Scio's rocky isle," she must add to the great epic a fiery ordeal and tragedy. The isle is only about the size of a New York county, thirty-two by eighteen miles, but it is big with renown! Cut off by a narrow strait from Asia, it looms upon the vision in three-fold mountainous magnificence. As we near it a breeze blows down the strait from the north-west. How do I ascertain this point of the compass? Not alone by the red, blue, and white Russian ensign, whose double eagle dallies with the wind and scorns the sun; not from the white plumes which shine upon the cloven helmet of the wave, but from the dozen Moslems on the deck, who, with unfailing piety, turn, by starlight or sunlight, toward Mecca, and "compass" our thought. One of these Moslems is a soldier, three are Caucasians, one an Iman, or priest, and all are pilgrims bound to Mecca. As Chios is more clearly sighted, one of this number calls to prayers! It is the Moolah. How strange and audacious his call, on this steamer of civilization! Soon the carpets are upon the deck, and the genuflections and monotones of the pilgrims begin. Ending their prayers with a splendid climax, and then pulling on their slippers, they, too, take a curious look at the celebrated and ill-fated island.

This isle is known to the Mohammedans, not for its wine, for they are abstinent; not for its figs, for other places are more prolific; not for its silk, for silken Broussa outvies all these isles; but for its *mastic*, the product of the lentisk tree, which, when incised, drops its gum about the middle of August. When refined, it is used by the Levantine females, who are too languid to knit like Penelope, but not too lazy to chew. It is to the female what tobacco is to our sex. It also makes liquor. This gum was the chief source of revenue to the mother of the Sultan, and the isle is said to have had some political and other advantages by reason of this peculiar product.

As we draw nearer to this isle, I look about to see the terrible work of the earthquake. What a catastrophe for ever so little a tremble! Looking away to the east for a moment, the mainland appears a rocky reach of high, clear-lined mountains. They are streaked with dark lines and vales. Beyond and above Scio the shade and sunlight alternate, and at the base of the mountains there are flat, green spots, deltas of mountain streams. A few villages are scattered along. The city of Castro itself, which once contained thirty thousand people, was the capital of the island when it had one hundred and ten thousand. This was before the Greek revolution of 1822. It now looks like a shriveled, twisted skeleton. Its very sea-walls give token of its shattered condition. As we approach still nearer, we perceive a hundred vessels in the harbor, if it may be called one by courtesy. The mountains above now seem topped by palisades, and still above them, and remote, are other dreamy Grecian mountains, full of myths and with little specks of green, where dryads and olives, and Pan and Nature once lurked. The sea never looked so blue in its bonnets of white. The ragged sea-walls give a still more desolate look to the harbor, to which the demolished castle adds its sad aspect. The city looks like a disordered body holding a crazy mind. There are trees amidst the ruins. They give even to the desolation a sort of sylvan Grecian beauty; for trees are now rare on these denuded Grecian isles. Now, as we come still nearer, the waves are seen to make cascades over and channels through the broken mole. Some windmills fly their sails on the lowest lands. A few other sails on the steadier element—the sea—ply their winged work in front of the harbor.

We are now in the ruined city of Chios. Before we left our ship the captain promised to go on shore with us. But he says that it is too risky, as this is an open roadstead and there is a fresh wind. "There may be a sudden blast," he says, "from the cave of Æolus, and I could not, in such a case, for love or money, get a boat from the shore to the ship." If we would risk it, he would see madam safely down the gangway. The truth was, that the boats which were dancing their highest flings about us, and whose oarsmen were vending their mastic about us and on board, were too small; and their men were not able to speak either English, French,* or Irish! The captain was equal to the occasion, and when the agent of the Russian line came on board, he arranged it so that we went with the agent. As we left, our steward, Simeon, cried out, "*Belle promenade!*" and we danced shoreward. We called back, "Au revoir;" but we left the ship with some misgivings. The agent at length found us a Greek who spoke English. He is one of the committee who have the funds in charge for the poor and houseless people. We found him exceedingly courteous and useful. Under his guidance we threaded the ruins and escaped the dangerous places, where the walls yet hang by a brick or a stone, awaiting a fresh shudder of Mother Earth. As we reached the landing we perceived wooden sheds for market-places and eating-houses, and some five hundred people eating, moving about, and chattering as none but Greeks jabber. They seemed to act as if the isle were fast anchored, and that there would be no more ominous "strange noises;" although only two weeks ago another terrible shock tumbled down many of the remaining buildings, and only last night there was another slight shock, which awakened my wife in Smyrna, so that she arose and reeled about to the window in her bewilderment to see what was up—whether Ephesus, or Paul, or Eunice, or Diana, or Timothy, or "a call of the House" in Washington!

We move amidst the eager crowds. They are in the Greek costume. We are not reminded of Homer or his heroes, but we are reminded of the old contest of 1822, '23, and '24 against Turkey, and of the destruction of this Hellenic people in that era of diabolism, when twenty-five thousand Sciotes were massacred, and forty thousand were sent into horrible slavery worse than death; for the trumpets sound from the dismantled castle and barracks, and the Turkish soldier appears on guard amidst the ruins! That splendid building yonder, as yet but partially in ruins, is another reminder. Near is a minaret, and we know its owner to be Turkish; and to be a Turk here, is to be a monster worse than the earthquake or the plagues.

These patriotic trials, fifty years or more ago, were more devastating than the catastrophe of God! Of the one hundred and ten thousand who peopled this island in 1822—after the war was ended by the deluge of blood—there were but two thousand Greeks left on the isle, and only fifteen thousand escaped into exile! Dearly, however, did the Turks pay for their cruelty; for one dash of courage of the olden time when Leonidas lived, came to the rescue, when Canaris and his little crew of thirty-three destroyed by a fire-ship the large Turkish vessel at Chios, with its two thousand Turks, who perished by flame and water! So that this Homeric isle has had its wild history, compared with which the calamity of the 22d of March last is insignificant. Yet even then there were seven thousand lives lost, and as many more injured. This is ascertained, although there is much exaggeration, and considerable doubt as to how many yet lie under the débris. We wandered over broken bricks, stones, and timbers for an hour or more. Some of the houses yet stand, with their gaps and cracks, unfit for residence. Others have their foundations turned up by the volcanic forces, and their walls lean perilously against other walls, in grim disorder. The "Court-house" was tumbled to pieces. It was a large building of two stories. Upon the ruins, and regardless of old boundary lines, shanties are being built of wood, and some better houses of sun-dried brick and frames, all low and one-storied. Donkeys and mules are carrying in their panniers fresh materials. Masons and carpenters are sweating in the sun, for the people must have shelter before winter. The old wooden structures were saved. A few Greek priests, in their black robes, and tall, rimless, black hats, are moving about; while strange oriental faces, with huge, black, sad eyes, and brown faces, peep from window and door at us under our umbrellas, as we survey the ruins. There are many tents on the grounds. They remind me of the day after the fire I once saw at Truckee, on the top of the Sierras. Everything seems improvised. There are signs of life, however, quite usual. Pigeons flutter in the ruins, birds carol, ducks squawk, hens cluck, and roosters crow, cats move about noiselessly and mew a little, as if fearful of something, and donkeys are heard from!

I ask the guide, Chooralos, "Did the animals make any outcry when the earthquake gave its premonition, or afterward?"

"You should," he said, "have heard them sound their songs of despair. It was at one o'clock in the daytime when the shocks began. The shocks made a noise—a whirring noise, and the upheaval was followed by a horizontal motion; but come with me to the monastery. There the worst is seen!"

So we followed Chooralos up the winding way amidst the rubbish and clutter, the lime, logs, and stone, to St. Felici's. This was a Capuchin Catholic monastery. It suffered terribly. On the threshold, if threshold it may be called where nothing of form and only chaos was distinguishable, we are met by a priest of the Capuchin order. He looked odd and good. Over his cap he had an old straw hat with a splendid brim, and under that a brunette face that beamed with goodness. He was Italian. When we were introduced as Americans he seemed to think we were friends. He is and was the head of the order here. His monastery is in ruins. He is loth to leave it. No wonder. It was but a few months ago a delight, in a physical as well as in a spiritual sense. Now, although the monastery is in ruins, there are the almond-trees, the grape-vines, the oranges, the olives, and other lovely shades and greeneries remaining. Father Antonio could not—cannot leave them. The donkey is still pumping water with a creaking wheel from the wells to feed the trees with moisture. The old clock, which stopped with the shock, now goes on as before. The cisterns remain, but "they hold no water." Dust and lime, stones and brick—through them, piles on piles, we wind our sad way till the good father takes us down into the dismantled church. Here his vivacity gives way. What a picture is this once exquisite chapel! The pulpit is now broken and the walls rent. The blue ceiling, with its golden stars, a pretty mockery of the Ægean nocturnal heaven, is twisted and cracked; the hands above the altar, once folded below the sacred cross, are all awry; but the spirit is still there, for there was the good Antonio still ministering! The pieces of the altar were rescued and removed to his own little room, which he showed us.

"See my bed!" he said, as he pointed to an old cupboard, which he had used to sleep in out of doors during the continuance of the shocks.

"Are you not still apprehensive?" I inquired.

"No, for the engineer says that I can remain here now in safety."

"What engineer is thus authorized?" I asked.

The question gave him pause; and I pointed to the motto above his broken altar, whose broken stone, lath, and plaster were all too apparent.

"Coronati Triumpha!" He smiled sadly as he repeated it in soft Italian. He went out of his little room, amidst the ruins, and bid us wait a moment, for he would like us to take a drop of mastic —or lemonade—with him. This we did, and, leaving a little gold to help him with the poor and destitute, we bid him a sad good-by. Then we wended our way amidst the ruins to the top of the tower—so as to overlook the disaster. It was sad, sad, sad enough. Over one hundred and fifty thousand pounds sterling, they say, have been raised to rebuild and resuscitate. It is but feeble help. However, it shows sympathy.

The steamer whistles us aboard. We go to the hospitals, and thence through a part of the city which seems at first look to be inhabited. I lift the knocker of one of the beautiful houses upon a street whose mosaic of white and black pebbles is as elegant as a Pompeii pavement, and as clean as that of a Dutch town. An empty echo is all that we hear. Not a soul on this long, pretty street of fashion and wealth—all deserted! Then we go down to the barracks. The oleander trees are blushing with flowers. We would pluck a flower or so. A Turkish bayonet says "no," and we retreat to the quay. But our boat does not come from the ship. We hire one. I take the helm. The madam is not certain of my maritime prowess and skill. I may not sleep, like Palinurus, but I may rush on the broken walls, or there may be sunken reefs or lifted rocks in this uncertain land and sea. The sea runs wild and high. We are not alarmed. Have we not been to the North Cape? We are perceived by the captain at last, as we are dancing away from the earthquake-rocked shores, on a very uncertain blue water. We are on board. "Thank God!" I said, as I had said before when we came safely out of other perils. We may still live to see Jerusalem! The mastic we bought is packed in the little classic jars as souvenirs of this Homeric and quaking isle; the breeze blows more briskly from the north, and our steamer speeds on, till a beautiful red and golden canopy covers us at evening between Nicavia and Samos, and sleep comes to us, as a great relief from a sad observation and a vivid experience.

Since leaving Chios the market for real estate has not steadied. The isle is sinking. Hot springs are appearing. One result upon which the Grecian world is to be congratulated will be that the seductive liquor of the isle, *raki*, will be no more. The Eastern epicure will regret, but the temperance societies of the Orient will rejoice.

The isle of Homer may not last. Homer will.

CHAPTER XVI.

AN EPHESIAN DAY.

Where is thy sacred fane, proud Ephesus!
Raised to the honor of Latona's child?
Like as the ship by stormy billows riv'n,
Sinks in the vortex of the whirling wave;
So the bright emblem of Ionia's state
Shall sink, confounded, in the mighty deep!
—SIBYL, *Orac., Lib. v. v.*, 293-305.

EOTHEN, whose volume about the East was quite the fashion a quarter of a century ago, dismisses the "Ruins of Baalbec" in a half dozen lines. He preferred that his readers should hold fast to their own dim meaning of the glorious sounds and airy phantasies which gather about those ruins. He disdained to give tall columns and their measurements in phrases built of ink. It is with some such vague and solemn thoughts that I have been occupied about the ruins of Ephesus. It has been impossible to settle down even to the incidents of the eventful day, so as to describe them for the gratification and information of friends. Other adventures have intervened—an earthquake or so; a dozen isles of Greece upshouldering their rocky crests into a sky of light and heat, and full of vague poesies and dim thoughts of yore and lore; and the beautiful, untainted azure of this Ægean Sea of marvels, not to speak of groves tenanted by old religions, and strange, calm men of the East, and strange muffled women, who follow them so tranquilly; but these interventions are only those of time, and the thought will wreak itself even in imperfect expression.

A day in Ephesus! Ah! could we but revert to the elder day of this prime city of Grecian art, Roman power, and apostolic eloquence—what a day it would be! Instead of a population of twelve camels and three persons, and four visitors, two from the Great Republic, "further west" than the "isles of the blest" of Grecian sires—what a day could have been passed two thousand years ago at Ephesus! In gymnasium, odeon, theatre, shop, palace, courts, and temples, what a throng of living wonders! How many people among them then? and now but a few camels and their drivers, and one "solitary horseman" besides ourselves, tramping under a fiery sun, through tangled grasses and prickly weeds, over broken columns and pulverized remains, down to a now waterless bay, with an extinct custom-house and an exchange where no voice is heard save that of a solitary sweet-throated bird! Looking down the departed centuries, and into the excavated pits where the skeleton of the great temple lies in its mutilated shroud of dust, what a crowd of bewildering thoughts arise!

This, in short, is the impression of that city whose praises are the theme of classic history, and where the great Apostle of the Gentiles made his tribune for two years, and made even the *smiths*, ever a numerous tribe of skilled handicraft, led by Demetrius, forget their cunning and cry out for their imperiled business.

It is hard to believe that the fresh blue waves of this sea ever washed the suburb of the grand old city. It is hard to believe that its now shoreless plain was once an inlet of liquid beauty, picturing at evening the twin mountains which made double the Ephesian acropolis; for now the plain is but a gloomy shore, and the *disjecta membra* of these stadia, theatres, and temples have not eveñ the honor of the ivy, nor have its arched aqueducts any longer the glory of the sparkling stream, nor its lone pillars the elder haughtiness of imperial greatness!

These thoughts are too dim for translation into English. The American reader will demand the measurements of the Temple of Diana, and the number of seats of the theatre into which the silversmiths rushed to raise a riot against the great orator from Tarsus, and the very number matriculated in the "school of one Tyrannus," where the Apostle disputed daily of immortality and salvation through his Great Master of Nazareth.

Must I, then, begin with our journey in its details? And must the Turk in his turban—the present degenerate keeper of these relics of old—sit, as usual, for his photograph? Yes. There is no other way to bring Ephesus and the Ephesians home to our people.

It has been one of our special hopes, in our long journey, to follow "the Acts of the Apostles" in their movements along these highways and shores; and, coming into Smyrna (one of the seven churches), and hearing of Philadelphia, Sardis, Laodicea, and other lamps of the early faith, as if quite near to our very feet, it would have been a remediless hiatus had we not sought out, at some risk, at least, the ruins of one of the scenes of the holiest of religions.

It is St. Paul's second missionary route that we follow, with some observations, physical and otherwise. After leaving Corinth he sailed into Syria. He visited Ephesus; then he went to Cæsarea; and thence to Jerusalem. After that he proceeded to Antioch. But much of his missionary work was here at Ephesus. It was then full of Jews, and quite Oriental. The people listened to him there for two years. He warned them without ceasing, and with tears. The seven churches received from him here comfort and ministration. He worked miracles at Ephesus, and rebuked sorcery and idolatry. The mystic Ephesian letters lost their magic, and the Word grew mightily. Johannine disciples were numerous. They were enlightened and baptized with the Holy Ghost. But these successes did not prevent the uproar in the theatre. The bears got the advantage, and silver shrines fell in the market. A mob was the result. It is the old story: Greed *versus* Goodness.

As I look back on this day of delight, I wonder that I undertook it. True, our friend the president of the railroad had advised that the trip was safe and healthy; but we were early in the season, the heat was still intense, the Syrian fever still dangerous, and, as there was no police yet organized for the vicinity, it was perilous in another way, which was not to be forgotten by one having regard to another's safety. Brigands are not the creatures of romantic fancy in and around Smyrna, or in the waste places of the coast and mountain. Within a few weeks captives have been made and ransom money demanded. Our lady friend from Troy, on the steamer, had a brother seized upon his farm (to his cost $7,500); and what would be the ransom for a live congressman, to say nothing of his precious wife—and that, too, at a time when parties are so nearly divided, and one vote, however humble, is worth so much!

However, we made our provision, through the aid of an honest dragoman, a Hebrew, Ibrahim by name. He met us on the steamer at six in the morning, and at once we were under his care ashore, a breakfast served, a lunch arranged, and by nine o'clock we were at the depot, *via* a tramway, and ready for Ephesus.

This railway is built by English capital and skill. It runs near the old city, and beyond it into and through a country of surprising richness and development for Asia. Quite a load of passengers, two-thirds in loose clothes and turbans, started with us. We wound up out of the town, under the shadow of Mount Tagus, upon which there is a splendid Genoese castle, in partial ruins. We pass, upon our upward way, through the valley of a mountain river, the Marles. Its waters are used for irrigation on its downward way, and for the city thirst. The cypress stands in tall array about elegant cemeteries, and over walls we perceive mulberries, olives, and figs. We stop at the camel caravan station for a time, where we observe these patient ships of the desert loading and unloading.

"What is it that those black horse-hair sacks contain?" we inquire of Ibrahim.

"Figs. Figs to be cured and packed and sent over the world."

These sacks are in such numbers as to excite attention above all other products—at least, now, when the crop is arriving. It is an unusual crop—180,000 of these sacks, worth $15 each; nearly double the crop of the previous year, as we are told. This railroad runs into and near, but not through or beyond, the great fig-land of Asia. Beyond Aidin the orchards just begin, and the work of the camel is there still indispensable. Dryness and sandy soil help the fig; and this garden of Asia Minor lies along the *meandering* Meander, which has a history and a philology of more interest than its thousands of sacks of figs. The railroad is yet to be run into this dale of beauty and plenty. There is one impediment. Its president tells me that the Arabs have an irrepressible impulse to throw stones into the cars and to place them on the track; not so much out of malice or opposition to the advancement of our locomotive age by steam, as curiosity to see some astounding results. It is their mode of acquiring intelligence. Still, with a growing commerce of imports and exports, now amounting to near a hundred millions of dollars in Smyrna, it is not to be expected that a few Arabs can get rid of advancing instrumentalities by throwing stones.

As we rise upon the heights above Smyrna, camels are seen in motion and at rest. It is curious to see their motions when they sit down. They make as many motions as a new member of Congress before he is sat upon. Some of them look cross in being loaded, and make ugly motions with head and neck, and show their pretty teeth. Along the road we see small huts, covered with straw; and in the melon-patches and vineyards improvised booths, under branches, where the watchful owners repose. The grapes are nearly all white and very sweet. They lack the size and flavor of the *Chousa* of Constantinople, which the honey-bees feed upon and follow from their hillsides along Marmora to the city stalls. Still, these grapes are grapes of the sun, and Smyrna is surrounded by their yellowish green fields, which are in beautiful contrast with the dark, silvery, bluish-green of the olives. As we pass along the trains of cars coming into Smyrna, we perceive the turbaned Turks, whose labor makes this part of Asia so fruitful, serenely sitting on the black sacks, smoking their cigarettes and guarding their property. Could the youngster at home, whose nether lip and saccharine tooth liquefy at the thought of these figs of the Orient, but see the turbaned, wild, and picturesque Moslem to whom he owes this luxury, he might add to his delectation a study in art and ethnology. Looking around from our car, we perceive the ranges of mountains, hiding, like the women of the land, their beauties under a misty veil. Nearer by in the fields are herds of black goats and big-tailed sheep. The houses are made of mud bricks, and are low, for has not Smyrna once trembled under the tread of Enceladus? It is easy to see why Smyrna now rejoices. It is not sun or soil; but these waters, which now, even in this heated term, have their small stream to make glad the earth.

"What," you ask, "are these black objects by the dozen, in groups and scattered over the plains—almost villages of them?". These are the dirty tents of the Turcoman. He is the nomad of this vast empire of unrest, over which, from the Chinese Wall to the Mediterranean, these herders wander, with their families and flocks. We see them upon the railroad side, gazing at the cars as if dazed at their movement. They look independent and happy. They have local government and rules of their own and are contented. The suzerainty of the Sultan troubles them little. Their Abrahamic ways are exceedingly paternal in the best sense of home rule.

It would astonish the souls of some of my old Ohio constituents to see how much sorghum these old plains raise; nor am I altogether sure that even the Scioto Valley could compare with this ancient historic dirt in making maize. Perhaps there is less of these staples here, because cotton, madder, grapes, pomegranates, figs, and melons pay better; for these products are only limited by the labor of the people. This labor is performed by both sexes, in field and hut. Stopping at a water-station we perceive, lying on the bare-swept ground, spread quite thin, plenty of grapes, being laid out to dry in the sun, for the black raisin, which is seedless, and for which Smyrna is celebrated.

The grain-fields have been harvested, and the fires are already burning up the rubbish, weeds, and shrubbery, rolling along with their clouds of flame and smoke over distant and near plains. Dusty clouds also appear in the fields, where are collected groups of horses and men, threshing. This is lively work, for twenty horses are rushing about in a circus of genuine utility, while the breeze blows away the chaff and dust of the grain.

On our way we have occasion to applaud the industry of these Turks, who raise grain and figs, grapes and madder, olives and oranges. We notice them and their women in the ploughed fields, breaking the hard-baked clods with their double-pronged hoes. Some of the fields (even those where the black tents of the Turcomans are) have dried branches for hedges, as if the real property were divided and segregated.

There is much to be seen along this route, if one could spend a week or so in the survey. What with rock cuttings and the Cave of Homer (for Smyrna also claimed him), the convent of the prophet Elias, the old aqueduct, the beautiful resort at 'Boujah, where mosques and gardens vie with Græco-Roman remains—" Paradise " is here and near, both great and small; for such are the pretentious names of these villas of delight in the heats of summer. Was it not here, among the cretaceous formations, where Mark Twain found the energetic oyster (I mean his remains), indicating to the scientific mind that at some era that delicious bivalve had added its flavor to this " Paradise " of grapes, melons, figs, and silks? He wondered how it had gotten up from its saline home below to this elevated spot. He forgot that even the oyster may seek for Paradise; and, although his sense of enjoyment may be small, yet he has a source of joy in giving pleasure to others.

We pass into plains, and amidst mountains, and through villages, where we are greeted by sights of camels, old and young; and by the old and young who, the world over, come out to see the movements of the outside world. There is occasionally seen a shepherd with his reed flute and pastoral crook. Strange people are seen, especially at Tourbali, thirty miles out—men of high turbans, colored and twisted like the pillars and domes of St. Basil's Church, in the Kremlin, at Moscow. Granite peaks appear, and evidences of winter floods over plains and in valleys; and inundations which destroyed bridges and track, but left fructified fields.

What a view one might have from that mountain on our left. Besides, it bears evidence of once being a stronghold. It is capped by a castle, which is so high that it seems very small. It is "Goats' Castle." It has its story. It was the defense of the tribes hereabout against the Ottoman Sultans. A shrewd native captain frightened its occupants away by putting lamps on goats and sending them up the high steep—a mighty host, with which it was vain to contend!

We are getting close to Ephesus. The path narrows. This is one of the gateways of history, as are all narrow mountain gaps. Alexander the Great (where did he not go on his conquering raids in the East?) here followed the paths of many former heroes. Here, too, are the ruins of cities made out of the ruined marbles of Ephesus. Some foolish people also locate, at a niche hereabouts, a miraculous dash of St. Paul's sword into the mountain side. It is said that, when he resided at Ephesus, he came out here to try its temper, and made this cave at a stroke. If this cave were alone and peculiar, we might give to it some little story of some prophet, saint, or king; but, the mountain being of limestone, the cave does not call for any supernatural exertion.

"The next station is yours!" says the conductor, to our inquiry. Our heads are thrust out of the car, to get a first view of the famous locality; for our Ephesus is not the station of that name, but it is near by, and, as we near Ayaslook river, there leaps into our eager eye a splendid mountain, decorated by an immense Saracenic castle. This, under other circumstances, and if it were safe from brigands, would make an attraction for excursion of itself; but this is only the Moslem vestibule to the old Græco-Roman-Christian temple of the first century. The cunning hands of nameless builders have sanctified this soil with relics. The very art which graced and lifted these once grand and now despoiled structures, mingles with the monuments they reared. A desert world surrounds us. Only one symbol of the new order is here! It is the locomotive. Very strange it seems amidst smitten temples and cities. The goblin of steam seems but "a dream half told," working its way into a land which Herodotus eulogized for its salubrity, toward a buried city, whose magnificence was the glory of the ancient world.

At length we reach the depot. A few people, in Eastern clothes, are seen in this feverish place. There is also a tavern. There is said to be near by, a Christian village, made up of descendants of the Greek Christians; but we saw but one person who looked like a Christian. He was a fine-looking, dark-eyed man (agent of the road), a Greek, who tendered us his services until he saw Ibrahim emerge from a "second-class" car, with his provisions. The day is hot. The camels are lying about at rest. It is high noon. We prepare for the trip. We look around and above for auspicious omens, as there is no certainty of our ever coming back from Ephesus, unless bought with a price. Naturally the flight of birds in the East is remembered; and there, sure enough, swinging in splendid gyrations about the Saracenic battlements above, are two eagles. Evidently they are typical of our native land, not to mention ourselves. How splendidly, as they circle, they seem to rest on the easy bosom of the air, a picture of lofty tranquillity above the ills, ruins, and breezes below. They give courage, especially as some of their flights

AQUEDUCT AT EPHESUS.

seem as cheerful as those of swallows before a shower. The worst may happen; but what is the worst? Heaven is just as near to us from the old prison of St. Paul, on yonder crag, as in the New World, about which neither his great teacher Gamaliel nor himself ever dreamed. Boldly we mount our horses, Ibrahim and myself, and to my wife is assigned a lively mule. The saddles are of a lofty wooden kind. Heavy rope halters burden the necks of the animals, who find them less cumbersome than the heat.

We pass under the arches of the ancient aqueduct. It is in good preservation and not far from the railroad depot. Its picture is presented. Without wasting a glance at the ruined mosques and minarets, which have for us *here*, and now, no allurement, it would be well to give, in a few sentences, something of that salience which makes Ephesus in its habiliments of decay leap out of history as one of the most interesting ruins of the world.

CHAPTER XVII.

EPHESUS—HER DIVINITIES AND HER DIVINITY.

The Empress of Ionia, renowned Ephesus, famous for war and learning.—GREEK ANTHOLOGY, iv., 20.

WE reach the suburbs of old Ephesus, and only halt to take a few breaths of inspiration. The reader of chapters xviii., xix., and xx. of the Acts of the Apostles desires no introduction to this favorite city of St. Paul. As an apostolic and Christian home it is better known than as a great capital and the site of the great pagan shrine.

Ephesus, in space, is or was situated on the Gulf of Scala Nova, and also south of the Caystrus River. It is now in, near, or over a very hot place. The caloric is mostly from below. A grand laboratory has been at work from the earliest times among these coasts of Greece. The recent evidences of its labors we saw, the other day, at Chios, and the cumulative, or, rather, tumulative, evidences of which are found from Smyrna to Constantinople, and from Athens to Adalia. Ephesus would not be quite such a pulverization but for the volcanic fires. Perhaps but for them the sea would still be laving its old walls and cheering its gloom. From the top of Mount Coressus, which was once a part of the city, could be seen the island of Chios and the promontory of Karaboumon, on the northwest; and on the south-west, set in the blue Ægean, the

THE CITY OF EPHESUS (FROM MOUNT CORESUS).

isle of Samos, and perhaps a dozen others, including Patmos and Scio. I doubt not that from the top seats of the great theatre, into which, with one accord, the people rushed, with Paul's companions in custody, the galleys of the Roman and Greek emperors could be seen going from or entering the bay to Ephesus.

Ephesus, *in time*, may have had more vicissitudes than she has had in space; but she took up a good deal of space once. From the time of Alexander the Great to the age of Cicero and Cæsar, its greatness rose and culminated. There is no way of ascertaining its population. It had no census bureau, whose records have been found; but, judging even by its vaults, where the superstructures are no more; by the size of the gymnasium and theatre; by the magnitude of its temples and their magnificence; and by its agora, tombs, mint, aqueducts, and their separate and joint dimensions and magnificence, the old city must be numbered by millions. There is no feeble, nebulous falsehoods about this grand old place. It is as much of a verity as Paris, London, Moscow, or New York. Through its streets surged a restless, intellectual, questioning, wonderful people; reaching out with their trident and worshiping no goddess more ardently than the fruitful divinity. It was next to Athens as a capital; for it was the metropolis of the Ionian Confederacy. It was next to Jerusalem as a school of theology, and to no other city was it second as a school of art. The city, as it was constructed by the highest refinement in its pristine beauty, is here presented to the reader, in the engraving; and as a contrast, a photograph of its condition as we see it to-day.

About its rocks, groves, shores, and caves the genii of Grecian myth played, as if festive, racy, and congenial with the soil. In fact, Apollo and Diana were born here. The silver tongue and silver bow—eloquence and adventure! Latona here had her seat of refuge, and, with Diana, from whose temples the fanciful icicles hung, guarded the sanctity of marriage. So that population, even by strictest economic tabulation and truth, must have increased. Metamorphoses—puerile but favorite kaleidoscopes, which brought out of the darkness of those early ages the richest hues of fancy, as aniline colors are transmuted out of coal-tar—here had more than Protean changes. While Pan, the symbol of Nature, did not disdain to lurk in leafy coverts upon hills and mounts, Bacchus did not venture very boldly where Diana was mistress, nor did Venus have here as much honor as Ceres and Jupiter Pluvius. The Amazons here found a pleasant asylum after a fight for their female rights; and in all that made up pagan rites, myths, ceremonies, and grandeur, we have the New Testament for testimony, that no small gain accrued by making silver images of the great goddess whose image fell from Jupiter, and whose worship here was "simply magnificent."

The worship in the Temple of Diana was conducted with great mystery and awe. Her great statue was clothed with symbols. There were signs of the zodiac, a necklace of acorns, a mural crown, and other emblems of her presiding and protecting power. The "properties" of the temple were as rich as the rites were imposing.

I present an etching of this Diana of the Ephesians. It is taken from Falconer's "Ephesus" of

RUINS OF EPHESUS.

1862, a volume of rare learning and research. It touches, with finest hand, all that classic history gives as to the origin and rites of this wonderful goddess, "whom all Asia and the world worshipeth." The cold and chaste huntress, who "chains in vestal ice the current in young veins," is not the Diana of this worship. The Bubastis of the Egyptians rather is the Diana of Ephesus; and her reputation is not up to the standard of the chaste huntress of the Grecian myth.

When the Temple of Diana fell in the third century, the spirit of St. Paul arose. "His word is more than the miraculous harp;" and it is still sounding down the centuries. Ephesus is noted not only for her great temple, but for her paramount religious connections. These were Christian. But like her arches and columns, they are now hid beneath the lush overgrowth of bramble and weed. The old haunts are places of resort for the owl and the lizard. The travels and companions of St. Paul, recorded in the "Acts," the conversion of Apollos by Aquila and Priscilla, the belief that John the Baptist here exercised his peculiar function, the schools of magic overthrown by apostolic influences, the work of Timothy and Tychicus, the prominence which St. John the Evangelist gives to Ephesus as the first of the Seven Churches, and the churches and councils of the early Christians gave to Ephesus this capital predominance.

This is a summary of the interests that cling about Ephesus, the last and not least of which are these Christian associations and the writings of the Apostle to his Ephesian friends. The elegant and earnest epistle to these men show how his heart yearned after those for and with whom he had suffered.

What, then, remains of this grand scene of other days and sacred lore? That we proceed to determine, and, being led by Ibrahim and the horseman who attended my wife's mule, we followed the path. Ibrahim has reserved the climax—the temple—for the end; and with proper taste. That climax we looked for at every turn; but the temple was not above ground. We thread our pathway, Indian file, for a mile or more over the dried bed of the creek known as Selenus, having started from the ruined aqueduct; then over rubbish, where old tombs, partially opened and heavy with marble tops, are apparent, down the sacred road to the gymnasium. This place is in area, 1,000 by 700 feet, and, as the surveys show, lies between the agoræ, or market-places, and the port, since filled up. The great agora is nearer the port and next to the theatre. This agora was the assemblage-place for the people. Corinthian columns, of which fragments lie about in great disorder, here formed a superb colonnade, while statues of the great Greeks and benefactors of Ephesus once lined the way. It is said that Antony here held a court of justice, and rushed out of it to pay court to Cleopatra, who was on a visit and happened to pass that way in her litter. We did not ascend Mount Coressus. We saw it plainly enough, and its great beauty, when clothed in verdure and covered with temples, was only equaled by its rival mountain, Mount Prion. Between them lie the odeon and theatre. A stream once played between these rocky acclivities, and the old walls ran over them.

As we trudged on and stumbled over the rough débris and amidst the high grass and weeds, holding our animals and our umbrellas, I could not,

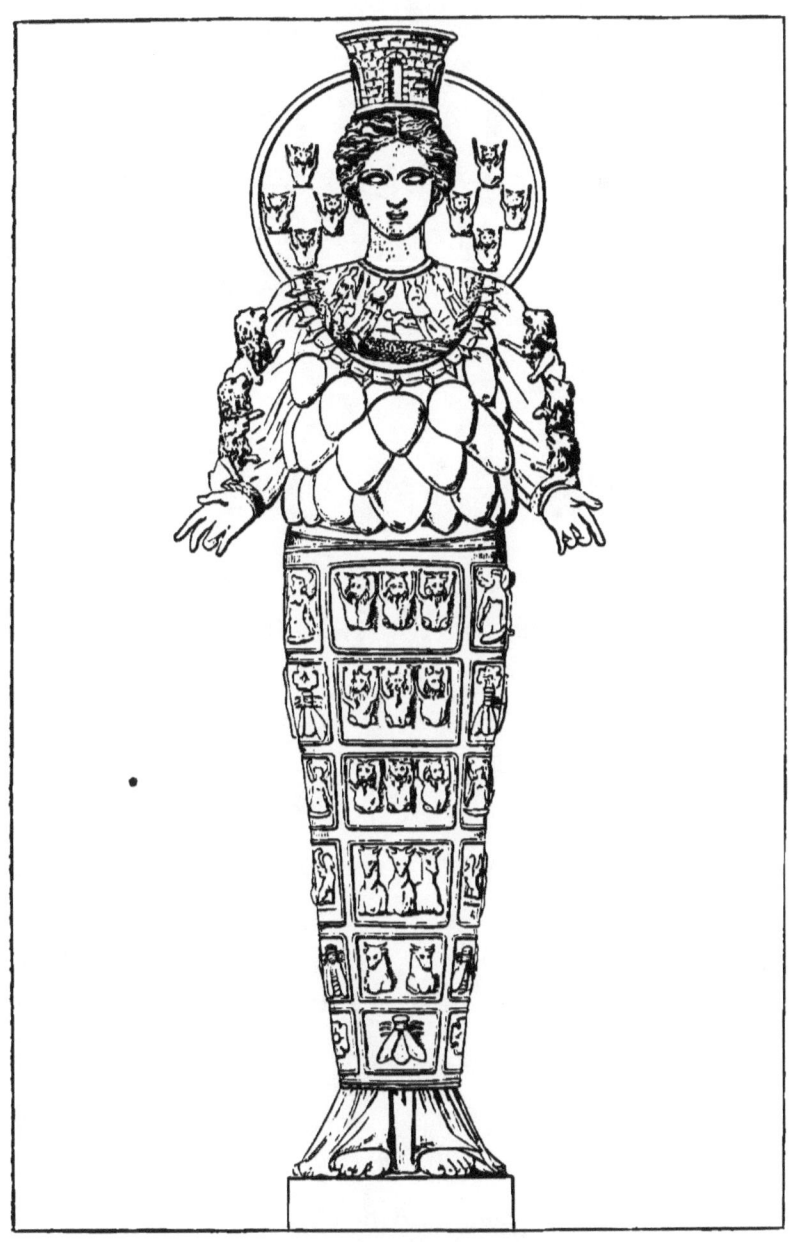

DIANA EPHESIA (IN THE MUSEUM AT NAPLES).

being behind, help noticing the unromantic and irreverent performance of my wife's mule. He was aware of the inutilities of his meagre tail in fly-time; and, like his American cousin, he used his heels with good effect—sometimes all four in the air at a time, and all directed at one fly. This caused us both much amusement, though it made the position on his back decidedly irksome, if not dangerous. My wife called a halt near the walls; and, remembering her experience in the Yosemite, arranged herself as an equestrienne à la squaw. This being satisfactory, and our minds fixed on the theatre (Acts xix. 29), made memorable by the riotous outcry against Paul, we were proceeding down the rugged and tangled path, when a small caravan of nine camels and three baby camels filled the archway. They were driven by two Arabs and loaded with straw; so that, if they had been posed for a picture in modern Ephesus, with the mule for local color and acrobatic vivacity, it could not have been better arranged.

This theatre was once, and is yet, immense. It held sixty thousand people. It is a great mass, but in ruin; not complete ruin, but complete with the aid of a very little fanciful architecture. The old semi-circle is there. Its arena is filled with strata on strata of accumulated dust, pulverized by time and shaken down by earthquakes. The grass and shrubs wave on its walls and over its seats. Some one has cut a small crop of tobacco near, which is hung up to dry. The old arches, without the superstructure, are there. The arches are of brick, and from beneath the weeds and broken stone peep forth delicate traceries in marble for architrave and pillar. We grow excited, having caught, after a couple of thousand years, the infection from the silversmith and his craftsmen. The perspiration rolls off from our animals, as well as from ourselves; but a cool breeze stirs the high weeds, and the shrubbery over the walls rustles. There is only one sound of singular sweetness heard. It is from a winged emerald, a "green canary," as Ibrahim called it; but really the honey-bird of Asia Minor. It flew forth from the theatre and sang its little opera, in strange contrast with the roar which once shook these walls for the "space of two hours," when Demetrius appealed against Paul; or with the growls of wild beasts which dashed forth from the dark vaults against the gladiators. Then we dismounted, if only to applaud the weird and winsome songstress of this historic theatre. No Patti, with her kissing lyrics; no Kellogg, with her sad, sweet warble, ever gave fresher charm. If upon the oldest roots the greenest mosses grow, so will this bird-voice be ever remembered as the sweetest of memories which cling to old Ephesus. Being dismounted, and pushing aside the shrubbery and weeds, we find inscriptions in Greek, and marble efflorescence in perfect beauty. These inscriptions, written for durance, are now only to be deciphered by some syllogisms drawn from the logic of that astute race whose schools were here in full play when Paul disputed. We did not stop to copy or endeavor to translate. It was no time.

We take a good view of the plain in front of this theatre, or what now seems a plain, where once rich argosies rode. Between us and the Caystrus river there seems a great prairie and some swamp land; while to the right and north of the castle there are grounds where the cotton-pod seems as

GATE OF THE CITADEL, EPHESUS.

happy among melon-patches as if it were "way down in Alabama." Leaving the theatre reluctantly (for we ever had a liking for the theatre), and stumbling down and around to the supposed port and custom-house, which no politics now invade and no tariff vexes, we gain one branch of the Sacred Way. There were two Sacred Ways. One is within, and the other is out and from the walls to the Temple of Diana. This first way is now our objective point. Passing by the Cave of the Seven Sleepers in the quarry (which is ultimate nonsense, unrelieved by any wit like that of poor Rip Van Winkle), and under the rocky cliffs of Mount Prion, whose imagined loveliness, when arrayed in Ephesian holiday, we cannot fail to picture, we ride up and down amidst scattered fragments, which are a few handfuls of dust or sand, compared with the measureless majesty of the proportionate temples of which they were once a part. Then we reach the stadium. This was splendid in its day. It was made prominent by being on the slope of Mount Prion. It gave convenient seats on its upper side, and these were cut in the rocks. It was larger than the theatre, and was arranged for seventy-six thousand persons. Underneath, it was equally immense. Everywhere we find tombs. Indeed, the whole city is a vast mausoleum. Along Mount Coressus they are strewn as thickly as along the walled heights of Constantinople. In the valley they were in plenty. On the sides of Prion still more, and along the Sacred Way from the Magnesian Gate to the great temple more and more. From the stadium to the temple, on the same Sacred Way, there are still more tombs. Into these the spades and hands of curious men have delved, with what results we do not always hear, as the Turkish exchequer is never full and ever greedy, and a proclamation of rich findings, as Dr. Schliemann found, leads to the lightening of the purse and the heaviness of the heart.

It is impossible by vague hints to portray the greatness of this buried city and its grounds. It is only when we remember the gorgeousness and numbers of these heathen temples to gods and emperors, and to founders of religion and empire, that we can recall in some fragmentary way the resplendence of this ancient metropolis, whose mounds are so magnificent. Thirty-three temples are plainly deciphered by ruins, coins, and inscriptions; but among them all in mien and gesture, beauty, purity, and elevation is that of "Diana of the Ephesians." It was on and below the plain between Mount Prion and the hill down which we started from the aqueduct. Its site was long lost beneath the soil of the ages. Falconer, in 1862, said that no fewer than seventeen travelers had mistaken the ruin at the head of the marsh (the great gymnasium), for the vestiges of the Temple of Diana. "One of the most glorious feats of excavating at Ephesus," he continues, "would be the discovery of the temple. It is an unexplored mine of antiquity. What gems, what statues, what bas-reliefs might be discovered in a city where a Parrhasius and an Apelles and Zeuxis—where a Praxiteles and a Scopas, besides a host of other artists flourished; and to the adornment of which we know that even a Phidias contributed."

It was reserved for a liberal archæologist, Mr. Wood, to find it. He succeeded. He began with the odeon and cleaned out the theatre, and, finding there a hint, he next found the Magnesian Gate. That way lay the temple. For three years he labored, till he discovered that the procession from the temple entered the city by one gate and went out by another. *Eureka!* The temple is at the junction of the two ways, and then he began to dig and dig. Ibrahim says that sometimes two thousand men were at work, and paid out of Mr. Wood's private funds. In April, 1869, he hit the happy angle, and the great temple was revealed in its height, breadth, and depth, though with its columns shattered and its *tout ensemble* materially destroyed; but still a form to enshrine a spirit, that of Diana the Great, whose image fell from Jupiter! It was the splendid shrine of her whose moonlight beauty gives to earth its selectest enchantment.

Looking over this ground, and recalling the scenes here enacted when the riot occurred which jeopardized Paul's liberty of person and speech, how much fresh and beauteous meaning bursts into flower from each one of the chapters of the Epistle to the Ephesians! When he dignifies and aggrandises the power wrought in Christ, he compares it in his first chapter with the dominion which was found in Ephesus. When he would grace the Christian with honors, he finds similes in the proud citizenship at Ephesus. When he would find a fit metaphor for the system of Christ, he looked toward the heathen temple, "fitly framed together, growing into an holy temple." He had but to look out of his prison upon the rock to frame his figure of a ship tossed to and fro, and carried about with every wind of doctrine. When he would travel through these hot vales and mountains, and longed for a cool retreat, he thought of the sweetness of the evening and would not have its ethereal mildness come "upon your wrath." Feeling the beauty even of the ambiguous service for Diana, he inveighs against that uncleanness that defileth. In fine, standing with the great concourse of the stadium, or looking upon the contests of the gladiators in the theatre, or seeing the exercises in the gymnasium, he might well cry out, with eloquent analogy: "Put on the whole armor of God;" "Ye wrestle not against flesh and blood;" "Stand, therefore, having your loins girt about with the truth, and having on the breastplate of righteousness, and your feet shod with the preparation of the gospel of peace." His allusion to the shield, the dart, the helmet, and the sword lifts the picture of Ephesus, even in its ruins, into a splendid illustration of this gentlest and bravest of all his epistles.

Slowly we return from our day of wonders, full of that weird mysticism which haunts the mind when such associations clothe the senses with their dim radiance. Coming under the walls of the aqueduct, we see three of the blackest of black negresses, partly clad in red robes. In tipsy glee they hail us for backsheesh. We fling a *para* or so in honor of the sex to which the huntress of the silver bow belongs.

"From Abyssinia?" I cry. No response.
"From Egypt?" Dead as the Sphinx.
"From Nubia?"
"Yah! yah! Nubia, yah! yah!" and the three Nubian priestesses, who serve Diana afar off and yet at her very gates, never heard of the beauteous Queen of Night, and know little of her peculiar mo-

ralities. Africa is watching by the grave of Asia, and America is endeavoring to penetrate its mysteries. One can only find expression for such eccentric changes of time in the quaint imagery of Sir Thomas Browne, who described Egypt as "the land of obliviousness, which doteth. Her ancient civility is gone, and her glory hath vanished as a phantasma. Her youthful days are over, and her face hath become wrinkled and tetric. She poreth not upon the heavens. Astronomy is dead unto her, and Knowledge maketh other cycles. Canopus is afar off, Memnon resoundeth not to the sun, and Nilus heareth strange voices. Her monuments are but hieroglyphically sempiternal. Osiris and Anubis, her averruncous deities, have departed, while Orus yet remains, dimly shadowing the principle of vicissitude and the effluxion of things, but receiveth little oblation."

Yet it is this doting old Egypt, this phantasm of the wrinkled face, this unresounding Memnon, whose monuments are speaking so feebly to the ear of this century, that keeps its dead watch, through Nubian harridans, over the ancient civility and vanished glory of Ephesus!

CHAPTER XVIII.

ON THE WAY TO DAMASCUS.

We heard the Tecbir, so these Arabs call
Their shout of onset, when with loud acclaim
They challenged Heaven, as if demanding conquest.
The battle join'd, and, through the barb'rous herd,
Fight, fight, and Paradise, was all their cry.
—THE SIEGE OF DAMASCUS.

A CITY which holds the ashes of Saladin and Buckle, and is the home of Abd-el-Kader—which had the glory of St. Paul's conversion and the honor of Mohammed's most oriental compliment—is not to be seen in a day, nor dismissed as a mirage of the desert. If it had not once been the capital of the Arab world, the Paris of the Orient, its claim as the elder beauty of the Abrahamic exodus from Mesopotamia into the Holy Land, would give added sparkle to each drop of its rivers, canals, and fountains, hallow every atom of its dust, and gild every object upon which its fierce sun shines.

Every rock seems familiar with the forgotten past. Upon its sides is written the history of departed armies—and although the record of the fire and stone are obscure, still they are penciled by the Mighty Hand. I have seen in these stony records, pictures of Egyptian and Assyrian, on the rock, with the names of Sennacherib and Pharaoh. Their deeds have lasted so as to confirm Holy Writ.

When we left behind the blue sea and the promontory of Beirut yesterday, and wound our way over the bare hills on hills, and bleak mountains on mountains which led us hither; and when we bade farewell to the heights and vales of that Lebanon by the sea, so much beloved, and the glory of its cedars, palms, mulberries, fig-trees, and vineyards, and began our long ride among the rocks, mountains, and plains of the Lebanon beyond the sea, we knew that there was a generous recompense in store for our travel. If our road was elevated and our path zigzag, were we not repaid by the shadows and splendors of the Lebanon ranges and the peerless magnificence of Mount Hermon? If our companions were of an alien race, were we not repaid by views of mountain vales and cones, and the wide, verdant plain at their base, not to speak of the ever-recurring vista of that Biblical sea which met our gaze through mountain defiles, and which ever lifts itself up as if it were a psalm?

What a prospect we have from these mountains of Lebanon! What memories! Yonder, in the south-west is or was Tyre, and there, somewhat nearer, was Sidon; and to the north, lined by a broad belt of sky and sea, which seem to mingle as one, are the ancient castles of Crusader and Paynim, and the mountains round about, which seem self-withdrawn, in perpetual grandeur! How could we bring our vision down to the details of the journey—the immense herds of cattle, goats, and sheep, and the caravans of camels, donkeys, and men—when at every movement we must turn to the marriage of sea and sky, under the white veil of the distant clouds? How can we condescend to tell of the beautiful kiosks, the Maronite monasteries perched on mountain summits, the picturesque fig-gatherers and raisin-curers, or the annoyances, the cost, and delays, when from the glen of Hummâna, with its bowering orchards and its vesture of vineyards, to the sublime gorge of the Abana, across the tawny plain of Sahra (Sahara), there is a gallery of pictures whose natural features are illuminated as well by the light from sacred truth as by the Orient sunbeams, tempered on the mountains by the most genial of airs? You may call it enthusiasm which takes the pilgrim hither and over three ranges of the two Lebanons. But is it not worth a striving to see the summits of these hallowed hills of the Bible? Are these bare heights, bursting in grandeur, although only here and there clothed with vegetation—are these dark gorges between lofty peaks and castellated walls—are these Druse principalities, all red with Christian blood, these streams silvery with the lymph which makes the fissures and plains fruitful in grape and fig—are these Syrian temples of Roman and Herodian times, these wild retreats and verdurous belts, these precipices of tanned earth and rock and terraces of blushing apricots and pomegranates—are these fountains of sweet waters bursting from cliffs of limestone—all nothing, that we should regret the heats and dusts of our way to the city of our promise and hope?

"Promise and hope?" Yes. When a boy, I read Lamartine's "Pilgrimage to the Holy Land." His stately poetic prose and lordly enthusiastic personality made a vivid impression. His picture of Syria as "calcined with desolation" did not detract from the aureole of holy light which he threw about these very mountains of Lebanon!

I wonder whether Lamartine saw these mountains in the spring, when they are said to be green and beautiful, or at the end of summer, as is our case, when all is umber and rock. But it is said that even when the terraces are tricked out in their finery of vines, olives, and mulberry, still the mountains look brown from below as you are ascending; but otherwise when descending, when the terraced walls are not observed. However that may be, we have now something of that contrast wherein lieth much delight. When the water supply here is full, then the spring and summer are generous of their graces and goodness. But it is not true—though poetically pretty, as our English Minister, Lowell, in his heyday of inspiration, once sung—that

> " 'Tis heaven alone that is given away,
> 'Tis only God may be had for the asking;
> There is no price set on the lavish summer,
> And June may be had by the poorest comer."

No heavenly beauty, no lavish summer, no leafy June, is to be had here gratis. There is a price which is paid in hard labor for all that the Lebanon gives to its stewards and toilers, either in loveliness or reward.

Something more than rhapsody is required to tell how we passed the day on the road to Damascus.

There is a good road, well macadamized. It takes fourteen hours in the French diligence. We started at the early hour of four. Our seat was not a happy one at first, for we were in the "interieur," and with us two Arab women, with child, food, and baggage, and two men. When daylight came I found my neighbor was a very black man, who insisted on sleeping upon my fraternal shoulder.

We soon rectified our position, for we had been cheated by the agent, who put us in the wrong place. Being elevated to the banquette, we had a better view of the gorgeous scenery, and more comfort.

In going out of Beirut, the scenes are so thoroughly Asiatic, with the square stone houses and terraced mountains, the palm-trees and the cactus hedges, the figs and the vineyards, the cisterns of water and the caravans of camels, that we felt, more than at Broussa, that we were within the realms of the Orient. We felt, too, that we were on the enchanted borders of the Holy Land!

Watching and waiting, gazing through dust and heat, we long for a glance at the city of our hope and promise; how can we help but anticipate? This emerald setting in the rough cliffs, between the far-stretching desert and the limitless sea,—when shall we see its seven rivers? When look upon Abana and Pharpar, "better than all the waters of Israel?" We are athirst for the vision!

Passing walls on walls of rock at the head of the great valleys, like those in the midst of our backbone range in Colorado, but decorated with vines in terraced culture; passing patient camels, horses, and donkeys in endless procession, overladen, as it seems, and trudging slowly up the steeps and down the windings; gazing at turbaned Abrahamic ploughmen, with their antique wooden ploughs and laziest of ox teams, driven by the old goad; peering into strange, bronzed Bedouin faces and veiled womanly eyes; and watching long companies of sealed metallic wagons, guarded by horsemen, fresh and alert, as if in a circus ring, we at length reach the plain of the classic river Leontes, now known as the Litany. Here are proofs of moisture in green fields and fruitful orchards and vineyards.

Our halting-place is Stora, where there is a hotel kept by a Greek, Andrea, which we find quite a comfort. Out of the coupé of the diligence leaps a splendid-looking man. He is an Arab, and all rush to greet him. A company of soldiers, Circassians and Turks in uniform, receive him. With quiet and elegant manner he embraces some and salutes others. "Who is he? Can it be Rustam Pasha, the Italian, the Pasha of the Christians, the ruler of the Lebanon?" We go within the hostelry of the Greek, and begin our late breakfast at noon. A crowd entered with the Governor, for he is a Governor or sub-Governor of these villages. His name is Halil Bey. He asks of his attendants the usual cigarette. I present my compliments and my cigarette case, and this leads to courtesy, and we begin to talk. Before it is done he inquires gently about our President—just dead! We invite him to America, and he tenders us his protection to Baalbec. This was well and pleasing; but we do not require protection here. It was well, because it gave us what is needed here, a little prestige. It helps us to other courtesy, and hurts none. In his retinue is the son of our former dragoman at Beirut. This young man gives us a card to his father at Damascus. His father is Ayoub Tabet. He is just from America.

We are now in the midst of that level, some ten miles or more wide, which divides the two ranges of the Lebanon, whose waters are shed on left and right, for over a degree of latitude, to fructify the plain, and which, breaking their way under the western shadow of Mount Hermon, debouch between the sites of Tyre and Sidon. Upon this level what populations once lived, when Heliopolis had its sun worship, or Baalbec had its millions and the coast its commerce; and when the land was not denuded of its forests or cursed with bad government!

We break the monotony of the way by talking to the conductor. He speaks French. He is a large and good-natured Arab, and has been trained by the Jesuits in the school at Beirut; still, he is an Arab. I inquire of him as to the effect of religion here. He replies, as he looks out upon Moslems on their carpets praying: "Oh, too many religions—not too much religion." It is a well-turned phrase.

I ask him again: "What good these pilgrimages to Mecca do? Every village has its man on the way now."

He laughingly shows his white teeth, and with an old maxim responds: "If a man goes to Mecca once, trust him: twice, don't: and three times, move out of his neighborhood."

We leave this place with some reluctance. It is a beautiful spot; but it is not Damascus. Our jolly Arab neighbor in the banquette halloos to the sleepy passengers, "Damask!" at every relay; but we are but half our way when we take a lunch and a fresh start at Stora, in the midway plain. Goatherds are hailed by the rowdy Arab; old sheiks are saucily chaffed by him; a small boy standing astride, like a miniature colossus, of our road is joked by him; the conductor of the diligence is even twitted by him, until the great shadow of our conveyance is thrown by the shades of evening down the mountain sides, and we are almost sure that Damascus is nigh. We have passed the pleasant vale, the fountains, and the ruined khans, called Meithelun. Gray hills of rock, with vines, which are the only relief to the eye under the suns of summer, usher in new views of villages on distant slopes, unromantic and flat, but with green about them as fringes; and then we strike the desert.

The road shines like a vein of silver across the arid plain. At its termination we dash with unexpectedness and delight into a defile of bewildering beauty. Foliage and fountains, and streams under sunshine, walnuts and willows, poplars ever so tall and elegant, give signs that water is here, working its magic and by its silver silences and murmurous melodies is beginning to make out of bleakness a beatitude.

Wherever there is water there is hope. Job tells us that even if a tree be cut down, there is hope that it will sprout again, and that the tender branch thereof will not cease. We have every sign here upon this road that the root has waxed old in the earth. "Yet through the scent of water it will bud, and bring forth boughs like a plant."

The mountains are white with the lime, and their contrast with the green of the descending vales is heightened by the appearance of cultivated villages. Our conductor begins to show signs of reaching for his horn. We drive faster and faster, until, lo! at a glance, as if the "scales" had fallen from our parched eyes, the road to Damascus narrows into a cañon, and becomes illuminated with a new glory. Out of the very bleakness of this desert, by the aid of irrigation and dams, leap the live orchards! Out of the river Abana, made by the snows and dews of the Hermon, but as if from subterranean lakes, come forth thick groves, still in strange contrast with the rugged mountains. Before we are aware of it, our road is again narrowed by walls, or blocks, made of dried mud, and held together by branches. These walls of brown clay, rolled smooth and compacted over, these branches (bricks with straw), appear more frequently; and then, still following the ravine with its laughing water, which is like a thread of silver in a texture of green, we find ourselves in sight of the Mosque of Selim, and hailed by crowds of expectant people. Gardens appear; willows with great trunks lean over the streams which they have scented. They run a race with us. Crowds of black goats and caravans of loaded camels, in strange contrast also with the white limestone cliffs and mountains; and then more houses with flat roofs; and baths with incoming and outgoing people; and rushing, roaring falls, and pictured houses; and then men in fine attire, on mules, donkeys, and horses, all draped in golden saddle-cloths; and we are under an avenue so warm and so thick with trees that the hot walls give us their spent caloric, and the branches of the trees fly saucily into the banquette of our vehicle. Horsemen with guns in hand, dash by; and the conductor cries out, "Damascus!" But he, too, anticipates. Some fields of maize, with a scarecrow; more canals and caves; cool depths of poplar and other woods; more old roots of trees by the water-side; plane-trees, spreading with time and hollow with age; and the conductor points to the last intervening mountain. Impatiently I ask: "Are we never to see Damascus? Are we not yet nigh?"

He responds: "Yonder! One more mountain!" We look up to it with gratitude. It is our beacon. Over it in faint, white crescent, emblematic of the Moslem, is the new moon. At last! Damascus is in our view. Then appear the six minarets—two black tipped—and domes innumerable bursting out of green environs. It is a splendid vision, for it furnishes to the famished eye signs of Damascus— the elder! Snap! Crack! Whisk! Tirrahlah! from the horn, and, amid a crowd of bystanders, open fly the gates, and we are within not only the city of Uz, the capital of Syria, the delight of the Orient, but within the precincts of the grand diligence establishment, and near the Hotel Dimitri. We find the goal of our ambition.

Preliminaries for return and a trip to Baalbec being settled, we are met by a courier, and escorted to our hotel. As we enter the narrow and low gateway, its court gives us an interior Damascene view, which has all the local color which trees and fountains, colored walls and arabesques of grace could give. It was a welcome place.

It is a grand old city; and we took it, not without some chivalric endeavor, for how else would one take the city which holds the tomb of Saladin?

Fourteen hours in a diligence, over a wonderful road! The heat was much, and the dust more; but the scenery repaid all, and the finale eclipsed the scenery. A French company owns the conveyances, and made the road. It is well ordered. It reminds us of Alpine passes. A toll of fourteen piastres (sixty-four cents, or three francs) on every animal—sheep, mule, goat, camel, horse, and donkey—supports the road. In winter it is much snowed, and the mails are in trouble in the wild gulches. Still, the road is now well protected. Brigands no longer menace in the defiles. The country of the Lebanon has had troubles, and ever since the war in 1860 it has been in unrest. But it has had a Christian Governor, and although Moslems are themselves restless under this arrangement, the "Great Powers" have kept this order in spite of all irksome outside pressure.

At our dinner at the hotel in the evening the father of our Stora friend, Ayoub Tabet, appears. He is full of his American trip. He makes us at home socially; and soon after we retire to rest and to dream of running waters, pleasant fountains, elegant kiosks and arabesques, flat-roofed houses set amid verdant bowers, and all crowned and overtopped by the splendid range of Mount Hermon— the first, last, and best vision of the Lebanon.

CHAPTER XIX.

DAMASCUS—ITS WONDERS AND GLORIES, MASSACRES AND MOSQUES—ITS TOMBS AND WALLS—ITS APOSTOLIC MEMORIES, AND GRAVE OF BUCKLE.

> *Between the foaming jaws of the white torrent,*
> *The skillful artist draws a sudden mound;*
> *By level long he subdivides their strength,*
> *Stealing the waters from their rocky bed,*
> *First to diminish what he means to conquer;*
> *Then for the residue he forms a road,*
> *Easy to keep, and painful to desert,*
> *And guiding to the end the planner aim'd at.*
> —The Engineer.

I WRITE by a couple of candles at midnight, in a land where there is no gas or midnight sun. By a certain motherly and necessitous invention these minor "lights of Asia" stand within the blushing bosom of two pomegranates, so that you may see why these letters from Damascus lack the electric light of other lands, and are rhetorically over-redolent of the aroma of the East. Besides, is it not worth while to sacrifice some convenience to unburden one's self? My memory of this city is already like an overladen camel. It refuses to "get up," or, when up, shows its critical teeth and spiteful lip. This is not my theory of pleasure or observation in travel; for, while I do not like to admire anything not intrinsically admirable, I do love to praise all that is praiseworthy. Hence, in despite of much in Damascene morals and annals alien to the Jewish and Christian mind, I may discreetly praise what is just, kindly, and honorable to them as a leading city in the advancement of our kind.

The bazaars and Bedouins, mosques and muftis, gardens and guitars, canals and courtesies, looms for silk and carpet, and forges for swords and cutlery, houses decorated by rare arabesques, and horses caparisoned with equipments worthy of Saladin—these deserve and have special places in its museum of memory. They displace much of the hateful and bigoted in the history of this city. Nor is it to be forgotten that, to make this terrestrial paradise, the same engineering skill which gave to Andalusia its irrigation and fruitful glory had its source in the race which invented arithmetic, algebra, and astronomy, the three big A's of the Moorish alphabet.

I remember well, when in 1851 I contemplated a trip hither, that I was warned that it was the city of the East, of all others, where fanaticism was so rampant that Christians were unsafe. No good conduct on their part, and no "safe conduct" on the part of the Government would then have protected us. Nine years after, intolerance broke out in zealous, bloody massacres. No returns have shown the number of Christians who fell. There were two thousand five hundred ascertained male adults alone murdered in this city. Some were refugees from the villages, and others strangers from Mesopotamia, Egypt, and Armenia. The Christian houses and bazaars were burned and pillaged. Worse than murder was the fate of many women. A cry of horror and of revenge was heard through Christendom, and steps were taken by the powers to punish the guilty and provide security for the future. So far as it is possible for me to observe, there is not much of this ignorance and intolerance left; although the Christians, who number in the city now some twenty-five thousand, out of the two hundred thousand population, say that the malice of the old enemy is only hidden, or, as the psalm hath it, "he sitteth in the lurking-places of the villages, and lieth in wait secretly as a lion in his den."

So far as my acquaintance goes, I think there may be some little to be said in extenuation of the crimes of 1860. I would not indict the whole race or a religion for the excesses of a part. The Arabs are a generous race, if unprovoked, and if decently led. Hospitable and frank, good-tempered and genial, we have found them, and in this respect they differ from their cousins the Tartar Turks.

Besides, was not Damascus the seat of the Caliphate, which it divided at one era with Bagdad and Cordova? And may I not commend to the student of toleration many of their precepts and policies, which have in them the essential toleration of our Constitution?

We visit the bazaars. They are like all oriental bazaars. The shops are very small. Their cross-legged proprietors are eager to sell. Other merchants go around the narrow thoroughfares, tendering you bargains. Sometimes precious stones are offered you. Pearls, turquoise, and diamond leap out of the folds from the bosom of a greasy old Turk, and are offered you. Now and then some veiled female, once a favorite of the harem, will tender the jewels she received in the morning of her life and beauty. You are sometimes invited to a seat and to coffee on the platform; and the goods are displayed to tickle your fancy. You are about to buy, when prayers are called from the minaret near; the merchant stops. He prays. After prayer he begins again to chatter and cheat.

What happens in these bazaars when two caravans of mules or donkeys, with panniers loaded five times the size of the animal, meet each other? What if a string of camels strive to "lumber" through; and what if our carriage, which can only go one way, and cannot be turned round, be caught in this Eastern imbroglio? This happened to us once or twice; and a mad camel,—and when mad they are very, very bad and mad,—dashed by us. His ropes caught our carriage, and but for the quickness of our dragoman we should have been upturned, or inturned into a shop. Fortunately there was but one step from the carriage to a silk stall; and we were ready for the step. Nobody here will get out of the way, if it can be helped. Not even a dog gets out of the way, though instant death stares him in the face. Like the people, he will gaze sleepily and half curiously at you; and, like them, he will cry on the least suspicion of trouble. You pick up a stone to hurl at a dog, and he howls till you throw it, or hit him, and then he goes off quietly. Although our cavass was a Moslem, and sat with the driver, sworded as a knight and pistoled like a Boabdil, and all recognized him as authority with the right of way, yet the dreamy turbaned folks about in the bazaars, cross-legged or on low stools, with their truck to sell or coffee to drink, never moved. We crashed in one of the four legs of a stool, and grazed the man who sat on it, but he smoked away as if nothing had happened. It was "Kismet!"

Our experience in the "interieur" of the diligence over the Lebanon has given me an insight into the inner life of the Arab, which confirms the kindly regard I formed when we sailed with crowds of them for eight days upon the coasts of Asia Minor and Syria.

Before a stranger can capture the interesting objects here he must have his dragoman. We are fortunate in having Antonio Sawabeni. He was the guide of the Brazilian Emperor. This he is proud to say. He is a Catholic, and has wounds, from boyhood, growing out of the massacre of 1860. He is well educated and speaks English intelligently.

Our consulate here is under the charge of Mr. Meshaka, who provided us with a cavass whose appearance was both authoritative and picturesque. His name is Selim El Havet, and his golden embroidered and braided jacket, above his widely flowing white pants, with his silken turban of red and gold, gave ornament to his genius. He had genius for command, and, if naturalized, would make an excellent sergeant-at-arms to Congress. Children gave way to him; grown people looked after him, and honored us because of him; and soldiers saluted us because of his relation to our Government. The bazaars, once unknown as pathways for carriages, now were free to our landau, when his presence was seen as its directing force. When he organized us for our observations this morning—it was with a carriage! A carriage is as strange in these narrow streets as a white elephantine Jumbo of the King of Siam would be in the Bowery. When, therefore, we went out of our hotel, under a low door, metallic, and four feet high, and mounted our carriage, we had no idea of the perils we would undergo and overcome from loaded camels and donkeys in the narrow ways.

These bazaars of Damascus are celebrated. They are, like those we saw at Broussa and Constantinople, screened from sun in summer and snow in winter. They consist of long, covered wooden sheds for each trade, and open stalls where goods are displayed. The smoking salesman sits comfortably on a rug in front of his little wareroom. There is no limitation on the kind and number of Asiatics who throng these cool, dark thoroughfares. What a medley of men and miscegenation of mankind! All colors, from ebony to ivory, in face and wardrobe; all shapes of matter, men, and women, and all sorts of movements, jabber, and cries! The fierce, dark Bedouin, with his light turban tied about his dark hair by a rope of black wool, and his weapons handy in his sash, is here. He is being measured for his clothes, trying his tobacco, or buying his shoes and saddles. We exchanged some civilities at a tailor's stall with a sheik from near Bagdad. My wife said to him that if we had more time she would like to visit the famous city of Bagdad, known so far and near. He gave a quick, honest glance, and said:

"We will assure your safety and ease. Go with us!"

These Bedouin promises are kept with fidelity, and but for trusts at home we should have "rushed under his belt" and taken his offer.

Our first venture was through the horse market, where the spirited horses of the Arabs are shown off and bought and sold by auction. Then we go to the great mosque. It is like many mosques of

Greek or other origin than Mohammedan. Inscriptions, quite ancient, in Greek show this. It adds to the Christian architecture the dome and minaret, arcade and pavement, and fountains of musical water, with their flexile columns in the light. These are Moslem. Taking off our shoes, we walked through its length, some one hundred and sixty-three yards, and across its width, one hundred and eight yards, and over its hundreds of carpets, on which a dozen Mohammedans were asleep in the cool shades by the murmuring fountains. Here, in and out of the structure, under the arcades, in the great court, and under the splendid dome, are arches and pillars of all forms of beauty and arrangement. Colored marbles and mosaics, and a thousand tasteful arabesque attractions make this mosque the most interesting — next to St. Sophia—of any in Moslemdom. Its site is sacred. Its library of choice books and manuscripts is lifted on columns, inaccessible except by a ladder. Some of its columns are from the Temple of the Sun at Palmyra, and others from temples of equal renown. The elder religion of Syria was that of Baal—the Sun—and there is much here, as well as at Baalbec, to illustrate the splendid dedication of art to this worship of the blazing deity. Here was once a marble tabernacle for the Sun, and it had a glorious litany. I remembered the story of Naaman and his love of the rivers of Damascus, and the worship of Rimmon, from which he was turned when cured of his leprosy by the Jordan and the prophet. I wondered, too, if this strange structure was not the inspiration of that beauteous altar which Ahaz had seen on his visit to Damascus, and which he had copied for his sacrificial offerings in Jerusalem. A hundred other associations of this worship gather about this spot, illuminated by Orient sunbeams.

After a promenade about its courts, where but a few years ago no profane Christian foot was allowed, we summon one of the imps of the place. He appears, not with Aladdin's lamp, but with a lantern some three feet by two. Open flies the creaking door, under the magic of a rattling. rusty key, and a Napoleon in gold! This latter magic, we find, is a special stipulation with the consulates, whose subjects were often taxed double for this privilege. The gate closes with a clang, and the lock is turned, so that no unholy intruder may enter. We ascend a devious gallery—our cavass in front—up the three hundred steps which lead to the main minaret and into the light. What a picture, bathed in shimmering sunshine! In its praise may we not sing a new song? Is it not wondrous in its strangeness, and strange in its loveliness? Turn whithersoever we will, high and above all appear the calcined mountains, as turreted walls of rock, guarding the treasures of this enchanted city. Lebanon and its glories lift their misty elevations under great shadowy clouds; and Hermon, the monarch of Syrian mountains, in his brown robes, sweeping down to the valley, is illuminated by a crown of snow. Turn wheresoever we will, this noble triple grandeur of Mount Hermon, with his tiara of splendor, overmasters all other imagery. Look below. The appearance instantly discloses why Damascus is the gem of the Orient. Its flat-roofed, whitish-brown houses are set squarely on the earth, amid orchards whose green is in pleasing contrast with the umber of the horizon surrounding it, above and beyond. Below us, on the west, is the old castle. It is itself a chief object, but in the whole view only an incident. Around us are the bulbous roofs of the mosques, baths, and khans. Do you see those old stones in partial arch, with rare ornamentation, hidden almost in the modern walls? That is an old triumphal arch. It is Roman; but, like many similar monuments, it serves only as a prop or aid to modern edifices of questionable taste.

Often had I heard of the remark of Mohammed, who, looking at Damascus from the outside, exclaimed: " I will not enter thy gates! My paradise is reserved for the next world!" With my glass I easily see upon the summit of the whitish limestone mountain in the distance, some four thousand feet high, a little temple or marabout, to fix and celebrate the spot from which he sighed and looked at this earthly Eden. Turning to the east we see white houses. They form suburbs upon the sides of the mountains, and to the west the canals and rivers are marked by emerald belts. Here is the Christian quarter, the East Gate, and the cemeteries. To the south there is a large area of groves; for, where water is so scarce and the brown and bleak are so common, verdure becomes exceedingly precious. Looking closely in our surrounding circuit, we are within hail—so clear is the sunlit air—of the other minarets of this old temple. Across the way, in the centre of the northern court, is the minaret of the " Bride "—white, with a few rosy colors. It is as graceful in its heavenward gesture as the beautiful woman in whose honor it is erected in this city of graces. Then, arising two hundred and fifty feet high out of this mosque, is the minaret—of Jesus! Truly it is wonderful—this apotheosis of our Saviour! But it is not so wonderful when we perceive within the mosque a splendid tomb which incloses the head of John the Baptist, he of the wilderness. He, too, is recognized as prophetic, and, like all these seers of the Orient, he came forth from the solitudes and silence of the desert to proclaim rules of faith and duty. As such the oriental mind recognizes them. It is not so wonderful, when we reflect that Jesus is recognized by the Moslem as a great teacher and prophet, and that the pride of Syria enshrined here does not disdain, in this emblematic way, to stoop in recognition of "the Judge of the World, Jesus Christ," who, when he comes, will descend upon this elegant minaret!

How the presence of our Saviour sweetens the associations of this place. A man once said to a lump of clay, "What art thou?" The reply was, "I am but a lump of clay, but I was placed beside a rose and I caught its fragrance." Yet, when we reflect, the seminal and capital idea of Mohammedanism, is only a projection of the Hebraic and Christian system. It is Oriental. Out of these deserts came that spiritual sublimity which knew no images in its worship. Zoroaster, Buddha, Moses, Christ and Mohammed, taught one truth in common. But it is strange that in this city of reputed bigotry toward Christians, Christ should be the judge of quick and dead!

It is my opinion that if the judgment should take place here, there would be some other "bloody and deceitful" men, besides those whom Lord Dufferin, the English Commissioner, sentenced, and punished for their persecution and massacre of the devotees of Jesus in 1860.

Then descending, we began our venture through the bazaars. We made considerable headway through the "street which is called Straight," and which has given rise to some profane crookedness of criticism, for which I have no sympathy, and by those who will not consider that all things are comparative. It was and is straight, as this world counts straightness. Its rectilinearness is one of the cumulative proofs of the story of St. Paul's conversion, not lightly to be omitted.

We pass the crowds of women who are in the bazaars to buy. The silk department is full of females. The Christian women are draped in pure white from head to foot, but their faces are not concealed. They seem singularly spiritual. The Arab women have their faces hidden—not *à la Turque*, with only those perilous, dreamy eyes shining out of the involutions of the yashmak, but under a dark-figured, square, gauzy veil, around which is a large, flowing mantle of varied hue. This dress is puzzling to curiosity. The "children of this azure sheen" have black eyes; and there are no children—especially the girls—to compare with these in beauty,—except those of my past, present, and future Congressional districts!

Damascus is full of Biblical associations. Its environs have villages and caves which have a record in the historical portions of our Scriptures. Tradition here, among the Arabs and Jews, is not to be despised as a medium of memory. Unlike the nonsensical nebulous myths of other lands, these traditions have coherency and reason to endorse them. Rock-hewn wells, tombs, and temples confirm holy sites, and even the ancient customs, as described in the Bible, are reproduced as they were three thousand and more years ago. Who can refuse to believe that Abraham once ruled in Damascus, and that he came hither out of Chaldea before he went into Canaan? Josephus proves it, and every Bedouin in the bazaar, on the road, tented in the fields, or ploughing left-handed with his rude wooden ploughshare, and driving his oxen with his antique goad, is Abraham's photographic similitude. The travels of the Apostles about these shores and lands are confirmed by geography. It is impossible to mistake the present Damascus, and its walls and streets, for other than the Damascus of Holy Writ. Roman remains mark these spots, as if they wore the signet of emperors, kings, tetrarchs, and prefects.

If you are sceptical as to the story of Paul's conversion, go with me to the traditional places, and, although you may doubt the miracle, and call it, out of courtesy, a fable, you will not doubt that right here—somewhere in, about, or on these walls—the scenes described in the ninth chapter of "Acts" are verities. The precise spot is shown where the slaughter-breathing Saul saw new light. It is near Damascus, and on the old Roman road. We know that it is a Roman road, and that it was at the eastern gate he entered, "led by the hand." If we are not certain that the spot we are about to visit is the house of Ananias, certainly it was in the eastern quarter, and in "the street which is called Straight," which was the lodging-place of Paul. Let us not be too critical. Certainly this is a spot of wonders, even speaking after the methods of men. This remarkable scholar and lawyer, Paul—whose name is sounded from every pulpit in Christendom; in whose name temples of the Lord have arisen for two thousand years, from Damascus, in the very home of his conversion, to proud old Rome which imprisoned him; and from Rome to New York; from the little church around the corner, in Hammerfest, under the midnight sun in Arctic Norway, to the mighty minster of Christopher Wren, at London—this grand teacher of the Gentiles certainly had great agony of spirit and darkness of mind until the scales fell from his eyes on this very road to Damascus!

"Go," we say to our guide, Sawabeni, "to the house of Ananias!"

Would you expect it to be above ground? Not after so long a time, for time will cover with its mounds all things sacred, even when the substructures remain. Winding among narrow streets and walls, whose heavy doors show significantly the precautions of these habitants of the Christian quarter, the cavass at length touches a knocker. We are quietly ushered through some rooms occupied by poor people. We pass down into a vaulted chamber where there is a little Catholic chapel. Several prints, representing the martyrdom by the cross of priests in China, and pictures of St. Jerome and St. Francis are upon the plain walls. Over the simple altar is a good painting of St. Paul. His black beard and hair and intellectual courage are well represented. He is kneeling before a fair-haired man. This is the good and truthful Ananias, who baptizes him. In one corner of the room is a large bronze lamp, which is lit after nightfall. Our Catholic dragoman grows eloquent over the scene. As the cavass cannot understand his English, he breaks forth in praise of his own father, who fell in the massacre of 1860, "cut in two pieces," he says, "by the scimitar of the Mohammedans. His last words were,'I die for my religion.' They asked me if I would not be a Moslem. I did not know then more than to follow my father, and so I said, ' No, I will die with father, and for the sake of his Saviour.' They wounded me here," as he pointed to his cheek, "and I am a living proof of that terrible time." A deaf and dumb boy makes his mute appeal to us as we enter the gateway, and we pluck some lavender and flowers in the court as we leave the house of Ananias.

Riding becomes impossible at this point; so we walk to the eastern gate to see three objects : one, the grave of Buckle ; another, the alleged scene of Paul's conversion ; and the third, the wall where he was let down in a basket. We come out under one of the three portals, for the "gate" is threefold, and find ourselves in the midst of a herd of black goats. Donkeys raise their dissonant music in the narrow way. Out into the grassless caravansary we come. It is a sandy plain, where there is a runlet of running water. There the camels, mules, and cattle congregate, after their journeys from Bagdad, with silks, dates, and carpets. It will accommodate four thousand camels. We perceive a hundred camels resting in the sun. As we pass they show their teeth, as if we were of the infidel order. My wife never forgives this patient beast since one of them ran away with her toward Timbuctoo, in Algiers, being frightened at her black dress. However, they are not more dangerous than the donkey, and we move amid them to see the cemeteries which line the place.

There is here a large mausoleum, where the

WALLS OF DAMASCUS.

bones of the massacred Christians of 1860 are deposited. Here, too, are the flat and dusty tombstones of the Christian cemetery, and near by is a rock. It is a mark of the spot where the great apostle received his new light. Altogether it is a rough and dusty spot, but a portion of the old Damascus highway is saved by the veneration of the Latin monks, who have celebrated it by distinguishing monuments. It may not be, however, so well avouched as the place on the wall where St. Paul was let down when he escaped to Jerusalem. This is pictured to the eye in the engraving. It was customary, in those days, to live upon the walls, and George—St. George, for he has been sainted—who was the porter of the gate, is said to have lived upon this wall. He kept this gate. The fact is briefly recorded by St. Paul in second Corinthians, 11th chapter, 33d verse. The spot is in an angle of the wall, which is fifty feet high, and whose old portions have been supplemented by Saracenic handicraft. The gate itself was long since closed. Near by, under the shadow of some walnut trees, is a tomb to George, the porter, who was beheaded for his kindness to Paul on this spot. An iron fence and a little temple honor his remains. The inscriptions are worn off, but a cross is there, and in a hole in the square tomb is a little antique lamp. This is lighted every night.

We cast some curious glances at the tombs around, and their Arab inscriptions. These were Christian Arabs. Their tombs, like all except those of Moslems, are not allowed to be erect! Their flatness is a sign of the subjected race. I ask the dragoman to read me one inscription.

"They each have on them," he says, "the God-Father prayer."

Here and there are conspicuous tombs of Arab chiefs—they are almost temples—square, with a dome. Around this open space are walls over which are seen bountiful orchards. "The dust of the wind" blows freely over the space, but the camels chew the cud regardless of it; for are they not born to the sands of the desert? A few Arab boys lie asleep in the shade of the walls, careless of the dust from the débris of the fires of the massacre days of 1860, which has been piled up outside the city. A few fierce Druses from the Lebanon, weather-worn and gray-headed, pass by on donkeys and horses. The sight of them makes our Christian guide voluble with indignation, for it was the "bad Druses" who showed themselves most bloody and vindictive in 1860.

We take a farewell of this singular place, solitary yet peopled with so much of which to think. We go round about these tombs, towers, and gates, and mark well the bulwarks. Alas! that it should be only a place for the camel and the trader. It smells of myrrh and aloes and cassia out of the ivory palaces. But it does not "make glad," for over yonder yellow wall, in the English cemetery, lies the body of the great philosophic scholar whose life was so prematurely clouded by disease, and whose light was quenched in this marvelous city, to which he ventured for health and repose.

Buckle died of typhus fever on the 29th of May, 1862. He had been overworked upon his famous second volume, and left England, and spent the winter in Egypt. He had recovered his health, and was traveling in Palestine on horseback, when he was again stricken down at Nazareth. He had reached Sidon, and overtasked his strength in the trip hither. Under the influence of opiates in his last sickness, he frequently exclaimed in his despair: "Oh, my book! my book!" He had every care from the English and American consuls, physicians, and missionaries. He was forty years of age. He had an ample fortune, but his delight was in his library. He was, *par excellence*, a student; a student with a philosophic theory. He was buried on the afternoon of the day of his death. The English service was read over his remains. For some time no monument marked his grave. Thanks to the sister of the English consul, at length there is an altar-tomb of pure white marble, framed within a border of black basalt, with a foundation of sienna-colored stone resting on a base of black basalt, to mark the spot. Around it is a pavement, overgrown by brambles and grass. An epitaph, written by his sister, Mrs. Allatt, simply gives the name, age, and day of decease. To this is added an old Arabic phrase, signifying that the written word survives the author. The Arabic inscription is in white on a black ground. The tomb is oblong and exceedingly plain.

Who among the princes of the East can be compared with the author of the "History of Civilization?" One great longing of my heart was to stand over his grave in this distant land. There it is, over that hateful wall. The wall is twenty feet high, with no ingress. Must I leave Damascus without my tribute at this tomb, whose occupant, when in his round full being won so many chaplets in the arena of philosophic analysis? Does he not deserve something more than a remote grave amid these rude Arab monuments? A niche in the Pantheon of Fame, along with the thoughtful worthies of mankind would be more fitting for his immortalization. I am resolved to see that grave. Our cavass mounts a lower wall, and brushes away the tangled briers; the coachman gives me his back as a stepping-stone, and with the help of the dragoman I mount. I see the grave. It is near that of Lady Digby, the English wife of an Arab sheik, who could not rival Lady Hester Stanhope, but who has just ended another eccentric career. The tombs of Shelley and Keats I have seen at Rome, and during the summer have visited many resting-places of the gifted in our literature, from that of Alexander Pope to that of Benjamin Disraeli. But to none do I pay such willing reverence as to his who welded the events of earthly history by links of gold, and gave concatenation and laws to the seeming chances and inconsequences of human conduct. And now all that is mortal of Buckle lies here in cold obstruction! The sweet breezes blow down from dewy Hermon, and wave the apricot and walnut trees which form the canopy of his tomb. Around are many other graves and flat tombs, amid the brown, uncut grasses, in this small God's acre; but his tomb is distinguished even here. It is surrounded by a railing of iron, but out of its plain slabs rises no column of marble, broken at the top, symbolic of his work and his fate. Amid the leafy luxuriance of the adjoining orchard rises one elegant, stately poplar, plumed at its summit, but, unlike the rest of the foliage, yellow with premature decay — another emblem of the lonely death of that elegant and rational student whose muse of history was a Minerva for wisdom, and whose simple eloquence was to me more than that of Plato for diction and dignity!

When Buckle was entombed here the Mohammedan bigots had destroyed the trees and mutilated the tombs. Vain, infatuate fury! They could not destroy the theses on which he founded his philosophy. How impotent seems a mob. Its unreasoning bigotry only adds to the glory of immortal natures.

Buckle gave us, after Adam Smith, the best science of wealth, natural and social. He discriminated between social and individual laws. In his method of averages he used almost mathematical theories; but they were, after all, moral probabilities. He aggrandized the intellectual in the social life; and the moral in the individual life. He was —in his enthusiasm for truth and liberty—a bigot against intolerance! "But he was a sceptic," says some superficial preacher. With tears in his eyes and his ambition discomfited by disease and death, he was able to exclaim: "Without immortality life would be insupportable. I believe in God!"

His weary star was here enlarged. He sought, from zone to zone, strength for his body, to complete his conceptions. Was he not guided—even when dying alone—by that Power which led his flight aright?

Perhaps it does not matter where the mere shell of such an intellectual soul as that of Buckle reposes. Perhaps it was his own wish to sleep beneath these whispering trees, under the influences of the beauty of Lebanon! Perhaps his spirit, as it took its leave of earth, rejoiced in yonder pale azure scarf and snow-crowned royalty of Hermon, and found the analogue of its studious life in the condensations of a higher atmosphere, from whose clouds of white, rivaling the snow in purity, comes down upon the thirsty land abundant refreshment, even "as the dew of Hermon, the dew that descended upon the mountains of Zion!"

My little band wondered that I lingered upon this wall, to muse over this to them unknown man, whose spirit seemed to breathe in the clustered trees, whose chant was a part of the infinite harmony in which his spirit found repose. Our dragoman became a little jealous of my devotion to the Englishman's grave, for the dragoman's sentiment was hovering around the tomb of the apocryphal St. George the porter, while our cavass cast reverent eyes toward the mausoleum of the Moslem hermit near by, as if all earthly good had lived and died with him.

"Antonio," I say, interpreting his thoughts, "St. George has gone."

"Yes," he replied, "and St. Paul is gone."

"But he lives," I respond, "in mighty words, spoken for all time."

To which he replies: "Yes, and but for St. George he never could have spoken or written these words at Jerusalem, Philippi, Ephesus, and Rome."

Marveling at the turn of his thought, I say: "And a greater than St. Paul never wore earth about him, save One!"

Truly it may be said that among those who were worthy to sit at St. Paul's feet, as he sat at the feet of Gamaliel, was the rare English scholar over whose tomb no vestal lamp burns, but whose analytic thought only did not reach apostolic exaltation.

Paul, the eloquent Jew, and Buckle, the accomplished Englishman, will ever rest in my mind together. One of them clearly saw the celestial light and heard the divine voice. The other was not unworthy to be a " chosen vessel " unto God, to bear his name before Gentiles and kings, and to suffer great things for his name's sake.

It would be impossible to leave Damascus without an attempt at least to see Abd-el-Kader, the famous Emir of Algiers, whose native city, Milianah, we visited in 1869. We were promised under our national convoy an interview with him if we visited Damascus. But he is absent at his country-seat, and we have missed the opportunity of interviewing the old hero of North Africa as to the recent and forthcoming movements in the Mohammedan world. I should like to have asked him what the Sublime Porte means by resuming its effete suzerainty in Northern Africa. I should like to have had his opinion as to the progress of that unity for Pan-Islamism which is giving occupation and anxiety to Western Cabinets.

CHAPTER XX.

A HEBREW HOUSE IN DAMASCUS—DAMASCUS MIRTH AND MUSIC.

And I will rejoice in Jerusalem, and joy in my people. * *
There shall be no more thence an infant of days, nor an old man that hath not filled his days. * * *And they shall build houses, and inhabit them.*—ISAIAH lxv.

IT is impossible, in moving about among these reminders of religious service and suffering in Damascus, to disregard the potential element of the Jewish mind. This reflection made me recall a promise I had made to visit an eminent Israelite at his own house. Even the most opulent of this race are housed in the Jewish quarter. Passing through this quarter we peep into the doors of many poor Jews; yet we find no beggars there. Cats and dogs, pigeons and children in plenty; some distaffs, and signs of dyeing and weaving, but no signs of discomfort—all in contrast to the poor Jewish refugees we saw flying to Turkey and Judea for safety from German and Russian bigotry and spite.

The Jewish quarter is in the southern portion of the city, within the old walls, and not far from the eastern gate. We enter the gate, and winding between the narrow walls, which give no promise of the sumptuous houses within, we are at length within the court of the eminent Hebrew of Damascus, Maire Effendi.

He was clad in the costume of the East, with the fez on the head and the flowing and furrowed garments to the feet. He was full-bearded, and beautiful in the expression of his eye and countenance. This was a visit worthy of a daintier pen than mine. I fail to recall the exquisite orientalism and luxurious taste which met us as we went, under the courteous guidance of the Effendi, into his audience chamber. All that I had read of Eastern poesy—all that I had seen at the Alhambra—seems here to be encrusted, painted, carved, decorated, in choicest arabesque. Tiny marble temples, and larger alabaster columns, rich in hue and exquisite in tracery; subdued light from " richly dight " windows; arches of Byzantine elegance; and fountains of silver droppings and jets; grand yellow Damascus silk hangings and ottomans, and tessellated mosaics in many-colored marbles furnish the feeble description of my poor pen and ink. One requires the delicate and gorgeous imagery of Keats or the pencil of Jerome and Meissonier in one of their oriental *intérieurs*, to give an adequate idea of the sensation which the bewildered eye bears within the brain for its entrancement at a glance of this sumptuous Hebrew chamber. Must I descend to the mercenary, and tell the thousands which this one chamber alone cost; or which the gold enameling of palm and pillar would weigh in minted pounds, roubles, eagles, or doubloons?

The Effendi does not speak English or French. He summons his son, who speaks the last; and while he tenders my wife all the welcomes, the Effendi, in Arabic—interpreted by the dragoman—tenders to me similar urbanity. My wife tells of the persecutions of the Jews in Russia and elsewhere, in which I had taken some public interest in Congress, and for which the Israelitish Alliance at Paris were pleased to thank me. Whereupon they remark that their interest is one with the Alliance, with which they correspond. Thus conversing—our family being upon the yellow ottomans, but not in oriental posture—we are served with a citron conserve, eaten out of a spoon of daintiest silver. Only one spoonful is the fashion. While the sweet waters murmur and the cool air refreshes, in comes a servant bearing cups as exquisite as those diamond delicacies with which Abdul Hamid honored us when, as a part of our Minister's retinue, we were received at the palace on the Bosphorus. Only this, that these Hebrew cups were set in filigree of silver; but the coffee had an aroma quite equal to that of his Majesty. Pursuing our talk, the Effendi inquired my title and office. He also asks my name. I give it. "Samuel! Samuel!" he repeats, with earnest gaze from his dark eyes. "Yes. It is customary for us to prefix the names of the grand Hebrew fathers to that of our own fathers." I did not leave him with the idea that I was a Hebrew; but I should be proud to have in my veins the blood of Isaiah and Paul, of Crémieux and Heine, of Treck and Moson.

I showed him my special passport as an "Honorable Member," with the sign-manual of Mr. Blaine and the seal of the United States. He asks:

"What is honorable?"

It was as puzzling as the old query, "What is truth?" The dragoman relieves me of the embarrassment. He designates me as a law-maker, one of the few among the fifty millions who make the law for all.

"Ah!" responds the Effendi, "a shereef!"

It is the phrase in the Orient which is the synonym of Honorable, and from it comes the name of our own sheriff; but I thought of my constituent, Major Bowe, "sheriff of the county and city of New York," and wondered if I were not entrenching upon his merited honor. Be it known that the highest honors in all Moslemdom is that of the shereef of Mecca. He is almost superior to the Sultan. He has charge of the mausoleum of Mohammed and of the sacred tombs.

"Have you," asks the Effendi, "tribunals in America who execute contracts, compel honesty, collect debts, and are they unbribeable?" This is the question of a successful man of business, and I make such answer as our chief judges would have sanctioned. I am asked to send a letter from America to the Effendi to let him know if we reach home in safety. Then I am tendered a smoke from the narghile of the Effendi himself. It is a special honor. He had ordered the servant to bring in his long, serpentine "hubble-bubble," with a live coal upon the tobacco. Its fumes, bubbling through the cool water, enrapture my senses. It takes me some time to raise a little smoke. The Effendi shows how to take the long, deep pull, which produces the result, after the method of the Orient.

The rest of the house is opened for our inspection. We ascend to the upper chambers, passing through the court of fountains into the synagogue. This is most interesting and curious, though plain. A reading-stand is in the centre;

a thousand volumes in Arabic, Hebrew, etc., are upon the shelves. The walls are lined with engravings, in nearly all of which the seven candlesticks appear. They are symbolic of light. Other representations of the ceremonies and elements of the religion of the household are about the sacred place. In a decorated desk are the books of the Bible, written in silver on gazelle parchments. A picture of Moses, writing the Ten Commandments, hangs above them. At every one of the score of doors we find nailed to the doorpost a silver box, containing the Ten Commandments, with some of the Hebrew letters apparent. A hundred other significant matters belonging to the law and to the prophets are here, but have now escaped my poor pen.

One thing remains to be said, prompted by the seven candlesticks. No amount of intolerance or detraction can dusk the luminous glory of Hebrew light. When that is obscured, religion, all religions, go out, in chaos. Dusk this radiance? In the language of Lamartine: "All the prevailing forms of worship have sprung from these solitudes, from the Star-deity who governs the worlds of Zoroaster, to the Allah of Mohammed; from the legislative Jehovah of Moses, to the True Word sought for amidst the obscurity of night by the shepherds of Bethlehem." May I not add, that out of the Hebrew Jehovah came all that we have of faith and devotion which takes hold on the invisible world beyond?

True, there are but six millions one hundred thousand Jews in the world. Of this number five millions live in Europe, one hundred and eighty thousand in Asia, four hundred thousand in Africa, three hundred thousand in America, and two hundred thousand in Australia. But their influence is not measured by population. Their thought permeates. It is eternal.

We ascend to the roof of the house. It is arranged for safety and observation. From it, as the soft light of the evening is drawing its mellow curtain about the brown bare mountains of the city, we see rising in supernal majesty the three peaks of Hermon, dominating the Lebanon range!

Beyond its limits is the land of Israel; beyond, even from "Hermon in the north, unto Tabor in the south," lies the home of the prophets and kings —the now unhappy land, once made so glorious by such lawgivers as Moses; such prophets as Elijah; such singers as David, and such sages as Solomon.

Descending to the court we are met by the ladies of the house, who give us greeting; and all give us a final farewell. An oriental salutation is expressive and graceful. The hands do not touch, but come nearly together, and are then raised to lip, head, and heart, signifying that by word and thought and feeling you are most tenderly regarded.

We went from that house with the impression of human brotherhood intensified, and the determination to do more for the eradication of that insatiate malice against this chosen race, from which our own boasted country, with its liberal canons of soul freedom, is not entirely exempt.

When evening came I summoned the dragoman for a stroll among the water-courses and gardens along the Barada, where the green Merj, honored in the Arabian Nights, displays its beauty to the new crescent moon.

It was a sweet and pensive evening, fitted to

make one think of dear friends at home, and the sadness which afflicts my country in its hours of bereavement and sorrow. I am not one of those who are ashamed to confess that the teachings of nature not only lead me to love my friends and my country, but in a larger sense to love the Primal Loving Cause of all our blessings. Nothing so binds me in "willing fetters" as the silver meshes of a brook, and these seven rivers of Damascus produce a pleasing acquiescence, to which the beautiful moon adds its fascination. There was a song in the groves of tall poplars and cypresses, like music heard in dreams. Besides, there were old plane-trees, whose branches have listened to many a story of the good Caliph's time. They spread their great arms in gestures of Eastern welcome while giving their venerable aspect to the mellow light and reflecting their shadows in the pleasant waters. We enter a garden where, along with the murmur of fountains, we hear the tinkle of the guitar and the thrumming of the tambourine.

The story-teller is illustrating some of the Arabian proverbs. He is telling the tale of a shoemaker whose name is Honein. An Arab came to purchase a pair of shoes at his shop. The usual bargaining began, the cobbler asking twice the proper price, and the Bedouin offering half; the son of the desert is impatient. Before the proper mean had been arrived at, he gave up the game of haggling. Honein thereupon resolves upon revenge, and hurrying forward upon the road where he knew the Arab would have to pass, he throws down one of the shoes. Presently the Arab comes past, and seeing the shoe says to himself, "How like this is to one of Honein's shoes! If the other were but with it, I would take them." Honein had meanwhile gone on further still, and thrown down the other shoe, hiding himself close by to enjoy the fun. When the Arab came to the second shoe, he regretted having left the first; but, tying up his camel, he went back to fetch it. Honein at once mounted and rode off home, well satisfied with the exchange of a camel for a pair of shoes. When the Arab returned on foot to his tribe, and they asked him what he had brought home from his journey, he replied, " I have brought back nothing but Honein's shoes." This is a common Arabian saying, and is proverbial for a *bootless* errand.

After the story came songs. They remind me of that olden drawling ditty of the Orient, heard from Morocco to Bagdad. Seated under the trees are some hundreds of Arabs, in every posture, smoking cigarettes and narghiles. They are old and young, but all grave as their tombstones. We order a chibouque and coffee, and listen. I ask the dragoman, "What is the song about?"

"It is the old love song," he says. "O heart! why lovest thou so much? Knowest thou not that thy beloved will fade as the roses? Come to me, beloved, before thou diest! Heart of my heart! come and solace me before the end cometh." This was too lachrymose for our jocund spirit; so we ask:

"Cannot you get up a jolly song, and make these solemn faces smile?"

No one smiles in this strange country. The dogs even partake of the general gravity. The way they howl, even before hurt, is a sample of the melancholy characteristic of all. Men—big men—burst into tears on the least occasion. They are tender and simple-hearted. I should infer, therefore, as humor and pathos are akin, that they would be pervious to mirth; and at this festive place I became anxious to know what resource this land has for any vent and vein of humor. The guide tempts the band with a silver mejideah (a dollar), and the band strikes up a roundelay, which was only a quicker variation of the same lyrical drawl. This music had words a little more sprightly.

I ask what they purport. "Oh, it is a song of a love-sick boy for a passionate girl, and the girl's anxiety to see the boy." A few old Arabs make a hilarious grunt at some of the verses, and some young men look at me askant with a curious smile. It was a song not at all fitted for ears polite, as I surmised; but, not understanding Arabic, I stood the embarrassment. The truth is, this Arab music has an Offenbach immoral twang, and much of his sweetness and characteristics in certain tones; but it is incapable of notation on account of its short or quarter notes and its irregularity and capriciousness. I have had enough of it. I prefer the sweet solace of the bray of the meek and miserable donkey to this "damnable iteration" of barbaric wailing.

CHAPTER XXI.

ON TO THE HOLY CITY!—JAFFA—LATRONE—RAMLEH—JERUSALEM.

He who, from zone to zone,
Guides through the boundless sky thy certain flight,
In the long way that I must tread alone,
Will lead my steps aright.—BRYANT.

AMONG the many anxieties of this Eastern travel we encountered two which thus far have not been realized. When we left Constantinople there was notice given by foreign consuls that the cholera was at Aden, on the Red Sea, and that quarantine would be established. As the time of pilgrimage to Mecca and Jerusalem was near, it was to be expected that the disease would be disseminated. The precautions against it were made drastic by the Turkish Government. An oriental quarantine in 1851 prevented our going to Jerusalem at that time, as then the literal meaning of the words, forty days, was the extent of the horrible lazaretto imprisonment, and such an imprisonment was not to be endured. When, therefore, we reached the ports of Syria and Judea, it was pleasant to know that the quarantine would only operate on vessels coming from the hot South, although it was not sure that going west from Egypt we would not fall into its clutch. The other anxiety connects itself with the state of the Mediterranean. It is in the fall, at best, an uncertain sea. We read the

107th Psalm, and thought how the sea looked to the psalmist from the Judean heights, and to one who had gone "down to the sea in ships, and who did business in great waters." Had he not seen the works of the Lord and his wonders in the deep? "For he commandeth, and raiseth the stormy wind, which lifteth up the waves thereof. They mount up to the heaven, they go down again to the depths: their soul is melted because of trouble. They reel to and fro, and stagger like a drunken man, and are at their wit's end. He maketh the storm a calm, so that the waves thereof are still. Then they are glad because they be quiet; so He bringeth them unto their desired haven."

It is no ordinary thankfulness, therefore, that we feel when we reach the haven which was, and is, the vestibule on the sea, leading us to the temple and city of our hope—Jerusalem! Indeed, we are thankful for a smooth sea ever since we left Odessa. In traveling about the Syrian coasts such serenity is indispensable, not merely for comfort, but for landing. The roadsteads are generally open, and when there is a harbor it is artificial. Jaffa does not boast of a harbor, and, unless the weather be calm, the landing is either dangerous or it is postponed for the return trip from Egypt. How many touring "souls have been melted" because of this trouble? We had tranquil weather and landed without a spray upon our garments, though carried ashore by sailors. Then we are ushered through the narrow and noisy thoroughfares of Jaffa, out among the gardens, where the Jerusalem Hotel is kept by the American Consul. A hurried breakfast and a short rest, and our dragoman, Mr. Floyd, who had come with us from Beirut, is upon his

Arab steed, and we are in a small vehicle on our route to the holy city.

There is not much of interest to be observed in Jaffa. Like most of these cities of the coast, it is built upon the débris of the furrowed mountains, which the winter rains bring down with their waters, for irrigation and vegetation. It rejoices in a fruitfulness which is partly concealed by the enormous cactus hedges; but here and there splendid orchards of orange and lemon and other fruits show their dusty foliage, cypresses and palms rise like verdurous minarets above the scene! The harbor facilities are in contrast with the suburbs; the former are as meagre and mean as the latter are luxuriant and delightful. The former are cluttered up with bales of goods, and camels, mules, and Arabs, and the bustle and business give no idea of the sylvan repose within the hedges and walls without the town. From the sea the town looks like a pretty picture of stone houses, here and there embowered in stately trees, but it gives no idea of the squalor of the people and crookedness of the streets. Where "Simon the tanner" once lived there is considerable improvement going on. There is here a German colony of great prosperity. It is a significant and sure sign of advancement. Besides, the locality shows that the traditional permanency of the tanner, at which Shakespeare hints, applies to the tanneries, for in this vicinage the business is still carried on as it was in the apostolic times. There is much tradition about Jaffa, and some Biblical history. Being the port of Jerusalem, timber for the temple came hither from Lebanon. From here Jonah fled. Here Tabitha was raised by St. Peter. Here, on the house of Simon, the apostle saw in a vision the grand object and future of that kingdom of which he held the key, and which was fitly named after that rock, which—if it be not a solecism—is as gentle as the plumes of the palm to the zephyr, but which, unyielding as granite, resists the approaches of time. What history Jaffa had under Roman, Crusader, Arab, Mameluke, and Frank, is easily remembered by those who have read or written the itineracy to Jerusalem.

But these are matters of the dead past. It is of more present interest to observe, as we did, the procession of fine-eyed, healthy Jewish children, who are out of their school for a holiday in the country. This indicates, as is indeed the fact, that benevolent Hebrews in other lands are raising up and training a new generation to instruct, refine, and elevate the coming youth of their race, who are thrown by persecution or poverty upon this their olden land.

Many curiosities are pointed out by the way. Yonder is a tree whose name we inquire.

"That," says the guide, "is the tree that bears the *husks* upon which the prodigal fed."

At every turn some natural object, with a Scriptural bearing, attracts the eye and memory.

We perceive on the road and in the suburbs sugar-cane for sale. It is cut in sections, and seems to be an article of food. We notice that the young Arabs take to it. They chew it just as the little negroes on the quay at New Orleans do, and in a style which they learned, unconsciously, from the monkey! Their plan, quadrumanous and otherwise, is to fill their mouth with the saccharine juice, supplied by a bounteous flux of the salivary gland, and then, when the mouth is brimful, to tip back the head and roll the cataract of sweetness down below the epiglottis into the regions where the diaphragm holds high, hilarious carnival over the festive scene. We pass many camels, laden with rags—rags for the paper-mills of Europe. These rags are *media* for sending out the plagues of the East, and there used to be stringent measures against their introduction into Western communities. Although the business is not as thriving as formerly, still it seems lively; but whether or not it lessens the bulk and number of oriental rags we cannot determine, as the ragamuffins seem to be as numerous in Judea as in Asia Minor.

We divide our journey to Jerusalem between two days, and rest over night at Latrone, and not, as is usual, at Ramleh. We are not frightened by stories of lepers at the last-named place; but our guide, who is the best in Judea, knows where and when to put us snugly away for the night, so as to refresh us for our entry into the holy city. It did not take us a half hour to get outside the sweet breath of the orange orchards, and into the wide, tawny plains of Sharon and the hardy region of the olive. Of course, in the fall, the fields look arid, brown, burned, and bare; but in the rainy winter and spring they are green and fair. The old maritime plain of the Philistine, which is another name for Palestine, lies along this coast, from Gaza northward, and it was considered a land worth struggles. This Joshua found. But in vain do we look for the "roses of Sharon and the lilies that grow" in this land, so renowned once for its floral beauty. Still, we are told that in the vernal season it is carpeted, like a Texas prairie, with flowers of various hue and loveliness. Along the dusty afternoon road we pass innumerable caravans of camels, led by Arabs on donkeys. The Arab generally sits on the remote point of the *os coccygis* of the animal, and without stirrups. He swings his bare brown feet and legs, while the little beast, like Iulus alongside of his father, trots *inequo pede*. Plenty of women, with faces here apparent, and in long, blue, cheap cotton mantles, and sometimes with head crowned with burdens of fruit, pitchers, straw, or wood, are met in the way. Some ruins, mostly of churches, here and there appear; while square, windowless, Turkish guard-houses are seen at intervals, at whose doors are the white-dressed, fez-capped Turkish soldiers, with guns and cigarettes. These are the police, who are supposed to guard the road; but to our observation no guard is needed, except in the dark mountain passes, and there Turkish engineering has been careful to have as few guard-houses as possible!

Latrone is only three miles from the famous valley where Joshua pursued his enemy. As we approach it, the moon throws its light and shadows upon the foot-hills and valleys, and we cannot clearly discern, except under its veil of witchery, the olive groves and cactus hedges, and wild scenery, which should show signs of the fruitful water and soil. From the balcony of our hotel at Latrone we take a survey of the leads of lunar silver, amid the enchanted rocks and hills. We forget, under its magical sheen, that it is named after a thief; but was he not the good thief? and has not his "penitence" removed from his supposed birthplace the stigma of stealing? This place has further and less dubious significance. It is only a mile from the Castle Emmaus, which the Crusaders built to command the pass to the Holy City. All about us here are the historic spots of the heroic Maccabees. In one word, it is the fighting-ground and the highway to Jerusalem.

There is not much to see on the road until you come to Ramleh. Beggars and backsheesh, and some old relics as crusading reminders are here, and one very conspicuous object. The latter is a square tower, with a winding staircase. It is off the road, and has a fine view of the surrounding country. It is over one thousand years old, and has many Moslem associations. Ramleh has been the scene of much contest. Indeed, every little spot here in Judea is full of memories, from the time Israel came down from the Moab mountains into the Jordan valley. The road is not to be mentioned for its convenience and perfection; only for its historic, religious, and æsthetic interest. It was built in 1869, by forced labor, and indeed its rough and stony incompleteness looks like anything but the result of cheerful work. It is supported by tolls, so much per head, on every animal on the road. One should not complain of the road when it is remembered that before 1869 there was not a bridle-path to Jerusalem. It is said that the Sultan promised the Empress Eugénie to build a road to Jerusalem if she would come that way; and this royal courtesy is the origin of the road.

Before we reach our destination for the night, and before the tower of Ramleh is lost in the distance, the moon comes out and hangs her silver lamp over the valley of Ajalon, which we were nearing; but it did not stand still any more than we did. The sun had already gone down to rest to "bait his steeds" under the blue waves, and we had no occasion or expectation of any marvel. Ours were peaceful purposes. Not an Amorite was to be seen; but some Russian pilgrims from the regions of the north were bent upon improving the silver light, and, along with numerous native pilgrims, trains, and footmen, were struggling to reach the cooler air of the mountain passes before the heats of the morning.

One excitement we found on the way not to be forgotten. "A jackal! See!" exclaims our guide, as in the light the animal creeps stealthily across the road. It makes good a retreat, in spite of the revolver. As it is said to keep company with the king of beasts, we felt better when it left.

Occasionally we saw the vine trailing from the fig-tree, both hanging plentifully with fruit, so that the Scriptural repose can be had under both and at once. Our repose, however, was under a substantial roof. It was undisturbed, save only by one incident. When we retire a scream is heard. It is from the moon-lit chamber. My wife is there! Good gracious! has she discovered another jackal? Ah! no. It is but the gentlest of lizards, which hovers in glistening beauty over her head, upon the ceiling. Before sleep is possible we marshal the household, and, armed with brooms and umbrellas, we succeed, like another St. George, in destroying the dragon, and thus allay the nervous intensity of our guardian angel.

To the distant and pious reader everything tending toward Jerusalem is interesting, and, therefore, it is not frivolous to say that our driver was a Frenchwoman. Her sex, owing to the mode of dressing here, we never suspected until we began our second day's journey, when we found her on the box, coaxing rather than lashing her team.

Our baggage is tied fast, and our equestrian guide is on his prancing barb. It is daylight, and the exhilaration of the bracing dawn is enhanced by the near prospect of the approach to the city of our hopes. But no pen can describe the beauty of the morning. On a spur of the mountain—bathed in the roseate beauty which we looked for in vain in the vale of Sharon—is a little village of square stone houses. It was not because the "Lion-hearted" Crusader encamped here seven hundred years ago; it was not because the mountains of Judah began to quiver with all the arrows of Apollo under the pink aurora; nor because each gray, rocky mountain became, under its effluence, a picture—or a statue, rather—forever indurated in the mind. But it was because through yonder winding glens, holy men of God, with the grandest thought and emotion, passed upward to the city of our hope! Up, up, still up, winding under the gleaming glare of the once-terraced elevations, through defiles that would not be so comfortable after nightfall for lonely travelers, we pursue our morning drive. At length we reach a point of vantage, and cast our eyes to the west. The blue sea is there in measureless content. It is thirty miles away, and the light falls on its bosom, evoking the subtle minstrelsy. This sings of hopes long deferred. Shall these hopes be disappointed? Our guide, ever vigilant, and with chapter and verse for each spot, curvets upon his steed about our carriage. What are the rocky caves and glens, and the high terraced slopes—terraced by regular and natural limestone ranges, and once terraced artificially and usefully, by man, with vine, olive, pomegranate, and fig? What are the gray, sombre rocks, tinged ruddy with iron? What the pretty intervales, full of the old, twisted olives, whose trunks are full of hollows and holes, as if riddled and stormed by the ages? What the lively little lizards, shimmering as they run into crevices over dusty rocks? What the blanched beauty of those desolated and bleak mountains, covered with prickly scrub-oak and shrubs of ilex? What the "animated nature," in the shape of the lop-eared pied goats, mixed with the large-tailed sheep and the donkeys and mules, camels, cattle, and Arabs, as they pass, heavily laden, desertward? What the lonely low houses, made of dried mud, stuck about the acclivities and in the glens? What the castles which top the topmost heights, and the stories of sheiks, like Aber Ghaush, who once commanded and robbed from them? What the succulent grapes which old Kirjath-jearim furnishes for our dusty throats, and the strange sight of a Gothic minster in ruins in this land of the Gibeonites, this boundary between Judah and Benjamin? What all these? Are we not approaching the city of our hope? Did not the ark of the covenant rest on yonder hill, in the house of Abinadab? Was it not borne hence to Jerusalem by King David, out of whose loins came those simple yet grand teachers and descendants, whose marvels of morality and miracles of heaven have moved mankind? Roman roads are here, and old pavements, and arches still spring buoyantly over dry torrent-beds. These are remnants of that Roman power which worshiped no god Terminus; but these are of mere passing interest; for yonder, upon our right, do we not look upon the birthplace of John the Baptist, in the "hilly country of Judea?"

All around are signal and lofty points, gesturing heavenward, and associated forever with the greatest names of the Hebrews—Samuel the Judge and David the King—and all pointing to the city of our long-deferred hope. As we look to the south and north, and through zigzags and glens—birth and burial places, fighting and praying ground of soldier and king, prophet and saint, command attention; while to the west we bid farewell to the azure sea, whose line is now marked by a long, steadfast range of white clouds above, but parallel with, its horizon. We prepare for the descent. Still more windings by the way, and more quotations from Samuel, the Judges, and the Acts rain in upon us from our Biblical genius upon the barb. These sacred memories have a sort of sudden confirmation by the instantaneous appearance of a venerable graybeard in gown of religious foldings. He has a grand escort. He turns around one of the zigzags as we turn down, and lo! the dignified form of the Coptic Bishop of Judea, upon a white mule! His attendants also appear, one bearing his silver-mounted stick, the mace of his authority. This vision appears as suddenly as if it had emerged from one of the many caves which shadow our pathway. It is as if Elijah had come forth out of the heart of Carmel. Our salutations are reverently made; and we drive with fresh impatience over a rolling plateau, at the top of the mountains, which begin to tell us that we are near the city of our hope!

The road grows more populous with beasts of burden. Arab women with blue tattoo upon their ugly faces, and dignified Arabs in their togas of striped brown and dirty white, come and go. The fruit-trees we perceive seem to add to the loneliness of the land. There are few houses in sight. We wonder who does the work here. The truth is, the ground is hardly scratched for the grain; and the grain is neglected till the sparse harvest-time comes. The terraces show more cultivation. The cactus again appears to shelter the gardens. Baskets of fruit, under green leaves, decorate the heads of the pedestrian women and load the dusty donkeys; and we rest, in disillusion and impatience, in front of a Greek restaurant, whose sign of " liquors and billiards " would disturb the oriental vision but for the sweet blush of the pomegranates out of the orchards, which give their tints to the rich garniture of the gardens. We understand from our guide, not that David was anointed or that Joshua fought here, but that General Grant here lunched in a snow-storm in February! A few lazy folk in baggy trousers are about to help our French female driver water the horses, while the unseen proprietor is making wine in his cellar, unconscious of our sacred anxieties. A cup of coffee and a fresh start, and only five miles to the city of our hope!

There is little time now to listen to scriptural texts as to prominent localities. Rags, refugees, and Russians, men of one religion or another, and of all qualities and costumes, are mixed up heterogeneously upon the thronged road, along with goats, sheep, camels, and donkeys. Water-carriers, bearing their sweating goat-skins, are trudging into the city precincts; but this only signifies a denser population. We perceive the Convent of the Holy Cross, a conspicuous object, and the new Jesuit college, and an orphan asylum. We quicken our pace. Then the suburbs—long blocks of Jewish houses, newly built, outside still of the city—appear; but these only serve to conceal, and not to show the view of the city. Then the Russian establishment, within walls like a fortress, and with its splendid appointments for pilgrims and sick, for poor and rich; and then a town itself, still outside the walls, from which you catch glimpses of the green slopes of the valley of Hinnom, and the old dusty graveyard and empty pool of Gihon, and the ancient aqueduct; and there, right before us, the far-famed Jaffa gate, with its moving mass of people. Then the western walls of Jerusalem, with their old gray stones and battlements; and far off, shining and seething in heat and light, and as regular in its sublime masonry as a wall built by the hand of man, full fifty miles away, is the splendid range of Moab.

The shops and market, and building going on about the Jaffa gate, and the groups of all nations which take their way to and from it, or saunter and jabber about it, do not impress one with any feeling of sanctity; but this one picture, nay, these two pictures, do. One is this weird Moabitish mountain wall of the desert, far off beyond the Dead Sea and the Jordan! The other is an unexpected, dramatic, and strange spectacle in the midst of the road. In sight of this holy city, on the first view, we perceive over a hundred pilgrim priests and their friends—all in black apparel—fall prostrate in the dust! As we pass they chant their prayers and kiss the earth. Who are they? Whence come they? They are pilgrims from the far-off peninsula of Spain. Their wives, sisters, mothers, and parishioners have caught the vision of the heavenly city, which their Saviour made the marvel of history, and they lie "silent as a nun in adoration," and then arise, giving glory, before the precious and hallowed home of the Incarnate Son of God!

If at first we were disappointed at the small size and meagre aspect of the city, we are beginning already to wonder and worship. The very air, the very stones, the very dust—and especially the rocks—seem sacred. Here is the sepulchre, not of a nation merely, but of a Saviour; not of dead, buried hopes, but of living and risen glories; not of an old and honored dispensation from Jehovah, but of a new and potential Evangel.

What wonders, indeed! It is said that time never works. It only eats and consumes, rots and rusts. But it does work; and such wonders! Out of this little span of Judæan land, fifty by two hundred miles only, and during the lapse of two thousand years—what wonders! Beyond yonder hills, now in our view, was born in the manger the God-man. It is the mystery of mysteries. This has worked these marvels. These solemn, dark-eyed priests of Spain, in their reverent way, recognize the wonder, even as the magi who came from the East. Suppose this ground gave not the most beautiful earthly vision of the sacred city; suppose the approach from the Jordan or from Damascus would enhance more the material attraction—was it not here that the swelling hearts of the Crusaders first beheld the city of their hope and their prowess? If they could sail and march so far, under helmet and mail, and all privation, to rescue the holy sepulchre from the Paynim, what wonder now that these men from the realm of "Isabella the Catholic," who gave her jewels to enlarge the kingdom of Christ upon our planet, should fall prostrate before the walls of that city which contained the grave whence rose the Redeemer! We pondered much this strange spectacle. Pilgrims from far-off America, whose geography was not known until the jewels of Spain found it—not known when these great transactions of salvation were here enacted—we could not refrain from sympathetic tears at the prospect of a city so hallowed by sacrifice, and so sanctified by time.

CHAPTER XXII.

WEST WALLS OF JERUSALEM—JAFFA GATE—HEBREW HISTORY—JEWS AND THEIR WAILING-PLACE AND HOPE.

Unto which promise our twelve tribes instantly serving God day and night, hope to come. For which hope's sake, king Agrippa, I am accused of the Jews. Why should it be thought a thing incredible with you, that God should raise the dead?—ACTS xxvi. 7, 8.
For the hope of Israel I am bound with this chain.—ACTS xxviii. 20.

WE were looking upon the western wall of Jerusalem. We had approached the city, as all do who come from the sea, and as doubtless Godfrey de Bouillon and the Crusaders did; for upon the west side the city is most vulnerable. It was upon this side the assault which succeeded was made. There is not much of a valley here, compared with the east and south. Here, within and near the Jaffa gate, stands the citadel. From it the red flag, with its crescent and star, waves. Near by and outside of this gate we are lodged. From it we have many fine visions. Twenty years ago one could not safely go outside the walls at eventide, if he were other than a Moslem. Now there is one-third of the population of Jerusalem outside. Its appearance is that of a new town undergoing erection and completion. The houses are of stone, and, though low, are substantial and cool. In the midst of these novelties is situated Feil's hostelry. Herr Feil is a German. He understands how to make pilgrims who can pay, happy. Outside the walls we were told to lodge. We were well advised, as the inside is not as fragrant as Arabic odors, nor as roomy as the mountains "round about." Besides, outside we are not so besieged; we are besiegers. That is an advantage. The city, like all oriental cities, walled and buttressed, looks more "comely" from the outside. But, from inside or outside, as we approach it, there is no lack of activity and population.

Whatever Jerusalem has been, after her several falls and frequent destruction, she does not now "sit solitary," nor is she "a widow," although she that was "great among the nations and a princess among provinces" is certainly now "tributary," as the Turkish crescent over the citadel doth testify. Jerusalem is, alas! only one of the places under the Pashalic of Damascus. How are the mighty fallen!

After our ablutions and lunch, we prepared for a superficial glance at her bulwarks and palaces, her " compact" buildings, and her ancient sites. From our hotel window the castle or citadel is in full view; but the city is not so high that many of its notable objects cannot be particularized. However, from this view the depression is apparent between Mount Zion and Mount Akra. Upon the latter are situated the "holy places," including the Church of the Holy Sepulchre. We are situated near Mount Akra, and still not far from Mount Zion. Indeed, distances are not so magnificent in the city, as at present walled in, that any point of interest is remote. Yet it is still "compacted together," as the Psalmist said. From the front balcony of our hotel the view is not inspiring. It comprehends the valley of Hinnom, and its waterless pool of Gihon. On either side of the dusty, white, and rubbly road, and intersected by stone walls, little green patches in the shape of olive-trees are seen, and some square houses. Rocks are everywhere, showing their irregularities and caves. A solitary windmill on the hill, which the Knights of the Crusade have not harmed, dominates the landscape; but its arms are maimed, and it has no welcome for the pleasant breeze which comes from the west. Beyond lie the bare mountains, whose " strong rocks and fortress " so frequently appear, as well on the soil as in the writings of the prophets of Israel. The valley bends to the south-east, without much depth or width. It is crossed by the aqueduct, which even yet, after three thousand years, bears water from the pools of Solomon, which are beyond Bethlehem. That way lies Hebron as well as Bethlehem; but the prospect is hardly relieved of its stony aridity and barrenness by the few orchards of olives. We are tempted to take up our staff and explore this valley to its outlet through Aceldama, the field of blood, into the vale of the dry brook Kedron; but we are reminded that Jerusalem, however small, compared with London or New York, Damascus or Constantinople, is compact with interest, and cannot be done in a promenade. She makes up in sacred places and grave associations what she lacks in immensity, so that we prepare for steady and organized work; and before we are through, we shall thoroughly go into, through, and around her.

While the donkeys are preparing, I fulfill a promise made to our Minister to Constantinople, and visit the Jaffa gate. It is but a minute's walk.

Along the hot and dusty path to it, the new outside city is making progress. I perceive the Arab women furnishing the stone and mortar, from their heads, to the masons in baggy pants and turbans, who are laying fresh foundations and walls. One curious thing strikes me. The ground is left within the rising walls of the building, so as to assist, without aid of scaffold, the making of the arches.

General Wallace, in his novel, "Ben-Hur—a tale of the Christ," has made a brief sketch of the Jaffa gate. He describes it, within and without, as a market as well as thoroughfare. This is as it was two thousand years ago. There was then, according to all accounts, what now I see, great traffic here. Traders came from Tyre, Sidon, Jaffa, Egypt, Bethlehem, and Hebron. Calling on alliteration's artful aid, he photographed the trading groups with their motley wear and different objects. "A pilgrim wanting a cucumber or a camel, a house or a horse, a loan or a lentil, a date or a dragoman, a melon or a man, a dove or a donkey, had only to inquire for the article at the Jaffa gate." This is a fair etching of the business folk who come, linger, and go, now, at this famous gateway. Outside, two score of camels are kneeling at their food, amidst baskets and smokers, babies and porters, prestidigitators and shoemakers. The camels are chewing the cud with satisfaction after their long journeys. Every kind of article, animal, utensil, and fruit belonging to the needs of this generation, here is being sold, and every kind of person, from a Bedouin to a bishop, seems to be chaffering. Women in white, some of them muffled, being Moslems; some in blue cotton garb, being in worse plight and lower grade; and others, Christian and Hebrew, in white and Frank attire, without the provoking yashmaks to hide their features, pass and repass as in a masquerade, amidst the noisy cry of the dominant and dissonant Arab voice. Here are women from Mount Sinai and beyond, with Coptic or Egyptian faces, such as are seen on old tombs in the land of the Sphinx, with necklaces of silver coin, flowing head-dresses, and ponderous and multiplied ear ornaments. Here are Nubians, tall and straight, some of them eunuchs, and all of them black, which is impressive for its dead, dull, unshiny color. Here are sheiks, graceful in mien and bronzed in face, with their robes sashed about them, and the long gun, decked with mother-of-pearl, slung over the shoulder. But why particularize further? Outside it is an oriental market. Inside, in the cool shade of the gateway, on the stone seat, we see some Arabs playing cards, and others casting up their accounts. Within the city, after leaving the gate, you are in the throng which is seeking its outlet to the market. The gate itself is of the height of the walls, fifty feet or more. It is somewhat soiled, worn, and torn, and here and there some plants cling to its rough places. It has now the Saracenic arch. Its counterpart, walled up, is in another angle. Evidently this gate has been reconstructed in parts since the scenes of " Ben-Hur " were acted.

But we must be alert for the afternoon's work, and so, being mounted on our donkeys, we proceed to the synagogue and wailing-place of the Jews. Why there? Because my first interest centres there.

The Jews of this country are increasing in numbers and in the quality of their immigration. Since Sir Moses Montefiore, Judah Touro, of New Orleans, and other Hebrews of means and benevolence have given their patronage and erected long blocks of houses without the walls, a better tone prevails as to their condition and the ultimate restoration of the land.

In Judea there are now over fifteen thousand Jews. They are divided between two classes, the Spanish and Portuguese, called *Sephardini*, and those from Germany, Poland, Russia, and elsewhere, called *Askenazim*. There are other subdivisions. But all keep the fasts and festivals with the same old ceremony and vigilance as when they were "chosen" of God.

There is something about the history and topography of Palestine which makes the land as "peculiar" as the people who gave to it such universal renown. It is, as a country, quite isolated. It is shut in by sea and desert, and only open at the north by a narrow pass into Syria. It is a strange phenomenon, this choice land of Jehovah. Almost treeless, riverless, and waterless, yet once the glory of the earth by the cultivation of its mountains and the culture of its men. It is belted by mountains, with one small plain by the sea, which has been the theatre of martial exploits from the time of Joshua to Napoleon I. The whole land is elevated, except this plain, along the sea from Carmel to Gaza. It does not contain more than twelve thousand square miles, and is only two hundred by sixty miles. Its population is about three million, and amidst its mixed races of Turk, Syrian, Arab, and Greek, there are now only a few thousand of its early inhabitants, who once numbered millions. It seems to have sunk out of sight, as a land of milk and honey. As a nation morally and economically it is not unlike the valley of the Jordan and the Dead Sea, which, physically, is sunk below not merely the level of the adjacent mountains, but below the average level of the earth and seas. Its religion is as varied as its costumes. Patriarchs control in it, what the Moslem does not, in connection with those things of time which take hold of the unseen world. What a history it has! Abraham, Isaac, and Jacob as rich sheiks; then the Egyptian sojourn; then the marvelous deliverance of their kindred; the battles of Joshua; the division of the land; the loss of the ten tribes; the elders, judges, and kings; the division of the kingdom between Israel and Judah; the struggles with the surrounding nations, Assyria and Egypt; the Persian conquest; then that of Alexander; the partition; the rule of the Ptolemies and of Antiochus; the patriotic struggle of the Maccabees; then the Roman imperial control, with its vicissitudes; then Herod, the Idumæan; the stately temple rebuilt with marble and gold; and then the birth of Christ, a descendant of Hebrew kings, before whose august name for two thousand years the nations have bowed! What crimes, famines, slaughters, crusades, insurrections, and devastations have since occurred! Judea is the pivot of history. What chivalry, sacrifice, tyrannies, butcheries, and bigotries, under all sects, since then, this land has witnessed! Are they not written on parchment, pillar, brass, and rock, pictured on canvas, and sculptured in bronze and marble, and sung by the muses of history and poetry of all time and every land? If, therefore, one were a liberal student of history, and recognized the splendor of the Jewish mind and morals, and the devotion to the great invisible Creator which these men of Jewish stock, whether prophet or apostle, whether of Carmel or Nazareth, have illustrated; and aside from the fact of their election by Jehovah as the medium for his revelations to mankind—would not the capital inquiry be, How do the Jews themselves now regard their relations to Judea?

Do you wonder that my first wish was to visit the scene of wailing? Before walking about Zion, or telling her towers, marking her bulwarks, or considering her palaces; before disputing about her streets or surveying her temples, her sepulchres, and sites, we mounted our animals and proceeded to the place of Hebrew wailing.

Through the Jaffa gate, past the citadel where the white uniformed Turk appears on guard, between the Christian and Armenian quarters, separated by the street of David, stumbling along amidst the quaint population, mostly made up of Polish Jews in their curious fur caps and dark robes, going the same way, on this Friday afternoon; omitting for the present the Church of St. John and the holy places on our left, moving due east in the narrow ways and in the busy and dim bazaars, we pass down, at last, a crooked lane to the right, and find ourselves within a close quadrangle. It is shut in between walls. On the west the wall is low; on the east it is the veritable and venerable wall of the temple. Its enormous blocks of marble, and the fact of its being below the streets, give absolute authenticity to the place; while sounds from the human voice break in dismal confirmation upon the ear. Every Friday, in the afternoon, this strange convocation here meet to celebrate their misery, and after that go to their synagogues.

When we reach the place, there are already a hundred Hebrews there—the old men and maidens, young men and old women—the Russian or Polish Jews predominating, as we discriminate by the long, straggling curl of hair brought before the ears, and the unmistakable fur cap, without rim, about the head. Some of the Jews have on old gabardines, with black caps or turbans. The women are in black dresses, and make the saddest lament. They stand, with faces bathed in tears, against the marble walls of the temple, and lift up their voices in such tones that it seems as if a fresh, present agony were torturing their souls. The old men sit on stools, or on benches against the west wall. They hold in their hands the sacred volume, or the Hebrew Psalter, or the Book of Jeremiah. These are generally large volumes. These, as is customary in the East, they read or chant, with the body swaying. This is no mere demonstration for the eye; it is the old lament. It is as old as those days when the stern Roman soldier allowed this refrain to be sung—for a consideration. The litany they chant is the very lyric of woe. Its burden is loneliness, departed beauty and glory, now ashes and despair. They dwell on the preciousness of the temple, now ground to dust by the ignoble feet of the pagan and spoiler. They utter such appeals for the deliverance of Zion and the return of joy to Jerusalem as never were wailed by the Rachels of this world weeping for their children, and refusing to be comforted, because they are not. To look at the marble blocks, beveled and polished, even worn into and at the joints, one might fancy that these lamentations had begun to wear and pierce the walls of the great temple itself. Century after century have these cries entered within these hallowed marbles: "How long, Lord! how long!" "Shall thy jealousy burn like fire?" Indeed, the words of the psalmist here find wonderful fulfillment, for are not "the heathen come into thine inheritance? Thy holy temple have they not defiled? They have laid Jerusalem on heaps"— literally and truly, heaps on heaps.

I was courteously permitted by some of the aged Hebrews, in the intervals of their prayers, to look at their old and well-worn volumes. The picture of such patriarchs in Israel may be found in every gallery of Europe where art has caught the features of prophecy, and in the Daniel Deronda of George Eliot, where the genius of fiction has hallowed the devotion of ages. But let it not be said—to the honor of the Moslem custodians of the temple—that any public scorn and derision is permitted to insult this congregation in this outer sanctuary. These sad inheritors of the great prophecies and psalms of the great race are undisturbed in their luxury of grief.

After this exhibition, and in the full blaze of history, one cannot help but feel that this is especially the city of the Jews. Christians may fight for and hold its holy places; Moslems may guard from all other eyes the tombs of David and Solomon; the site of the temple on Mount Moriah may be decorated by the mosques of Omar and Aksa; but if ever there was a material object on earth closely allied with a people, it is this city of Jerusalem with the Jews. In all their desolation and wandering, was there ever a race so sensitive as to the city of its heart and devotion? All the resources, native and acquired, of this rare race, including its love of music and domestic devotion, have been called in to summarize and aggrandize the soreness of its weeping and the tearfulness of its anguish over the fate of Jerusalem, and the restlessness of its exiles.

Imagine, for a moment, the exiled children or emigrants of other lands returning to their ancestral homes with such patriotic and pious loyalty to the past. An Austrian refugee would not be found weeping about the Cathedral of St. Stephen's in Vienna, or a Norwegian over the tomb or well of St. Olaf in Trondhjem; and if an American should be found dropping tears over the bones of Canute in Winchester Minster, or over the relics of the Plantagenets and Tudors in Westminster, the mockery would be as funny as that of the lachrymose Twain over the grave of Adam. There is only one people whose devotion to its old home can be compared with this of the Hebrew to Jerusalem, its temples, valleys, and sepulchres. It is that of the Irish to their antique altars and beloved isle. This unexampled devotion finds its expression in this wailing-place. Referring to it, in some remarks in Congress apropos of the persecutions in Russia and elsewhere, and recalling my own picture, I felt an irresistible impulse to witness it, in spite of the painfulness of the spectacle.

What plummet ever sounded such a deep of desolation? What wine-press was ever trodden by such weary feet? What promise of an Eden was ever so blighted into a waste? Yet these stricken souls lift up their souls in ecstasy. They see the fountains silver in the sands; marble cities, pillared in proportion, rearise; the crown again upon the bared head of Judah; song, timbrel, and dance, and flowers from Sharon, grapes from Engedi, and a new dawn on the towers of Salem!

And the word comes back to them, in their doleful wailing, from the outer world—a world regenerated with the new and strange forces of steam and electricity; a new civilization born of progress and enlightenment, and dashing by their ancient haunts with a chariot more fleet and fiery than that in which their prophet ascended—"Not long, not long, ye wandering ones of Israel. Your day of enfranchisement is nigh." If not in a physical, yet in a spiritual sense, comes back the hymn, which new voices are raising the world over:

> "Rise, royal city; Zion, rise!
> Thy king's approach to hail!
> Long has thy night of mourning been
> In sorrow's gloomy vale."

Whether it shall ever come to pass that this remarkable race shall repossess the land of their ancestors; whether the temple shall again arise within the walls of Zion; whether the teachings of their religion and all the elevated thoughts of their poets, prophets, and priests shall be sung even "within thy gates, O Jerusalem!" one thing is to be conceded, that in America, under our free institutions, they are permitted unmolested to worship the Jehovah of their fathers, where at least they have a highway out of Egypt into the promised land! Wherever may be their local habitation, from the summit of Mount Sinai still radiates the eternal lesson cut in stone; from the calcined soil and the sacred mountains of Judea goes forth an effluence, to civilize, cheer, and bless. No one can be so darkened in his understanding as not to see the wonderful power of that little land through which the Jordan flows, with a population not larger than one of our own counties, which for two thousand years and more has held the world in thrall by its teachings and by its worship of the invisible Jehovah. Its people have carried the ark of their covenant into many lands and climes; and though bigotry may still be pleased to think that their dispersion as a people is a curse, still from their migrations humanity has been beautified, justice purified, and liberty glorified! Out of their rigid and austere code there springs and flows forever an influence as gentle as the dews that fall upon Hermon, and as potential as the quaking of Sinai, out of whose throes came the great moral law of mankind!

Finding the preparations for service in the synagogue incomplete, and desirous to get a glimpse of the city from an elevation before nightfall, we were permitted to ascend to the roof of the synagogue. The picture enhanced the solemn and grand thoughts which are beginning to grow and supplant our first feeble impressions. Although not the best point of observation, yet from it the main features of the city can be defined. To the northwest are seen the domes of the Church of the Holy Sepulchre and the Church of Queen Helena, and beyond the walls and the Damascus gate are the tombs of the kings; to the north-east, Mount Scopus runs southward into the Mount of Olives, with its church and point of the ascension on the east. Between it and our view is the Mosque of Omar, desecrating under its dome, and with its mummery of Mohammedanism, the site of the great temple.

Scattered trees are about the sides of the Mount of Olives, and minarets aspire from Mount Moriah, where two mosques hide the sacred temple. Turning our eyes downward, to the south are the narrow streets of the Jewish quarter, upon whose roofs we see people preparing booths for the coming Passover; while beyond, in ever-enduring magnificence, is that cynosure which first caught our vision here, the mountains of Moab, made enchanting by the dreamy evening lustre, and the attenuated and fairy scarf of distance! Jordan and the Dead Sea are not seen. Bare mountains of "the desert" are seen, between Moab and our vision. The house of Caiaphas, the Protestant cemeteries, and the tomb of David—a strange, incongruous company of localities—are pointed out, just outside the walls. All about us are the walls —battlemented and antique walls—and without them, tombs—tombs in caves, tombs cut in solid rocks, tombs whose stones lie in flat and wretched disorder on hill and on vale, tombs everywhere! To the south-west is Zion gate. It seems to be the highest place. It overlooks many ancient and modern tombs, as well as the Montefiore cottages; and to the west the Armenian convent and its few palms, and even the valley of Hinnom.

The general impression of the holy city is that of square, whitish houses, with many domes. But what we see is not the ancient city and walls; it is the outer shell of shells. These are but the foundations for the "heaps" of two or three thousand years. To touch the sacred soil, you must do as many engineers and enthusiasts are doing, excavate a hundred feet or more. But where the rocks protrude, and in the great mosque, on the temple's old site, you find solid substance, which has defied the tooth of time and the vandalism of man.

Retiring from this scene, we content ourselves for the present with a hurried visit to the Holy Sepulchre, Golgotha, and Calvary. The confusion of so many creeds and rites here, celebrating the divine benefactions and sacrifice, with the intricacies of the "places," jars upon the mind and soul. It renders this visit all too brief and unsatisfactory. It requires another and more exhaustive study.

Following our guide through mazes of narrow streets, consciously going over the ground once familiar to prophets and saints, and threading the Jewish quarter, we make our exit from the Zion gate on the south-west, and thence due north, under the shadow of the western wall, which is gilded with a pensive light, we find rest from our first day's observations.

If at first we were disappointed at the small size and meagre aspect of the city, we are beginning already to wonder and worship. The very air, the very stones, the very dust—and especially the rocks—seem sacred. Here is the sepulchre, not of a nation merely, but of a Saviour; not of dead, buried hopes, but a monument of living and risen glories, not of an old and honored dispensation from Jehovah, but of a new and potential Evangel.

CHAPTER XXIII.

THE STAR IN THE EAST—WHAT BETHLEHEM IS TO-DAY—SCENES OF THE SAVIOUR'S BIRTHPLACE.

> *Like a pall at rest on a pulseless breast*
> *Night's funeral shadow slept—*
> *Where shepherd swains, on Bethlehem plains,*
> *Their lonely vigils kept;*
> *When I flashed on their sight the heralds bright*
> *Of heaven's redeeming plan,*
> *As they chanted the morn of a Saviour born—*
> *Joy, joy to the outcast, man.*—WILLIAM PITT WALLACE.

THREE chapters, I propose, for Bethlehem, Jerusalem, and Bethany; birth, death, and ascension. I begin at Bethlehem.

The distance from Jerusalem to Bethlehem is but a half dozen miles. We propose to go to and from it in a morning. Our vehicle with its female French driver, which brought us from Jaffa, was retained for the purpose. Although the road was rough and stony, and the streets narrow, we risked the carriage and ignored the donkey on the pledge of the guide. The sequel showed that there was some risk, as many of the streets were impassable for a carriage.

We leave the Jaffa gate, pass under the upper aqueduct and over the upper part of Gihon, and then drive nearly due south. The bed of the Kedron, in the deep valley on our left, pursues its empty way to the Dead Sea; while on the right, and to the west, along the horizon, in broken and gray masses, lie the mountains of Judah, shutting out the Mediterranean. One lonely person we meet in the unaccustomed path between the stone walls before we reach the direct way to Bethlehem. He wears a stove-pipe hat. Its strangeness and awkwardness in this land of robe, fez, and turban, create a smile. When we reach the main road, and leave the "hill of evil counsel" on our left, we find the way filled with laden camels. Under the lash of our guide these give the way, and with considerable malice both they and their drivers fumble and tumble about awkwardly amid the rubble of the road. The olives are thick, perforated, and old, in the fields, within the stone walls. "Where," we ask of the guide, "do they get so much stone for the walls?"

They are ten feet wide and three high, and like the Dutchman's wall of the anecdote, "when they fall down they are higher than when they stand up!"

"Why do you ask?" says the guide. "Don't you see the fields are full of stones?"

"But no one could miss any stones out of those fields," we remarked.

"Oh! a few are left over," responds the guide.

How the hardy olive can find sustenance on such "stony ground" is a miracle.

But for the olive the best of these fields of cultivation would seem desolate and lonely. The olive does not stand in any regular row, like our apple-trees. The fences and boundaries, whether of cactus hedge or stone, are as crooked as the olive trunks and branches, and these are twisted from their sapling youth to their gnarled old age. The peasants, when they plant the olive, set their sticks in the ground and twist several of them together; and as are these twigs, so are the trees.

We are happy in a breezy day, which mitigates the fierceness of the sun. What a crowd of people now are upon the road, going to Bethlehem and Hebron, and to Beersheba, and even further south. Nine out of ten of these are upon donkeys and camels; and more than three-fourths have their eyes sore or shaded; and these are Arabs, whose suit is sometimes gay in color, but generally of stripes, brown and white, which reminds us of the dress of our penitentiaries, barring the long robe of the wearer. They carry the long Damascus gun, and a plentiful pouch, for the desert and danger. Cactuses, with their big stocks and leaves, furnish some of the hedges, and "turn" the animals from the fields. We meet some people, who are blue-eyed and good-eyed, in European dress. These are of the German colony, which here thrives upon the old soil, and makes its crops of grape and grain in their season, or several crops in one season. Some herds of black and white cattle of Dutch breed are seen picking up a quiet rumination from the browned herbage and the green leaves left on the trees.

The land is not unlike the dress of the Arabs—brown and white. It is burnt with the sun of the now departing summer, and white with the lime of many summers.

"Ah! this is fine land!" we say ironically to the guide.

"Good land! I guess it is," responds the guide, who is from the State of Maine, "or it wouldn't hold up so many stones and rocks. Good deal of heft about it."

But we notice that where water runs the vineyards of the Germans appear, and the walls have a trim look. Thrift, Teuton! thy name is thrift! Old olive roots for fuel, as twisted and as difficult to unravel as the philological roots of our college days, appear on the backs of multitudinous donkeys going up to the city; while going from it, for the terraces, on the heads of blue-robed, tattooed Arab females, are baskets of manure gathered in Jerusalem. The plain of Rephaim is spread around us, two miles wide by three long. Here David defeated the Philistines. Here also many associations cluster. Among them the cave of Adullam has been verified, which another Samuel has described, and the well of Bethlehem, "which is by the gate," for the water of which David was athirst, comes in for an explanation from our Biblical guide, with apt quotations from "Samuel." These, however interesting, must not draw us aside. We had passed the traditional tree where Judas hanged himself, and the rural abode of Caiaphas, the high-priest; but these nebulæ of tradition detract from the main object—Bethlehem. The Well of the Magi, however, is one of the incidents of the main object, and a pretty story is told of it, although it is not recorded in the second of Matthew; for did not the wise men, after leaving the presence of Herod, here stop to draw water? Was it not here that the reflection of the star which led them was seen in the well?

Then we pass the Greek convent of Elijah, where other stories are told, not now worth the repetition. But from this point the cities of Bethlehem and Jerusalem are visible—" twinned in mutual being," birth and death. From this eminent point, too, can be seen the sugar-loaf mountain called the Tomb of Herod. It is high and round. It is the scene of a massacre of Franciscans; but it sinks into nothingness, as Herod did, compared with those he persecuted, along with that dim vision, shining hard and bluish like steel, twenty-five and more miles away, through avenues of dark and gray sun-bathed mountains. That is the Dead Sea. This is our first glimpse of this famous laboratory and sport of nature. Below and around is something more attractive to both eye and memory. It is the field of Boaz and the scene of that sweet story of love.

"Ruth and Luke!" cries out our guide.

"Ruth and Boaz, rather," I respond, with a pleasant thought, too, of Naomi, the mother-in-law, as we gaze with curious eye over the rolling, bleak, and now dry fields, where the ever new, ever old tale of female devotion is located. Then Bethlehem appears more clearly. Its prominent object is the Church of the Nativity within its semicircle. On the right is the old Knights Templars' castle, now the house of the Austrian consul. The landscape begins to show much grape and olive. The square, solid houses of Bethlehem, and terraced hills, gardened and groved, amid ledges of limestone, make as pretty a picture in its frame of rock as artist could desire to delineate.

Our guide calls a halt at the foot of the hill. We are at a singular square tomb. It is not unlike those domed temples which we have seen for the burial of holy men in Algiers and Syria. It is the tomb of Rachel. Surrounding it are the slovenly tombs of Mohammedans, with their rough gravestones lying loosely in dirt and dust. It was built by the Hebrews. Here they come on Thursdays to wail and burn incense. There is no doubt that here not only was Benjamin born, but Rachel died. All agree to this; and it is pleasant to have brothers—both Hebrew and Moslem, both of whom claim a fee-simple in all that concerns Jacob—agree upon something. Here Jacob set a pillar to memorize the last resting-place of her whom he won after such a romantic, though dilatory, courtship. Seven years was nothing "for the love he bore her." "And as for me"—how sad the simple story —"I buried her there, in the way of Ephrath—the same is Bethlehem!"

Who is the strange man we see sitting wearily at the arched door of the tomb? What brings this pilgrim here—he of the grisly beard, and long, unkempt hair? He is no Arab—no Hebrew. He wears no bournous of stripes, and no dark gabardine; only a plain black garment, dusty, like his bare feet, with travel. We ask him, through our Yankee-Arab guide, not altogether incurious at this sad, strange, and lonely warder at the birthplace of Benoni—"son of my sorrow"—Is he, too, like us, a pilgrim to this tomb and shrine of the elder day? Yes, he is a pilgrim, like us—and from Russia. He is a Greek priest from the Volga, and lives spiritually upon Jordan's stormy banks, waiting for the peaceful shore; and really upon Jordan's arable banks, waiting for the rains to fructify his fields. He owns property here also, and has come hither to make his new leases. Thus was our illusion of the pilgrim at Rachel's tomb dissipated; for even here the cause of the pilgrimage was a *causa lucri*. Near by, on the west, in the village of Beit Jala, live the Greek and Armenian patriarchs, so that this is a pious precinct, and land is none the less valuable because it is not cultivated by Arabs or overrun by Bedouins; Christians till it. At this point you may go to Solomon's pools. They are one of the wonders of this vicinity, and worthy of minute description for their beauty, size, history, and permanency. From them yet, waters flow into the mosque which is built over the temple. Here is the "Sealed Fountain," referred to in Solomon's Songs. It is said that these pools were repaired by Pontius Pilate; but that would not make their waters more agreeable. Maiden-hair ferns abound about them, and swimmers of an archæological turn can take a plunge and come up beaded with antiquities. We had no occasion to study in that fashion, and were content to see the Arab women fill their goat-skins from one of the openings of the aqueduct.

The hill-tops show little villages after we leave the Hebron road, but none look as blithe and prosperous as Bethlehem, as she sits crescent-shaped upon the mountain side. How or whence come its vine, fig, and olive luxuriance I cannot see, except that the water comes mysteriously from the pools of Solomon; for is it not said in Ecclesiastes, "I made me pools of water to water therewith the wood that bringeth forth trees?" Or perhaps this white soil hath dews. Certain it is that in and around Bethlehem something else was grown in early days than the sheep which David tended hereabouts, or the lion and the bear which he fought. Here were once the fruitful barley fields which Ruth gleaned after the reapers, when the great love arose in the breast of Boaz, out of which grew the stock of Jesse and David—a line ever made benign by having as its pleasant places the vicinity of Bethlehem, and its ancestress Ruth, and its descendant Jesus, the son of Joseph and Mary! Here is the source of the kings of Judah and the world's Saviour!

We halt at the gate of the town. We are, owing to impediments, compelled to abandon our carriage. We are surrounded by a bevy of Bethlehem girls. One is exceedingly pretty, and does not degrade the neighborhood of Ruth by unseemly screeching for alms. She plies a little pair of pincers, and turns in and twists upon the wires olive beads for rosaries, with a "property of easiness" which Shakespeare commends in the "hand of little employment," meanwhile chatting with easy grace. My wife buys one, and contracts for another rosary, to be made before we return.

These dozen girls, of whom "Eothen" makes an extravagant picture of coy and debonair loveliness, are vivacious and somewhat pretty, and would be more so if not dirty and sore-eyed. They wear little, close, cottage caps, with two or three rows of coins lapping closely on each other, and in the sum making quite a dowry. They jingle merrily when shaken. I would not depreciate these Christian maidens, for these are not of the Moslem religion, whatever their blood. But I cannot fail to portray one beautiful woman, a young mother, who, be it said reverently, recalled, if not the Madonna, the picture of her by Raphael—"La Perla"—in which the magi are offering gold, frankincense, and myrrh. She sat apart upon a stone under the shade of the archway, nursing a babe. Her hair had that rich auburn and ethereal fineness with which Murillo favors his Madonnas, which are likenesses, by the way, of his Andalusian wife. I wondered if, peradventure, this beautiful Bethlehem mother might not have in her veins some of that precious blood of the house and lineage of David that escaped the murderous decree of Herod.

Bethlehem has four thousand people and five hundred houses. Many of the houses are substantial. The streets are so narrow that our guide has to ride ahead and employ people to move impediments out of the way. It is said the people are handsome. That reputation may come from the ruddy cheeks of David, or the graces of Ruth, or the pictures of the Madonna. One thing must be said of the town, and that is, that if it has any beauty or good in it, it is Christian, for it is *par excellence* the Christian town of Judea. In 1834, after an insurrection by the Arabs, Ibrahim Pasha, then ruler, riddled the Moslems unto death after his peculiar methods, quite worthy of a successor of Herod.

Before purchasing our olive-wood, beads, mother-of-pearl, and other souvenirs, where many such are deftly made by exquisite art, we make our visit to the most attractive place of Bethlehem. The place of the Nativity has been often described, and the church above it. Every object and personage here and hereabout have been the special object of gifted pens and impassioned eloquence. Make a catalogue simply of the names; and each name will be set to music like a psalm. The anointing of David by Samuel; the family of Jesse and their exploits; Joab, Abishai, and Asahel; "the city of David," as Bethlehem is called, Rehoboam's stronghold, the habitation of Chimham; the story of Joseph coming from Galilee out of Nazareth; in fine, the incarnation of the Word here in all its mystery, each and all are a poem which resounds from the simple cave in Bethlehem, with a sweeter and louder chorus than that of the Hellenic *epos* of the blind old man of that Scio whose shaken rocks we left but a fortnight since.

Let us enter this place of the Nativity. It has been honored, as is well fixed, since the second century. Over it, in the third century, the mother of Constantine erected that church which is the oldest in the world. Some of its columns are from the temple. Here in one corner of the church we perceive a lonely hermit. He is insane. He has been twenty-five years in this place, drawn, like many others, by the wildness of his vagaries about the unknown world. He is a Chaldean, and, it is said, was a sheik of his tribe. Amid the forty old pillars of the porch of the temple, brought to decorate the birthplace of Jesus, sits this strange man. Had he lived in the time of the Saviour, and had his faith been then as now, perhaps the demon of insanity might have been exorcised.

But it is the crypt we seek. There are two chapels here, leading to the place of Christ's birth; one is Greek and the other Armenian. On the north side there is a Catholic convent and church. From this there are steps to the holy spot. We choose to go by the Latin way. There are many reasons why the Latin way in the Orient is preferred. No traveler can fail to note the learned, modest, and elevated tone of the Latins, compared with the Greeks and Copts.

The priest at this spot makes his drudgery divine as well as intelligent. We are welcomed to the convent by him. Like most of the Catholic priests in the East, he speaks French. Our guide seems to be a favorite with him. He invites us to a glass of native wine or tea, and under his direction, and with lighted taper, we take our devious way below. Many tombs line this dark path, and among them is the tomb of St. Jerome. It is to his patience, goodness, and scholarship the world owes the Vulgate, or Latin edition of the Bible. It was here that this early and great father gave his forty years of seclusion for the glory of God and the benefit of mankind. Approach the chapel of the Nativity. You will know it by the Latin inscription and the silver star in the centre. We are led into this vault by the priest. He shows us the manger. It is explained to us that in "those days" stables were not unusually found in the caves so common in the hilly places of Palestine. This cave is many feet below the floor of the church. It is thirty-three by eleven feet, and decorated with marble. Precious lamps burn before figures of saints, chief among them St. Jerome. Sixteen silver lamps burn over the spot where the silver star indicates the place of birth. Another recess shows the place where the wooden manger, now in Rome, was found. Other spots are shown, as the chapel of St. Jerome, and the chapel of Joseph, where the angel appeared to tell him to fly to Egypt.

If these are apocryphal traditions, they do not detract from the fact established by scholars and antiquarians, and confirmed as well by what St. Jerome wrote as by his selection of this spot for his duties and fasts. He believed it to be the place, as his life and death bore witness. Never did art consummate so splendid a representation of self-abnegation as that wherein Domenichino portrays the last scene in the life of this Dalmatian saint and hero, who verified as well in his life as by his death his faith in the goodness and glory of the Gospel, whose good tidings were chanted first in the starry vault of Bethlehem!

Doubt as we may as to the Milk Grotto, the Shepherds' Grotto, the Magi's Well, David's Well, and the burial of the twenty thousand innocents murdered by Herod here; doubt as to the Shepherds' Fold, the Altar of the "Wise Men"; doubt—doubt that Christ was born immaculate and miraculously; but one thing is indubitable—that Christ was here born, and that from this nativity arose an orient sunbeam, for the faith in whose beneficent and heavenly guidance thousands have perished as martyrs, and millions have risked their souls' salvation! What place can be more holy, unless it be that consecrated by his death!

There are said to be only two places in this Holy Land superior in sacred associations to this place: Jerusalem and Nazareth. To my mind, Bethlehem has no superior, unless it be Jerusalem. "Why?" will occur to the learned Bible student and to the veriest child who has read the Gospels. Bethlehem is not one of the mountains which encompass Jerusalem, but it has its lofty thought. It is a beauteous pearl in the diadem round about the royal city. It is not the scene of sacrifice and sepulchre; but it is the scene of the nativity and the magi, and of the angelic song which ushered in the purest and greatest life ever clad in flesh.

Among the hundreds of books of travel and description of this country, the Bible is the best guide-book after all, and in many ways. In no one way is it more so than in its references to this spot, over which the star shone and the angels chanted of peace. No amount of degeneracy, superstition, tradition, or pollution, no surrounding, however disenchanting, detracts one beam from the orient radiance of that star, or gives one dissonant note in the seraphic hymning which here filled the heavens with a new-born joy! The genius of painter and sculptor has illustrated the story of the manger, with its gifts and worship, the choir of angels, the awestruck shepherds, the flight into Egypt, the beautiful face of the Madonna, with its golden aureole, and the majestic, masterful, and melancholy features of Him who became here the genius of love unto mankind. What place, therefore, in all this calcined country, now so many centuries made desolate, is so alluring for its fruitful themes, whether for studio or library, for the orator or artist, for the disciple or crusader?

Although Bethlehem was called "little among the thousands of Judah," and at a time when Judah fed her thousands of thousands from her well-tilled terraces and valleys, she is great among men, and will be great so long as her story remains. How often has the story been told to loving hearers! From the little Catholic church at the North Cape, but a year old, which we visited under the midnight sun and amid the summer snows, to the splendid church of St. Sophia, which dates fifteen hundred years ago; across wastes of time and oceans of space, over dark continents and isles gilded by an oriental summer, this story of the manger is a theme as sacred to kings as to peasants; as dear to the leper of Ramleh as to the emperors of earth.

The *locus in quo* of such a story, even though it were almost lost in tradition, must be a part, the first act indeed, of that wondrous drama. Even sceptics cannot ignore the fact that the event has, as the apostle phrased it, "turned the world upside down." Well might Gamaliel say that this work, proceeding out of this little village, if it were of men, would come to naught; but if it were of God, could not be overthrown. The evidence is that to-day its results appear in civilizations! What a moral and religious work has been accomplished by its energy! Beginning at this small fountain, what a fruitful spreading stream of light for the irradiation of the dark problems of our life!

As I came from the church I did not hear the angels above chanting the millennial dawn; but nevertheless I did not cease to believe that in "this city of David had been born a Saviour, which is Christ the Lord." Nor will I unto my last moment believe otherwise than that for this advent—the greatest upon our star—"glory should be given to God in the highest," and that out of it shall eventually come "on earth peace, good will to men!"

Forgetting for the moment that we are from the starless land of the unsetting sun, I blessed God for the stars—for the Star of Bethlehem; for rest and hope; for Night!

What but night can give this comfort? Contemplations and wonders, far-reaching thoughts come to us with the night. The faintness of the day ceases with the night. New vigors are imparted; more joys, more hopes, less grief, less hurry and worry. No wonder that some tribes of the East worshiped the stars, with the same fervency as those who worshiped the sun! Night was to them all opulent and thick with lustrous beauty and unfevered salubrity. It was not like the day—the symbol of hate—garish, full of infection and evil. Mystery and beauty—ever inspiring and ever renewing.

Tully speculated on the future life with rapture; Socrates taught that we live hereafter; Horace—epicurean though he was—sang that "we did not all die." What then shall be said of the authentic prospect painted by Divine Hand of that eternal bliss, when we emerge from the tomb to join the friends we love, and to lose ourselves in the ecstasy of an assured immortal future? This hope cometh from the Night—from the Star of Bethlehem! It has in it the flush of the dawn and the purity of its dew.

CHAPTER XXIV.

THE HOLY PLACES OF CHRISTIANITY—OLIVET AND BETHANY—THE SCENE OF THE ASCENSION.

*The dew's last sparkle from the grass had gone
As he rode up Mount Olivet. The woods
Threw their cool shadows freshly to the west,
And the light foal, with quick and toiling step,
And head bent low, kept its unslacken'd way
Till its soft mane was lifted by the wind
Sent o'er the mount from Jordan. As he reach'd
The summit's breezy pitch, the Saviour raised
His calm blue eyes—there stood Jerusalem!
* * * * * How fair she look'd—
The silver sun on all her palaces,
And her fair daughters 'mid the golden spires
Tending their terrace flowers, and Kedron's stream
Lacing the meadows with its silver band,
And wreathing its mist-mantle on the sky
With the morn's exhalations.*—N. P. WILLIS.

"ARE we fresh for Olivet this afternoon?" asks our guide, after we had spent the best of the day since its break in going to, seeing, and returning from Bethlehem.

Yes; and by three we are upon our donkeys and off. There must be secular methods about sight-seeing, even of the holiest of places. Leaving our hotel, outside the Jaffa gate, we take the path around the walls eastward, past the Damascus gate. The road, if it be one, follows the walls to their north-east corner, near St. Stephen's gate. There we descend into the valley of Jehoshaphat. I confess that ever since childhood, either owing to the rattling of the dry bones in Ezekiel's vision, or something ghostly, my impression of this valley was of the sombre kind. It changes as we descend into it and look from its many-tombed cemeteries. It is very like other scenes in these Eastern lands. There is no feeling of horror; on the contrary, we are quite jocund even up to the chapel and fountain of the Virgin's tomb. Even the grotto of the Agony and the garden of Gethsemane do not impress with melancholy. Our Arab donkey boys sing their roundelays as we go down, across, and up. The old olives, gnarled, gray, and dusty, do not appal. The bells of the convents and churches make no cheerless music. The children, who are picking fruit from the olives, have the "flichterin' naise and glee" of universal childhood. The Arabs who follow us with antiquities, old coins, and pottery to sell, do not unnerve us.

We have passed around that part of the old, or rather the newest part of the old city, Bezetha. Part of it is within and part without the walls. It is here that, in Herod's day, the city grew beyond the walls. It is now the Mohammedan quarter. We are passing the dry bed of the Kedron, and are in the valley whose name, Jehoshaphat, means the judgment-seat where Jehovah will judge the heathen for their treatment of the Jews. We are opposite the site of the temple. Across is the place of Solomon's throne and the Golden gate. We are called on to descend into the grotto. It is there our Saviour is said to have been betrayed. There is a chapel of the tomb of the Virgin here, and it is very old. This grotto and chapel are under the charge of Franciscans.

A good brother joins us to show the garden of

Gethsemane. The garden is inclosed by a stone wall, and still within is an iron railing, which incloses the very, very old gray olive-trees, each one a picture. Formerly visitors were permitted to go beneath the sacred trees and gather souvenirs from their branches, but now the sprigs of the old trees are collected and arranged by the "Sisters," and we were permitted to purchase them, exquisitely arranged.

As we leave, the guide informs us that we are pursuing the path of David, "when he fled from Absalom and went over the brook Kedron toward the way of the wilderness." He went up by Olivet, his face covered, barefoot, and weeping. Here we commenced the ascent of Olivet. Our guide, being on foot, makes a demonstration quite Oriental. He meets in the way some old Bedouin friends from the east of the Jordan, under the shadow of Moab. They mutually embrace and kiss with a will and fervor quite unusual with our sex.

"Who are they?" I ask.

"Some robbers; good robbers, if you pay them honorably; otherwise, not. They belong to a tribe whose sheik is trustworthy when he gives his word. I have employed him often for parties. This sheik has killed his hundred men, and is proud of it. He can mount fifty thousand men. He has some pretty daughters, and has vowed that they shall marry the men who kill the most. The Turkish government can't manage him, and let him run; but he is faithful when his word is out, and without his escort no one can go down to the Dead Sea. If they do, they are dead, sure."

We reach the summit of Olivet. Leaving for the present the old tower on the left, the tombs of the prophets on the right, and "ruins" near the brow of the mountain, we go to the old, crowning mosque. There is a sheik here, too. He is in command, and levies his tribute. They all do. Near is a church to commemorate the ascension. After our guide has embraced and kissed this sheik also, we mount the dark, winding stairs of this minaret. It is called Tur. The wind blows quite cool. The view on every point is superb. It is the finest prospect about Jerusalem. As it is seen from every part of the city; so from it all the prominent objects are visible. Below us immediately are the trim terraces where corn is sometimes raised on ledges of rock; but the olive-trees are not plentiful, but sporadic. There are enough of them, even unto this day, to vindicate the name of Olivet. There is a clear sky. No haze obscures the sight. The mountain is a ridge, and rises above Mount Moriah some two hundred and twenty feet. The walls of the city and octagonal mosque on the temple's site, and a few cypresses and the dark dome, seem under us, though across the deep ravine. Here Jerusalem with its churches and holy places is indeed "golden" Jerusalem. From St. Stephen's to the Golden gate, and from the Golden gate to the south-east corner, the magnificence of the eastern walls is appreciated in all their beauty and strength. We cannot see the tombs on the hither side of the valley of Jehoshaphat, nor the multitude of flat Jewish gravestones awaiting removal when the dry bones of Ezekiel shall rattle for the judgment; but the massive masonry of the old walls shows grandly, although one hundred feet of it is still concealed by piles of rubbish.

The city, in its four elevations, with their angles

and gardens, towers and domes, stands out and up in its lights and shades. Wrap your coat about you, for it is cold on the minaret, and take your glass for the far-off eastern view. Not yet—wait! Below you, to the east, is the beginning of that "wilderness of Judea," which no one who ever saw the Sahara around Damascus can mistake for a smiling land. Over white, hot hills, and over gray, verdureless vales, in involutions and convolutions, and swathed in shimmering sunshine, the bleak landscape descends for miles, until it melts into the valley of the Jordan, whose course can be traced by its zone of greenery. The glare is not too great in mid-afternoon to see the line of the valley or the dark line of the river as it enters the stark, still Dead Sea, a portion of which, like a bluish cadaver in an immense sarcophagus, is discovered between the brown hills and cliffs of the intervening wilderness and the range on the horizon's verge. A few olives break the sameness of the color till the pale azure of the Dead Sea is reached by the vision. It lies over thirteen hundred feet below the tideless Mediterranean, and double that below the Mount of Olives, from which we observe it. Above it is a massive wall, so remote as to seem like an exhalation, and yet so near that its shadows and ridges appear. These mountains are fifty miles away. They are the ever-beauteous mountains of Moab.

Our guide tells us stories of his capture in these mountains and his release. He has still an abiding faith in the Bedouins who took him; and, being a "well-spoken man" in Arabic, and knowing human nature "down East" in the States of Maine and Moab, he is preferred in many ways by all except those who are now endeavoring to monopolize the travel in Judea. We notice that in our expeditions, where the good-will of the sheiks is required, Mr. Floyd, the guide, is at home with them. We met the one hundred and ten Spanish pilgrims—three-fourths priests, in black, wide-brim hats and long robes. Ever since they have been in Jerusalem these pilgrims have been on our track or we on theirs.

When we enter into the mosque and church of the "Ascension," the Spanish company, for once, are in advance. They are kneeling in prayer. The slab is shown which has the impress of the Saviour's foot on his ascent into heaven. All kiss the stone fervently. Many pass their rosaries over it, and the last pilgrim, a devoted woman in black, touches it with her sleeves, shawl, veil, dress, and all she wears and has on that would reach the sacred place. Soon the trumpet of the Spanish guide sounds without, and the Spanish host rallies to the sound for a new crusade upon other holy places.

I have not discussed any of the mooted points about these holy spots; but it seems to me, without going beyond the New Testament, that it is very clear that the ascension was not from the Mount of Olives. The verses in Luke xxiv. have this most explicit statement:

> "And he led them out as far as to Bethany, and he lifted up his hands and blessed them. And it came to pass, while he blessed them, he was parted from them, and carried up into heaven. And they worshiped him, and returned to Jerusalem with great joy."

In the first chapter of Acts there is another description, but it is indefinite as to the precise place. Unless it be corrected in the "revision," it is misleading, as it says that after the ascension the apostles "returned unto Jerusalem from the mount called Olivet, which is from Jerusalem a Sabbath-day's journey." The truth is, that Olivet is not a half hour's walk, and even if the ascension were at Bethany, which is beyond Olivet, it is not an hour away. But whatever be the fact, Olivet is holy ground. It was chosen by the Saviour for his most confiding utterances. Was it not here that he talked of what would befall Jerusalem, his disciples, and himself? Was it not here that he spoke some of the wisest parables, and prayed and rested at evening, after the moil and toil of the city and the day? Was it not here that he agonized, and gave up his own to do his Father's will? If his ascension was at Bethany, certainly he passed —even as we are now passing—over Olivet to reach Bethany.

On the summit of Olivet we find a newly-built cloister for nuns. It is built by a French princess, Mme. Latour d'Auvergne, and is to be eventually her tomb. It is said to be the spot where our Saviour taught his disciples to pray. In the inner court of the cloister is arranged on tile tablets the Lord's Prayer in thirty-three languages. As we enter, our Spanish pilgrims crowd the court and surround the tomb of the princess. A life-size figure in white marble lies at full length over the sarcophagus, and is said to be a good likeness. The face and figure are those of a beautiful woman, mute and angelic in death. Sweet lavender and other flowers ornament the garden, and give their aroma to the shaded walks, and all is in neat and dainty contrast with the dirt and slovenliness of the city. The princess is absent now on a visit to France, her native country, but her workmen are perfecting her future mausoleum.

Before we leave Mount Olivet, our guide would fain have my wife go into the sheik's house, near the mosque. "Be careful that his seven wives steal nothing," was his admonition.

As evening is coming on, we hasten toward Bethany. There is evidence of a Roman road here. The rocks are solid, but worn with old chariot wheels, and by time and travel. Many Arabs live amid the hovels and caves in by-places, and come out upon us unexpectedly. Pursuing our way, Bethany soon appears down and around the mountain, almost hid in a nook. Some cultivation appears. Dusty fig-trees are seen over rocky fields, once terraced, fruitful, and beautiful. Bethany means "house of dates." Palms grow here; for was it not from this place that Christ entered the city in triumph? The Arabic name of Bethany is Lazarus. It is made of old houses. Along the way we find dumb monuments, in the shape of trimmed stones and fluted pillars, which had once some structural dignity. Lazarus lived here, and his sisters Mary and Martha. Here Jesus often slept, and here Lazarus was raised from the dead.

Here was the home life of our Lord and Saviour.

It is almost a domestic thought, this association with Bethany:

> "Come, let us leave these noisy streets, and take
> The path to Bethany; for Mary's smile
> Awaits us at the gate, and Martha's hands
> Have long prepared the cheerful evening meal."

The localities are pointed out, with painful, because doubtful, particularity. Even the tomb of

Lazarus is shown, and the débris of the house where the sisters lived. The appearances do not confirm the tradition. The people look seedy and distressed, and we leave the old place, desiring to have only the memories with which it is bedewed by the gospel narratives. We turn our faces Zionward by another road. Evening is beginning to draw its veil. A few pink clouds, with the cool breath of autumn, fill the air. We remember that on this path Jesus made his entry into Jerusalem, and that there were eager multitudes awaiting his triumphant coming after the miracle of Lazarus, filled with the religious fervor of the Passover.

We are startled from the deep hush which prevails, and from the solemn thoughts which it inspires, by a hail in Arabic from another company of the wildest Bedouins. Their faces are sinister in the gloaming. Our guide responds, and again there are embraces and kisses.

"These, too," says the guide, "are no better than the Jericho thieves you read of. They belong to Jericho, and are on their way home, and they will steal anything, unless they have given their pledge."

We look at their long guns, and knives in their belts, and the loneliness of our situation, and feel relieved at the *entente cordiale* between them and our guard. As we see them depart down amidst the rocky declivity, the moon comes out over the distant Jordan, and just then the sun departs with its last lingering light. The very caves, and the tombs in the solid rock, and the grandeur of the Mount of Olives make the scene weird; and the memories of the past, with its city of Zion, once the "joy of the whole earth," and so gorgeous in gates,

TOMB OF ABSALOM, VALLEY OF JEHOSOPHAT.

palaces, and temples, and over whose future desolation and woe Christ here wept because of its unbelief and ignorance, leave an impression none the less emphatic, tender, and melancholy, because from this point he gave his last directions to his disciples, before the " cloud received him from their sight!"

In descending into the valley again, we pass Absalom's tomb and others, including that of St. James. They are cut in the rocks, and look like temples, with rounded columns of alabaster, in the moonlight. Even from the shadowy valley of Ezekiel's vision the walls of the city are silvered into new beauty. We look up and realize how high they are, and why the besiegers preferred their attack upon other points than this. Yet there, now hid by the rubbish of ages, once arose the steps which led by the Golden gate to the temple and city. Passing under the shadow of Gethsemane, we cannot enter by this gate. It is the one by which Christ entered in triumph. It is sealed now, and the moraine of the wear of centuries also conceals what may remain of its ruins. We enter by St. Stephen's gate, whose two lions, cut in the stone in *bas-relief*, look down quaintly on either side of the archway. We enter St. Stephen's gate, to pass through and return, as our route takes us round the wall by the path we came. It is upon the east. It lies in the shadow. It is sepulchral and gloomy, and but one sound besides that of the donkey-boys urging the animals disturbs the stillness. It is the voice of an owl, hooting as mournfully as a poor whip-poor-will, as we pass the grotto of Jeremiah.

On our return to the hotel we meet at dinner our accomplished consul, Colonel Wilson, and talk over the sadness at home growing out of the President's demise. The day has been one most eventful, but it is the more memorable because upon it seemed to hang, in spite of orient sunbeams and moonbeams, a shroud of woe, and around the city there seemed to stalk the very spectre of despair.

CHAPTER XXV.

THE HOLY PLACES OF CHRISTIANITY—A SUNDAY IN JERUSALEM—TOMB OF DAVID—THE CRUCIFIXION AND SEPULCHRE.

Speak, history! Who are life's victors? Unroll thy long annals and say—
Are they those whom the world called the victors, who won the success of the day?
The martyrs or Neros? The Spartans who fell at Thermopylæ's tryst,
Or the Persians and Xerxes? His judges or Socrates? Pilate or Christ?
—W. W. STORY.

IT is past the middle of October, and our excursions partake of the coolness of the heights and the season. We give to them a half day each; but how much is compressed in these two halves! They require that we should be up early and come home after nightfall. The mornings and evenings are cool, and even the midday is not too hot. As fall approaches, the breeze blows its salutary comfort, and although we have no rain, and have had none since we left Norway, in July, it is not unpleasantly dusty. The donkey is the charm of these excursions. He is a relief and a comfort. Besides, he is safe, and with the aid of the guide on foot and the two donkey-boys in the rear, he is sufficiently prodded to his duty. We should gladly have gone to church to-day, but it is our only day to see the Mosque of Omar and the site of the temple. To omit these is to omit Jerusalem from the programme of Judea.

On our way we stop at the Armenian convent. It is near the Jaffa gate, and the street to it, though like all the rest in narrowness, is exceptionally clean. In fact, the Armenians of Jerusalem, though few in number, are rich in purse and in charities. The Armenian church is called "St. James," and as a representative of "St. James" in the old Seventh Ward, with its five thousand parishioners, I felt bound, after seeing his mausoleum in the valley of Kedron, to look upon the place of his martyrdom, and the methods of worship under the auspices of that most moderate, just, and wise disciple.

We dismount in front of the church. Over the walls opposite, and in the court, large tamarisk and pine trees give their cool shade; birds, *raræ aves* here, fly and twitter; while the bells from the Russian quarter, outside the walls, call to prayer upon this sweet Sabbath morning. While waiting for the custodian, we examine the plants which cling to the old walls and the Arabic arches of the large edifice; but cannot admire the poor daubs of pictures at the door and in the vestibule. Some Armenian characters, likely the Lord's Prayer, are written over the archway—a common usage in the East. Standing under the porch are solid boards of wood and pieces of metal, which, when struck, answer for bells! The stones of the pave are worn glossy by time and pilgrims.

This convent was founded more than eight hundred years ago by Georgians. The Turks taxed it heavily, and the richer Armenian Christians bought it in three hundred years ago. Next to that of the Holy Sepulchre, this is the largest church in the city. The Armenian school is here, and we hear the buzz of the scholars reciting their Sunday lessons as we await the appearance of the warder with the church key. He does not come, and we are disappointed, not because we fail to see the rich vestments or the extravagant pictures which the church contains, for these are said to be so tawdry and highly colored as to be barbaric; for it must be recollected that Armenians are Asiatics. But we did want to bear home to friends a mental photograph of the chair of St. James, which is here preserved. We content ourselves with going into the convent and through its corridors. Within its vaulted and capacious rooms there is an extensive printing establishment. It is under the control of the Armenian patriarch, who lives on the premises. We were allowed to go upon the flat and stony roof of the convent. From it we look down on the barracks and castle upon the north, and over the exquisite gardens of the convent on the south, and to the east—for we are in the very midst of Mount Zion proper—we look at the other mounts which make Jerusalem so celebrated, but whose elevations are not so apparent, owing to the masses of building. On one especially, crowned with the dome of the sepulchre, we look, for it is proudly eminent.

Upon these roofs, under which three thousand pilgrims can be accommodated, are many conveniences. We see an Arab servant drawing water from a well on the roof; he is filling his goat-skins. We look at him curiously, as he is using a small skin funnel to fill his quaint sack. Would you believe it? He asks us for "backsheesh" for looking at the operation! "Attend to that at sunset," says the guide. He responds in Arabic, "Morning is better.".

This was a reflection on my pet name, which I resented by withholding my piastres. Grape-vines grow about on the roofs and out of the very walls in the courts below. Jessamine festoons the angles. We are reluctant to leave so exceptional a street and quarter. Its neatness is fascinating.

As we pass into the streets out of Zion gate, at the south-west corner of the walls, we meet a company of Circassians. They are Turkish soldiers, and in the peculiar uniform which we saw in Russia, with their shining metallic cartridges on their breasts. "A murdering crew," says the guide, as we pass the hirsute group. They look it.

Those familiar with these ways of Jerusalem, in and out of the walls, will anticipate why we leave by the Zion gate. Upon an eminence on the extreme south end of the city is David's tomb. It overlooks the lower parts of the city, and is as well authenticated as most of the main objects of the city. There has been much logomachy and demonstration as to this and other spots for the royal tombs, but it is generally thought that David's tomb was on Zion, and above the valley of Hinnom. Certain it is that when Peter spoke as to David he said that his "sepulchre was with us unto this day." Certain, also, it is that Solomon, when he buried David, placed treasures in the tomb, a great temptation for its rifling, and it is equally certain that others besides Herod were guilty of the sacrilege. All these tombs of royalty were hewn out of the solid rock, and, eliminating all the legends, we come to the solid fact that among the groups of tombs in these valleys and hills, none are so imposing as those alleged to belong to the kings David and Solomon. None have been, or are now, guarded so sedulously. Only one person not a Moslem has seen them. This was Miss Barclay, daughter of the author of the "City of the Great King," who, for the services of her father, a physician, in curing a pasha, was allowed to go down and see them. The account of what she saw, "is it not written," says our guide, "on the two hundred and twelfth page of her father's book?"

We are not allowed to go into the tombs, but only into the temple over them. We look through a grille, and see old, moth-eaten, and ragged mantles, red and blue, covering something. They are made like the tombs of the Sultans and Caliphs. A large coffin is placed over the tombs, which are in the rock or earth below. This outer covering is all we see, and for it we pay quite a sum, which leads to a fight between the sheik's son and another attendant. This fight for the spoils about this abode of the royal dead is lacking in decency as well as in pluck. No blows are given—only a choke, a pull of the hair, a collection of saliva and a spiteful spit at the enemy, some clawing out, and only one belligerent at it at a time. This is the general Arabic way of settling controversies too complicated for their jabber. It is the anticlimax of the desperate fight described in the verse:

> "So frowned the mighty combatants, that hell
> Grew darker at their frown, so matched they stood."

Once a year the Catholics are allowed to worship in this temple. Why? Not because of David, but because here is the "upper room," as is alleged, of the Lord's Supper. It is to this tomb that Peter is supposed to refer in his oration related in the second of Acts.

The Arabs think more of David than of Solomon; but they hold both in such esteem that they desire a monopoly of their bodies. As we pass out of the court of this mosque, tomb, or temple, four camels crowd us closely. They are bringing in charcoal—and of such is the glory of Solomon!

Returning then to Zion's gate, we find a colored brother and a brown Arab boy playing cards. There is quite a throng at this gate. We are stopped, and have time to note that it is tricked out in places with gaudy paint. Its pillars are daubed red and green. Our donkey-boy gets into a mêlée with a crowd of laggard donkeys and horses and their drivers. He let his stick have full play on other people's beasts, and his tongue on the people. "What does the young Arab say?" I inquire of the guide. "It is an expression here, 'Why don't you go on like people!'" Sure enough, my young turban, why not?

Then we go to the door where Peter knocked, when the little maiden, Rhoda, came, and running back announced to the friends his enlargement from prison. The Syrians have this church. It has curious green gates and crosses. We go through the Jewish quarter, into the old Syrian church, with its sounding boards as bells also, and pass down David's street. I am attracted by a sign, "Photographs by Nicodemus." What an anachronism! What gaps of centuries between Nicodemus and this new art, never dreamed of by Hebrew or Greek. It being Sunday, we meet many Germans coming from the Lutheran church; for let it be known that there are some Protestants in Jerusalem. The cheery, cherry faces and bright blue eyes of this race are in radiant contrast with the sallow and bronzed features one meets here at every step. How well dressed they are—men, women, and children! They are of the German colony. The German consul, who lives at our hotel, tells me that there are over one thousand five hundred Germans in Judea. They worship here on the old site of the Temple of the Knights of St. John. The grounds and ruins are adjacent on the south to the Church of the Sepulchre. They were made a present to Prussia in 1869 by the Sultan. The old church is being excavated, as for fifty feet the rubbish covered its arches and walls. There has been much work done, but one-third only of the excavations are completed. The walls are already dressed in vines. Going up amid the antique cloisters of the famous knights, we see upon what "heaps" Jerusalem, as now known, reposes. We look into a hole fifty feet deep. Down in its darkness we see the old street ways of Jerusalem in the crusader days! Enough stone has been taken out and piled up to build the new church which is being erected. Some of the old arches are elegant in shape, and keyed with a skill that defies destruction. In the courts up the stairs—whither we are guided by a tall Nubian in white burnous—there is much taste in the growth and arrangement of the flowers, for the sun shines in upon the cool balconies. We enter the vaulted chapel, once occupied by the knights. It has its lace-covered altar, embroidered chancel, polished wooden pews, Maltese crosses, baptismal font, and plain pulpit, recalling the anomaly of Lutheranism in the grand old Catholic cathedrals of Scandinavia. We look for the blackboard, with chapter and verse and number of the Psalm for Sunday. These are not here, but the Bible, hymn, and prayer-book are. We open the last. "Herr, höre meine wörte," is the first line of the hymn we see. Were we Teutonic now—but this is no place for singing psalms, for, as I listen, the murmur of loud voices pierces the wall from the noisy street. It is not Sunday for the Arab. We hear him in the bazaars below, measuring grain and counting its prices. There is a "corner" in grain even here, judging by the Sunday racket. Excuse these details as to this extraordinary illustration of the vicissitudes of time. Here is this fair-haired race, whom we meet from Castle Garden to Holland, and from Hamburg to Hammerfest, under Providence, resuming peacefully the old cloisters of the crusader. Preparation is already made for their religious devotion, and a Prussian hospice is provided for all who need its care. Even a descendant of the Sultans clears the way by a notable gift for the Teutonic immigration into the heart of Jerusalem!

We had already made one hurried visit to the Church of the Holy Sepulchre. As this is the Sabbath-day, we keep it holy by renewing our visit. Here are seen Golgotha, Calvary, the tomb, and other unmistakable memorials of the Saviour. Each spot, however apocryphal, is of moment. Hundreds upon hundreds of years, good men, kings and scholars, soldiers and priests, have regarded them as authentic. From the street we descend by a flight of steps into a paved court. Here are columns in rows, and chapels abound— Greek, Latin, and Armenian. This is the entrance. A Romanesque façade is upon the north side of the court, with sculptured illustrations of our Saviour's life. We enter the south transept, which looks like a vestibule. Here is the stone of unc-

THE HOLY SEPULCHRE.

tion. It is a large, red and yellowish slab of marble, inclosed in a railing, directly fronting the entrance. It is adorned with suspended lamps. This is the spot where the body of Jesus was anointed. We pass into the divisions of the church, and enter under the dome of the sepulchre itself. The dome is blue, and spangled with golden stars. Over the tomb is a canopy of reddish marble. It seems old and worn. The pavement is glossy and slippery. On either side of the canopy are two large round holes, used for the holy fire-miracle by the Greeks, who have its monopoly. The Catholics discountenance it, and very properly.

Every volume on Jerusalem has its chapters descriptive of this edifice. It has played a great part in history, from the time of Constantine, whose mother, Helena, inaugurated the investigations for its verification, and that of its sacred rocks. Whether Golgotha, Calvary, and the tomb should be here located or not, has been a theme for quarto on folio of controversy. Whatever may be the merits of the question, this spot has had, since the early centuries, the favorable verdict. All now seem to acquiesce in the decision. Our consul, Col. Wilson, has made an exhaustive study of the question, and has confirmed the general sentiment, which is the opinion of Drs. Robinson and Prime. Let us not quarrel as to the precise spots of the crucifixion, the rent rock, and the anointing of the body; the apparition to Mary after the resurrection; the seat of St. Helena, and the place of finding the cross under her superintendence; the spot where He was crowned with thorns; the rock of Golgotha, or the tombs of the crusading kings of Jerusalem. Whatever may be their topography or history, it is known that He was crucified near by, and here He was entombed. Let others, who are critical and cynical, dispute to their hearts' or heads' content. It is enough that the powers and learning of the earth have fixed upon this as the holiest of places. Here, too, have they fought, and are ready to fight again, for its vindication as the holy of holies!

To avert these contests, of which the Crusades are a sample a thousand years ago, and the Crimean war the more recent one, and that Christ's disciples of every rite should dwell and worship in some unity under this dome, there has been much diplomacy; and to reconcile jarring Christians, much tact and some show of Moslem force.

We are allowed to go up and down the various stairways in the rotunda, notwithstanding the diverse quarters of various creeds. Above are the Armenians, looking down on the canopy. In a secluded spot the Copts have their chapel. The Syrians are allowed a place by Armenian grace. The places are numbered, as pilgrims sleep here frequently, and this order is indispensable for peace and rest. The Greeks and Latins seem to have the largest space and liberty, the former making the most demonstration in shrines, pictures, and jewels, but scarcely as much devotion in ceremonies and services as the Latins.

After looking at the outer forms in the rotunda, the lamps, pictures, tapestries, and shrines of jewels, silver, and gold, we take our tapers and go to the left down into the dark. Here is solid rock. It is no counterfeit. We are shown the tombs of Nicodemus and Joseph of Arimathea, and others not yet opened. Then we enter the sacred place. Descriptions given in the early centuries correspond with what we see. It is a cave hewn in the rock. It is above the level ground. It is some six feet square, and one-half is occupied by the sarcophagus. The mark of the workmen still shows upon the hewn rock.

As we enter we hear the chant of the Franciscans sounding in the Latin church, and perceive a priest renewing the lamps over the tomb. We reverently draw the curtain; he motions us to enter, and then retires by another way. It is a narrow place. Age is upon everything here, except upon the fresh, pure, white, stainless marble, which covers this sacred place, and upon which our Lord's body lay. Some pilgrims are here praying. It seems a place for hush and prayer. I find in my wife's journal this brief sentence, for I cannot describe the impression: "The hallowed spot seems, indeed, holy ground, and we, too, with reverent lip touch the cold stone with loving, tearful awe."

Never since I have had a consciousness of the soul that rose with my life's being, and which has ever seemed, to my best meditation, to come from afar—from God, who is its home—have I had such uncontrollable and worshipful emotion. It is useless to reason about it; and to avow it, why should one be ashamed? In this far-off country one is very near his highest and best thought; and at the very tomb, or at least in the very precincts of the spot where He suffered, agonized, and died, the utter helplessness of one's condition, without divine aid, subdues all pride and humbles all worldliness. What Whittier said so tenderly came to my memory with new, unutterable meaning:

> "I know not where His islands lift
>   Their fronded palms in air;
> I only know I cannot drift
>   Beyond His love and care."

It is meet that we should close our Sabbath here and thus. We thread the *Via Dolorosa* homeward, pondering the problems of this life, which these scenes, however wondrous, only serve to make more recondite to the finite mind. Alas! we can see only in part. Here in Jerusalem it may be said, with more meaning than elsewhere in the world, " From mystery to mystery."

CHAPTER XXVI.

SITE OF THE TEMPLE OF SOLOMON — MOSQUES AND MOSLEMS.

The moon has sunk behind the Mount of Olives, and the stars in the darker sky shine doubly bright over the sacred city. The all-pervading stillness is broken by a breeze that seems to have traveled over the plain of Sharon from the sea. It wails among the tombs, and sighs among the cypress groves. The palm-tree trembles as it passes, as if it were a spirit of woe.—B. DISRAELI.

NEXT to the Holy Sepulchre, if not above it in sacred interest, is the Temple of Solomon. In what I have written its site has been designated. Societies have been organized, tomes printed, surveys made, moneys spent, and firmans procured, without exhausting the interest, resolving the problem, or making absolutely sure its exact situation and salient features. Many years ago, when in London, Mr. Morrison, then M. P. for Plymouth, furnished me with all the plots and plans of the temple, made under the auspices and pay of the London Exploration Fund Association. But as I did not reach Jerusalem then, they remain in my library at home. Since that time much progress has been made, and many have been enabled, like architectural Cuviers, from a few fragments to construct anew the temple as it was in its best estate. The various walls, exterior and interior; the substructions, constructions, and superstructions; the style of its masonry, the extent of its piazza or platform, its square or nearly square figure, its inclosure and spaces, its rock on the extreme top of Moriah, and all the facts, measurements, history, and traditions of this rarest of structures form a large part of the literature of travel and Biblical disquisition.

Whether the lofty situation was used by Abraham as praying ground, by Ornan the Jebusite as a threshing-floor, and by David as an altar; how its porches and reservoirs were sustained and arranged; where were its entrances and outlets; what were the plans and uses of its vaults and cloisters; what part of the area it stood upon and how it stood with reference to the walls; who destroyed and who rebuilt; what became of its columns, and what are the sacred and secular associations in all the changeful events of its history and that of Jerusalem, may be brought out in that good time when the Sultan shall regard more heedfully the wishes of the Christian "powers."

There is now one disfiguration upon its ancient mount. It is the Mosque of Omar and its companion Aksa. I may have been surfeited with mosques this summer, and may find now little grace in their meagre decorations, although these mosques on Mount Moriah have many graceful arabesques and much refinement of art; but when the son of Vespasian overthrew the glory of Solomon, and the temple fell, the pride and pomp of Mount Moriah departed. The Kedron, even, has no mournful meander, as of yore, to celebrate the desecration of the mountain which rises out of its waterless bed. The land of prophecy and parable, the very *religio loci*, is profaned by the turbaned spoiler who keeps guard over the marble plateau whereon once the wise men of Judah held council and worshiped Jehovah.

Arrogating to themselves the supreme glory of Solomon, these Moslems have placed their octagonal pagoda over the sacred spot, and have surrounded it with cypresses. They hold the Mosque of Omar to be next to Mecca in sanctity. It is *El Harem*, The Sacred. It is only within a year or so that the unbelievers could obtain entrance here.

The precious place for which David paid fifty shekels of silver—as an altar to the ever-living God—is held by them aloof from the profanation of the infidel, who, though he may believe in all the patriarchs and prophets, is not accounted worthy unless he accept Mohammed as the head of the faithful.

Even now, when we visit Mount Moriah, we must have government conduct. Accordingly, Colonel Wilson, our consul, sent his cavass, all accoutred with sword and whip, to clear the way and assure us safety. We have found this institution of the cavass quite ornamental at Constantinople, and indispensable at Damascus. Here it is both. By 8 A. M., under his guidance and that of our dragoman, Mr. Floyd, we are on the Dolorosa Way to the temple. As we approach Mount Moriah the trumpets of the citadel sound near the Jaffa gate and ring out a "tirala." It gives a sort of triumphal *élan* to our entrance. A feeble echo from the mount is heard. It is the horn of the Spanish dragoman calling his hundred pilgrims together for a similar onset upon the mount. These Spanish pilgrims are not so exemplary here on this Hebrew and Moslem ground as they were in the holy places. They bustle about with impatience and noise. I think they feel the indignity of the Turkish patronage over the sacred temple.

The site of Mount Moriah is well ascertained. It is on the western side of the valley of Jehoshaphat. There was a rock protruding at its summit, and this, having had some grading down, is still there, and the marble area is around it. It is a sacred rock, and over it is the mosque called "The Dome of the Rock." Still, Moriah is isolated. On the east it looks sheer down two hundred feet on the valley of the Kedron. As the Second Chronicles, third chapter, says, it was here that Solomon erected the temple:

"Then Solomon began to build the house of the Lord at Jerusalem in Mount Moriah, where the Lord appeared unto David, his father, in the place that David had prepared in the threshing-floor of Ornan the Jebusite."

Josephus confirms this, and the Jews generally believe it. Excavations make the proof strong as the holy writ which they confirm. The description in this and subsequent chapters of "Chronicles" gives the "bill of particulars," with measurements and cost. There was the cherubim and nails, precious stones and chains, purple veils and embroidered fine linen, carved pillars and pomegranates, molten seas and caryatidean oxen, flowers of lilies and baths of beauty, lavers, candlesticks, and basins of gold, courts of brass, and the chapiters, basins, wreaths, censers, pots, and shovels, and crowning all a golden sacrificial altar! How the king moulded the ornamental imagery in the clay of Jordan; how he dedicated the rich and gorgeous structure for the ark of the covenant, and how the two tables of Moses were reconsecrated; and standing before the altar upon the brazen scaffold, how he prayed with outstretched hands to the Lord God of Israel, is it not "chronicled," in dainty and elegant detail, among the annals of his remarkable forty years' reign? What a sublime orison that prayer was! "Behold! the heaven of heavens cannot contain Thee; how much less this house which I have built!" How large and liberal his prayer for the stranger, who might "come from a far country for Thy great name's sake!" How patriotic and loving for Israel exiled in foreign lands! Was it wonderful that fire from heaven should come down to light the altar on the solemn sacrifice? Was it wonderful that from far-off Sheba came hither its resplendent queen, with a very great company, and camels that bore spices and gold and precious stones, as tributary to his wisdom? Or that harps and psalteries welcomed other sovereigns and their tributes?

No wonder that pilgrims now come to this ancient shrine, and that Jews "wail" for its restoration. No wonder that Mohammed is alleged to have ascended here, where a little tower marks his observatory. No wonder that Omar insisted on making his name immortal by building on the place and fame of Solomon.

It is a shame that these Moslems could not keep its precincts and platform cleaner outside, as they are so particular against defilement inside of their mosques that they will not allow any one to enter without slippers on his feet. Our first examination is at the Golden gate. It is a part of the eastern wall, and it does make one giddy, as Josephus said of it, to look through the apertures of the battlements upon the vale of graves far below.

It is doubtful if the present material of the gate is as old as the gate. The vestiges are there, and the memories; but Saracenic work has been done, even at this Golden gate.

We enter within the Mosque of Omar unsandaled, under the guidance of our dragoman and one of the servants of the sheik who has it in charge. The hundred Spanish pilgrims have their dragoman, hurrying them from point to point, and they still keep up quite a noise. The sheik himself is attracted by the unusual stir, and appears on the scene. He is fat, gross, and chunky, with a rubicund face and a bulbous, fluffy form. He is in his element showing off to the Spanish infidels his supreme control of the place. We slide on our slippers around the railing which confines the sacred rock, and under the pendant ostrich eggs; look at the script from the Koran on the glazed tiles; count the pillars of the mosque; step off the sixty odd feet of each of its octagonal sides; admire its various marbles and colonnades and arabesque patterns, modeled after those of Damascus and copied by those of the Alhambra, as well as the pointed, stained-glass windows and the gilt crescent in the dome; open our startled ears at the hollow sounds produced by stamping over the caves and vaults, and our eyes at the last footprints of Mohammed before he ascended; all this, and no interruption from our Boabdil sheik. I modestly ask the Moslem guide if he will open one of the large, illuminated Korans upon a stand in an angle near the pulpit. He acquiesces. I ask him to read a sentence. He does, in Arabic.

"Mr. Floyd, will you translate?" I ask of our dragoman. He does.

"This is the book of God, and I am a sure witness."

That is the text; and just as I am reflecting about the Mormon Bible and other apocrypha, the blustering sheik rushes up, exclaiming in bitter invective and harsh voice against me, using the word "*Kelb*," signifying, as I knew, a dog. Now I like dogs, but do not like to be called one, however faithful. I knew that he meant me, and that he used the word in an opprobrious sense. Did I get angry, profane, belligerent? Not a bit. I inquired in English of our dragoman:

"What does the incarnate old Diabolism say?"

"He says, 'Shut that book! No dog of an unbeliever shall look upon it.'"

"Aha! he said that, did he? By—" but the expression stuck in my throat. It was unparliamentary, and being better up in the rules of decorum than "familiar with the rules" of this Moslem body, I withdrew it—in my mind.

I began to say, however, that the old curmudgeon must have got up wrong end foremost this morning, and that his breakfast must have disagreed with his dyspeptic interior, etc., when I caught our guide's eye. He looked scared. He said to me, *sotto voce:*

"Our guide there is the sheik's own son. He understands some English. We will be thrust forth. Beware!"

Then I began to think better of the noble sheik. Was he not a devoted Mohammedan? Was it so strange, therefore, that he should seek to honor its record before men, especially before Spanish priests and strange interlopers? Does he not accept many of our prophets, teachers, and patriarchs—Noah, Abraham, Moses, Jesus, and others—and ought we not to be grateful? Although he believes that their separate dispensations are fulfilled, and that all heavenly wisdom is merged in Mohammed, does he not have a religion with a Scripture as well as a system of architecture? His creed might not be as spiritual, its symbols as beautiful, or its sentiments as sublime as ours; still there is to him a spiritual life beneath the letter of his Koran, and an iconoclastic grandeur in the very letters with which his mosque is adorned, and on which I have presumed to set my profane vision.

Thus reasoning, I excused his zealotry, and felt a pride in the excessive commotion which agitated his doughty stomach. When, therefore, he prepared with flaming eye to order me out of this sanctuary of the prophet, and with that guttural cry called me a canine unbeliever, and especially when I found out that our own Moslem guide, before whom I had vilipended the Sheik, was that sheik's own son, and being anxious to see more of the site of the temple, having come six thousand miles, I smothered my feelings, cultivated the *suaviter in modo*, with a view to the *fortiter in re*, and said sweetly to the son of the irate parent:

"Tell your noble and distinguished father that I have not met, in all my wanderings from Indus to the Pole, a form so commanding as his, or a face so radiant and benignant with holy light. If a darkness of intellect has led me to ask for the illumination of the prophet from this great book under his illustrious keeping—why should it be accounted unto me for unbelief, and why should I be likened to a sceptical quadruped? Tell him that!" My five minutes not having expired, and no previous question pending, I added: "Moreover, tell him that if ever I am compelled to seek light, it will be under the magnificent shadow of his wide-spreading arborescence, of which he is the tallest specimen since the time of the Caliphs."

This speech, I fear, was but feebly translated and delivered; but it was effective! Were we not at once ushered around with profound condescension? When we left the presence of this swelling son of a prophet we would have bowed to the ground in response to his abysmal grunt of salutation, only that one foot got tangled in the cane matting, and the slipper of the other came off with inconvenient profanation.

The other mosque on the temple's site is visited before we leave the mount. It is called Aksa. It is on the south-west corner. It is vast in size. Its central arch is of the Norman zigzag kind, indicating its origin. Its columns are fine, and it is probable that they were rifled from some of the Greek churches or classic temples. Its pulpit is ornate, and, as we see by its style, is Damascene. There are many traditions and much nonsense about this mosque. We indulge in some of the latter. In the outer court in the wall is a black stone. If you can, with eyes shut, march across to it from a pillar twenty feet off, and strike it, you will be saved; and if not—not. That is what they told us. I tried it and succeeded. My wife, being suspicious that I peeped a little, insisted on a second trial, and pushed me a little to one side. The Moslem son of the sheik, who had a vein of fun, and rather liked these whimsies of his faith and tradition, exclaims:

"Your wife sends you to hell with your eyes shut."

I tried again, and succeeded in getting, as it were, into Mohammed's heaven.

Another test this Moslem joker asked me to try, and I was not averse to this renewed frolicsomeness.

There are in the court two pillars near each other. The person that can go between them will go to paradise. I "ordered tellers" and squeezed through, but it was a tight fit.

Some of the old tombs here are covered, like those around Constantinople, with colored rags, which are placed on the surrounding vines, to keep off the evil eye and cure disease. We walk out into the marble plateau and look from and over the parapet and across to the sacred Mount of Olives. Some fig and carouba trees are around the open plateau; some negroes from Nubia on wooden platforms are praying toward Mecca; some Arabs are drawing water from the round wells; and then, under the convoy of the son of the sheik, we go below into the vast vaults, where the stables of Solomon are. It is said in the Bible that "Solomon had four thousand stalls for horses and chariots, and twelve thousand horsemen, whom he bestowed in the chariot cities and with the king at Jerusalem."

There is enough light below to see. The holes in the old pillars are for the halters of the horses, and the number of stalls is just four thousand. It is said the knights of the crusaders here bivouacked. It is a cool, nice place for horses. We observe the roots of a fig-tree, a foot thick, running down the walls from a casement. It shows how vital is the tree, and how little water it requires.

Coming out of this old place, which is on a level

with the ancient temple, and reaching the plateau again, we find a pillar protruding from the wall. Opposite and below are the thousands of Jewish graves in the valley of Jehoshaphat, which I have already described. It is on this pillar, as it is told us, that Mohammed will sit to judge the world.

The ghosts, or bodies, of the resurrected must walk across the valley on the most attenuated gossamer; and woe to him who has not the acrobatic agility. This is the Mohammedan tradition. It is likely a distortion of the description in our Bible, and is doubtless garbled from the thirty-eighth chapter of Ezekiel, where the prophecy is made of a restoration of Israel from all lands, as well as the restoration of bone to bone, and of the sinew and flesh upon the bone. It is a most remarkable prophecy, and fitted to this valley of dry bones, if ever words of vagueness suited a marked place, for there is here a dramatic sublimity which they illustrate worthy of a Miltonic epic.

While looking about upon this plateau, we perceive the excavations made by Captain Warren. If he had not been stopped he would have been enabled to make many intensely interesting discoveries. Since visiting this place I have been gratified to see by an English paper that the vast revenues of these mosques, which now go to Constantinople—yearly a quarter of a million of dollars—are to be confiscated by the Sultan, or converted, rather, to the noble purpose of excavating, so as to bring to the light the "wonders of the deep" beneath these profane strata of Moslem structures. Where, then, will my sheik be? Where will be this doughty commander of the faithful?

There is not as good a view from the western and northern parts of the city here as from Mount Olivet, but certainly the view is not to be ignored. The tower of Antonio, the minaret of Omar, near the twin domes, black and white, of the Holy Sepulchre, and the few palms and many domes over khan and bath, convent and church, are here seen; but each and all, with the city and its walls, subordinate to the grand and ever-pleasing vision of the Moabitic mountains, now under a haze of blue.

It is always meet to close one's last view from, if not of, Jerusalem by a look at misty, distant Moab. Out of this mist issued, more than three thousand years ago, the chosen people of God, who drove the Canaanites from their possession, the land of promise, and who, after many years of conflict, a thousand years before Christ, extended their dominion from the Euphrates, on the north-east, to the border of Egypt; and who in the meridian of their power were indebted to these very Canaanites (or Phœnicians) for much of the material and skill wherewith to erect upon this selected spot the greatest and richest marvel of architecture of the elder world.

Engineers have delved to ascertain its routes and bounds; architects have endeavored to reproduce its angles, walls, pillars, arches, foundations, and domes; painters have pictured it on canvas under the shades and lights of genius; but it is left after all to the reality of actual excavation to do what was done with the temple of Diana at Ephesus, and what money and power have done for Pompeii, so that we may verify by unveiling that which the Bible and Josephus, prophet, apostle, crusader, scholar, and theologist, have said of the glory and opulence of the temple. Over it now hangs the witchery of the unknown, and therefore of the wonderful; and in the absence of facts, as exploration will give them, imaginative men resort to the subtlety of the supernatural for the existence of its supernal splendors, and are prone to believe—

> "That devils and the genii wrought
> These everlasting walls:
> That Solomon designed the plan,
> And they built up what he began."

CHAPTER XXVII.

A WALK ON HOLY GROUND — THE SOLDIERS, PILGRIMS, TOURISTS, AND MONEY-CHANGERS ROUND ABOUT JERUSALEM—THE POOL OF BETHESDA—A VISIT TO THE TOMBS OF THE KINGS.

> *One spirit—His*
> *Who wore the plaited thorns with bleeding brows,*
> *Rules universal nature.*

WE have done what we could in our limited time to "encompass" Jerusalem. Not only have we made excursions to Bethlehem, the birthplace of the Saviour, and to Bethany, the place of his ascension; but have seen the "holy places" of his teaching and life, his sufferings and death. But how many delightful intervales of association lie between these lofty themes, in and around Jerusalem. The very streets—rough, dirty, and narrow, and covering the old ways with the accumulation of centuries—are nevertheless sacred. How can a person of sensibility stop to reckon the number of feet below which he walks, as the place where the stations of the passion of the Saviour are located? We have passed and repassed the *Via Dolorosa* and the arch of the *Ecce Homo*, where Pilate pointed out the Saviour to the multitude. In fact, there are two arches where a staircase leads to the "Judgment Hall." Opposite is the alleged place where Christ was scourged. Some say it is the place where the crown of thorns was placed on the Saviour's head.

What matters it to fix in these raised streets the actual scene of these agonizing associations? How much more comforting to do as we did, call on the "Sisters of Zion" opposite, and see what the good sisterhood are doing in following the Master's advice? These places are now as familiar to our eye as home scenes. How can we dispute about the exact sites when we know of a verity that very near, if not along this path, he bore the cross, that he met the virgin mother, wiped the sweat from his brow, and fainted and fell; and that at still another place, almost surely fixed, he bore our sins upon the tree? Here Turkish soldiers in white attire, much more meek and courteous than those of Roman days who crucified him, saunter with nonchalance; and here money-getting still goes on, and money-changers and venders of doves still ply their trade. Here, within those jalousies and flowered lattices overhanging the narrow streets, Arab women chatter about Christian dogs, where once sad-eyed women wept over the humiliation and sacrifice of Jesus. But in spite of all this, and all that the sceptic may say, good and devoted people of every rite are here, loving even the supposed footprints of their Saviour, and ready to lay down their lives as martyrs of their faith. Here are noble women, worthy of association with those who bore the ointment and spikenard early to the tomb, and who, when apostles shrank, were last at the cross and earliest at the grave. Here are those Sisters of Zion teaching the young, and not omitting in their teaching the great transactions upon these hills.

We visit the pool of Bethesda. It is full of benevolent, nay, angelic memories; for did not the angel here go down at a certain season and trouble the water, so that those who were diseased and waited along its five porches for the moving of the water should be made whole? Did not the impotent man here receive from the Saviour his cure, for which he was reproached, it being the Sabbath day? Now, how changed! There is no water in the pool, save a little green pond in a corner. As we enter it, the air is dusty and full of the cries of boys and men driving donkeys within, loaded with the refuse of the city, and whose basket-panniers are full of dirt, to be emptied here, to make room elsewhere for buildings. But to our mind it is now, as ever, blessed with the sweet waters of healing. An English engineer offered to the government to clean it out, connect it with its olden sluices, and fill it with pure water. The proposal was rejected. This tender shows that these sacred memories are not all dead, nor is the land altogether left desolate.

We do not pretend, in thus bidding farewell to Jerusalem, to make more than an etching of its external scenes. Scientific men, sent out by our government, have made exact many of the facts and sites of this remarkable land. There is a surveying party of the British Palestine Society now doing excellent work across the Jordan. Ruins and cromlechs, monuments of dead religions and sites of elder cities,—names familiar with early Hebrew history, and methods of building, long a puzzle to the learned, are being brought to the light. Others will record the results of their researches, under the prompting of learning, science, and religion. We can but give our last and best impression of this holiest spot on our planet, before sailing for the historic land of Egypt, which our Bible associates so nearly with Judea.

Go with me for a final survey of these sacred spots. Around the walls let us go, in the pure air, and out of, and aloof from, the sores and sorrows of the poor, crippled denizens of the town. Would you see the tombs of the kings? Ride over rocks and rivulets, north of the Damascus gate, a mile or less. There, overlooking the head of the valley of Jehoshaphat, you may go down into immense cisterns or areas, that now hold no water, and enter within the dark caves hewn by human energy thousands of years ago. There you will find not only the vast tombs, almost rivaling the pyramids, if not in solid magnitude, in historic interest and ingenious contrivance. The tomb of Helena, the mother of Constantine, is here located. On going down, we perceive that some one has been cleansing the spot, although we are saluted by a sudden whirlwind of dust, as we enter the broad, rock-hewn trench. We pass, stooping, under a low archway through a rock seven feet thick, into an excavated area nearly one hundred feet square. The walls are smooth rock. This leads to other chambers. There are evidences of columnal elegance, with carved grapes and garlands. On the southern side we go into the tomb itself. The door is small, and the rock has been shattered; but the ingenious arrangement to seal the tomb from lurking rascals would do honor to a Yankee. The door was covered with a heavy round slab running in a groove. This is only movable by a lever. The door looks like the solid rock, and there is another sliding slab at right angles to the door, which bolts it. There is also an inner door still, so hung that if pressed from the outside it gave way, but immediately shot back and inclosed the intruder. Now, it may be understood what is meant when it is said that "the stone was rolled away from the sepulchre." Yet how inane and useless all the contrivances of kings or men to preserve their bodies from Time the Despoiler.

Then we will convoy you through groves of olives, on "stony ground," into Jehoshaphat, and patiently bear you about the city. Many other tombs of prophet, saint, and prince, Zachariah, James, Jehoshaphat, and Absalom, are here on the left, cut in solid rock on the mountain-side; while below them, by thousands, awaiting the final summons, are the thousands of buried Jews beneath the rude, dusty graves. Look up to that walled gate on your right. It is the Golden gate, whose steps have been trodden by the Saviour. They are now hidden by the "heaps." A little more opulence of fancy and you may see the Man-God—he who was "acquainted with grief"—ascending and descending here, going to and from the porch of the temple, where he was wont to walk and teach.

Hearken! You hear the bells of the mules and the cries of their drivers; they are off for the Jordan, a stream sacred to our faith. They are bearing the luggage, under Bedouin conduct, of a camping party of archæologists. Above is the village of Siloam. It is half in the rocks and half in stone huts. The bray of donkeys and the cry of children salute your ear. On the hill, above the tomb of Absalom, a sweet voice is rendering some Arab refrain. It approaches the edge of the cliff, two hundred feet above us. What is she singing or doing? Hers is not a pleasant occupation, for she is picking up, for fuel and manure, the chance dirt of the beasts which go that way to Jericho. Our donkey-boy answers her roundelay, and we momentarily forget, in the simple duet, sung from hill to vale, that these Arab children have a language and a music which, born of the Orient, echoed in these caves when the Saviour and apostles, with heavy hearts, wandered over this vale to Mount Olivet.

"What—what is the girl, and what is our boy, Hamed-Evad, singing?" I ask of our guide.

"Oh! my love is far, far away," he sings; and she responds, "I cannot come to you, my beloved."

Are they improvising? What a simple romance, amidst these monuments of the great dead past! The tombs grow denser as we pass down the valley, as the Jews strive in life to locate their tombs as near in death to Mount Moriah as they can. Now we enter the dry brook Kedron. We see Arabs digging in the piles of gravel and rubbish for old pottery. What for? To pulverize, for cement. It makes rare and valuable cement, and thus the ruins of one age become the habitation and support of another. Then we turn down the rocky, meandering Kedron, to the Fountain of the Virgin. It is said that here the Virgin washed the clothes of the Child. Various rubbish is told about this fountain, and various modes to account for the appearance of the water are given, until some little science was brought to bear upon the phenomenon of its irregular flow. We seem any women here washing clothes in a most motherly way, and filling their goat-skins for the irrigation of their little gardens below. We retrace our steps, and go up out of the cave into the sombre light of the valley. Tombs of the "Judges" and tombs of "Prophets," old and new, surround our steps. There are tombs on every side. Indeed, we begin to find the place populous with others beside the dead. There are waters flowing here, and some green results appear. Old Arabs in striped mantles appear with antiques to sell, in the shape of coins in the time of Titus, and pottery in the age of Herod. We buy much doubtfully, for ever so little. Now, we are under the south-east corner of the temple plateau. How finely the battlements stand! This is indeed Jerusalem, and fills every expectation! From the village opposite comes the sound of a rude flute and the jabber of multitudes. The hills opposite are terraced and tenanted to their tops. In the valley below are some olives, some cabbages, and a cow; also a few carouba trees and many caves, a few vegetable plots and many donkeys. From another point Siloam seems a larger village. We pass a well; there is a bronzed Rachel at it, filling her goat-skins with water to irrigate her patch below in the "King's Garden." The lime rock and soil are very white, and the dust and gravel very thick, and the wonder is that, even with water, anything can grow here. Here we are called on to examine some excavations recently made by a German palæontologist. He had found the old wall of the city, and was proceeding to make out of his inner consciousness the temple, in all its parts and majesty of proportion, when the good pasha called a halt on his enterprise.

It is said that one of the chief agonies of the Saviour was, that "all forsook him and fled." So they did, and it was the bitterest drop in his cup of misery; but now, after two thousand years, his name is in the household of hundreds of millions of the race! Out of this desolation, sacrifice, and crucifixion there is ascension for these millions, as there was for him! Who can describe the healing and consolation which have emanated from these scenes of suffering and salvation? Now, as then, there is the same deep meaning in the beautiful verse:

> "Sad one, in secret bending low,
> A dart in thy breast that the world may not know,
> Wrestling, the favor of God to win,
> His seal of pardon for days of sin;
> Press on, press on with thy prayerful cry,
> 'Jesus of Nazareth passeth by.'"

If the streams, woods, grottoes, hills, and mountains of Greece were peopled by imagination, with naiad and nymph, dryad and god, illustrating the aspiration of our nature after the spiritual beauty with which we are surrounded, and if these mythic haunts still allure us to arid, dead Greece by the fascinations of fancy, how much more entrancing the caves, pools, groves, mountains, and rocks about Jerusalem, which are instinct with that wondrous benevolence which lived to bless and died to save. There may be no romance in the dry and dead scenery here; Jerusalem, Nazareth, and Bethlehem may not be cities of palaces, like Vienna or Paris; they may have no flowing Propontis or Neva, like Constantinople or St. Petersburg, but here there is a history, illumined like a sacred missal, and clasped in the everlasting rocks—for the vindication of which kings and crusaders have fought, good men like James, Peter, and Paul have died, and

Chrysostom and Jerome have fasted, studied, and prayed. There is yet to be a better epic of "Jerusalem Delivered"—delivered not from the Saracen or Turk, but delivered from the grossness which envelops it, so that its high estate on earth may correspond with the glory of its spiritual effluences.

CHAPTER XXVIII.

EGYPT'S FADED GLORIES—ALEXANDRIA AND CAIRO—THE VIEW FROM THE CITADEL—A DRIVE TO HELIOPOLIS—A GLANCE AT THE PYRAMIDS.

All were but Babel vanities! Time sadly overcometh all things, and is now dominant, and sitteth on a sphinx, and looketh upon Memphis and old Thebes, while his sister, Oblivion, reclineth demi-somnous on a pyramid, gloriously triumphing, making puzzles of Titanian erections, and turning old glories into dreams. History sinketh beneath her cloud. The traveler, as he paceth amazedly through these deserts, asketh of her, Who builded them? and she mumbleth something, but what it is he heareth not.
—Sir Thomas Browne.

IT was quite a puzzle whether we should omit the first days of Congress, until the holidays, or content ourselves only with glimpses of Egypt. Could we have reached Congressional duty for the December session, or have presumed on the forbearance of the constituency, then we might have had time to stem the current of the fruitful river to the first cataract, and to revel in the temples and tombs of Karnak or Luxor, or have ventured into Nubian wadis, or even rested under palmy oases in Upper Egypt. This was not to be.

Egypt still holds for us much of her mystery. We have failed to pluck out its heart. These wonders, like the enchanted Dulcineas of Don Quixote's fancy, fly from us like the whirlwind, and hide in Montesino caves of Egyptian darkness.

After our good-by to Jerusalem, and our fortunate boarding of the Austrian steamer at Jaffa, and a day and night on a smooth sea, we awake in the harbor of Port Said. It is the northern terminus of the Suez canal. The land about it is low. We wind in and around the artificial moles until within fifty yards of the artificial quay. These artificialities are made out of the bottom of the canal—conglomerates of sand. There is some trepidation as to our sojourn here; for had there not been rumors of cholera, and quarantine decrees, and vessels in limbo? Is not the Levant full of cursing at the prospective impediments to its commerce? Do we not see the yellow flag floating above the dead level, and the crescent with a star —under yellow auspices—floating at the end of a busy boat about the narrow harbor? Can we go ashore? I did go, while my wife dreamed of her sojourn at Jerusalem. I found a "*cosmos*" of a town. It does not show largely from the sea or harbor; but it is lively. It has a census of ten thousand, or had when the canal was building. The principal occupation of its many-tongued people seems to be to watch the canal, deal in Indian and Egyptian goods, drink liquor, smoke, and play billiards. There are in port a score of large steamers, loading and unloading, and others finding their way cautiously into the waters of the canal, on their way to India. Two-thirds of these vessels are English. Looking about, I see on a rear street the flag of our country. I salute it mechanically, and make for shore, regardless of cholera rumors, and when on shore make several angles to reach it. Stirring up some colored sleepers at the postern, I am directed through a garden of palm and clematis into an upper story, where a handsome young man, in a vast looseness of garments, is writing invoices and giving information to distracted sailors and shippers. This was our commercial agent. Recognizing my American ways, he invited my German companion and myself to his parlor. There was a library, a gallery of rare prints, a home, yet a homeless home, for the young Englishman had lost his American wife; but, under the inspiration of his library and cosmopolitan genius, he was fulfilling American duty. His courtesy leads me to commend him. His name is Robert Broadbelt—a comprehensive name. He laughed at our fears of epidemics and quarantines, and I returned to the ship with a determination to see the land of Cleopatra, Pompey and his pillar, Cairo and its cafés, and old Nile, with its pyramids and sphinxes, even though I caught the cholera from Yedda, or lingered at quarantine in close time for the session.

The next morning Alexandria is in sight. As we enter, the military bands of the war steamers play, and I distinguish the French as the liveliest. The world knows now what these iron birds of prey are after in this old and superb port of this eldest of nations. The world knows now of Arabi Bey and his revolution, and the Chamber of Notables, which has raised the banner of Egypt for the Egyptians, and no Egypt for the alien. The English are happy with Suez, the French with Tunis, and both very, very happy in Egypt—"except these bonds." The Egyptians would be happy if either dear charmer were away. This is the meaning of the late revolution in politics, the meaning of the Sultan's intervention—and of the ironclads in the harbor.

The material for the breakwater at Alexandria

is artificial blocks, made of stone and cement, composing blocks of twenty tons weight. The cost was twenty-five thousand dollars. An Englishman made the harbor. The blocks were made on the ground, hoisted on a car, run into the harbor and dumped there.

Alexandria is worthy of its namesake and history. It has had its schools of philosophy, its grand library, its columnal and royal glory, and its grand conflagration. Its Pompey's Pillar remains, on high dusty ground, where there is no water and much dirt, and where black torsos of sphinxes lie around amidst sleepy Arabs and flea-bitten dogs. The pillar is one hundred feet high. It is a single shaft. It shares with the famous Pharos lighthouse, of polished granite, the attention of travelers as they approach the city. It is supposed to have been built to honor Diocletian. The palace of the pasha is worthy of the city, which has now 300,000 population, and an increasing commerce.

Most of the houses remind one of Arabic Spain. The streets are unpaved and dusty. Date-palms and donkeys, camels and dusky people; wide trousers for the men, and loose blue jean gowns, black head-cape, and dark or white muslin veils, supported by a bamboo stick, for the women; with occasional white veils for the higher class, attract our attention. The dun, smooth-skinned, curly-horned buffalo, with nose up, drawing cart or plough, such as the fellahs in Pharaoh's time used, with water-wheels served by buffalo, donkey, and men—these are prominent features in and around Alexandria.

But Alexandria has its drawbacks. Fleas are one of them. We had much discomfort in Judea from sand-flies and mosquitoes; but for fleas, Egypt bears the palm! What some one has said of the regions of Galilee, as to its congregation of fleas, applies to the cosmopolitan cities of Egypt. The smug, steady, importunate flea from London; the pert, jumping puce from France; the wary, watchful Italian pulce, with his poisoned stiletto; the vengeful pulya of Castile, with his ugly knife; the German floh, with his knife and fork insatiate, and the swarms from all the Russias, and Asiatic hordes unnumbered—all these are here, rejoicing in an international feast, of which America is the victim.

From these annoyances what a relief to ride and walk, out of sight of the canal and the sand, amidst the Hesperidean gardens of Alexandria. Never since I have been traveling, either at Kew or Versailles, Peterhof or the Hague, has there appeared such tropical luxuriance of flowers, fruit, and foliage as in one of the magnificent gardens we visited in this city. All that grows under glass with us, blooms and spreads, shoots, effloresces, and tangles here in the air of winter. The palms are plumed wonders, with golden-red dates in luscious clusters. They seem to be the supreme object of the landscape. After watching the diabeyahs upon the grand canal, and the canal itself, running its Nile water lazily for the irrigation of fields of corn and sugar, and these incomparable gardens, we begin to wish for more time, and to think of Cairo and its dreamy beauty. Pictures in our own library at home, of the Libyan desert and the pyramids, of Heliopolis and its lonely obelisk, begin to arise in the fancy like rosy auroras, to which the recollection of the "Howadji" of George William Curtis adds its soft, balmy charm.

At Alexandria we have a day of festivity and courtesy from our consul, Baron Mannasce. He is an Austrian baron, of immense wealth, one of the richest of the rich men of Egypt, counting his millions. He is happy in taking upon himself the honor of representing the United States. At his residence, which is the finest private house in its appointments and articles of vertu and art which we have seen abroad, we were welcomed and breakfasted.

We are off for Cairo on the first evening train. We pass, in four hours and a half, over the darksome lowlands of Egypt to a grand depot. The omnibus takes us to the grand new hotel, itself a picture of the Orient in regal magnificence.

Here we are, at length, in the Cairo of the old and new—Cairo of a recent bloodless revolution—Cairo of the Mamelukes and Mehemet Ali—Cairo whose palms ever wave, whose "dates" are older than our Christian eras, and whose five-thousand-year-old sarcophagi and mummies come forth more fresh and fragrant than the cadavers of our merchant princes.

Being here, how shall we employ the time until equipped for the pyramids and the Sphinx? There is the citadel of the new mosque of Mehemet Ali. It is equal to anything of the kind in Turkey. It has domes, columns, arches, and half-domes. Alabaster, for which Egypt is celebrated, furnishes the material.

The view from the citadel is the best in Cairo. The lonely obelisk which marks Heliopolis, and the tombs of the Mamelukes; the quarries of the Mulcattem hills, out of whose abundance came the pyramids; and Cairo itself, the Nile, the isle of

Rhoda, an emerald in the yellow stream; and Ghizeh and Sakkarah, and beyond the unknown desert —these furnish the panorama, while the heroism of the scene is remembered in honor of the brave Mameluke, Emur Bey, who leaped, horseback, from the wall and escaped the massacre. Above all the objects, however, are the pyramids, in interest and age. Distance lends its charm to them, for they seem like pictures unreal and strange upon the edge of that trackless desert of sand!

The drive to Heliopolis was interesting. Since we cannot see Memphis, it being in the "abyss of time," and under the freshet of the river, and since Thebes is out of the question, as we have no time, the next feasible thing is to visit the ancient city of Heliopolis, the seat of the university where Plato studied logic and beauty. There is but one obelisk left here, and its counterpart is now in Central Park. Still, five miles or more from Cairo is the spot where "Orient Sunbeams" were worshiped, three thousand six hundred years ago, with great pomp. This worship was celebrated. The road is dusty, but shady. Some of the pashas have made avenues about Cairo, and they deserve honor for it. It is the land of the sun, and the shadow is indispensable. But of the solar worship only this one obelisk remains. It has its Biblical association, for it looked down upon Joseph at the time of his marriage with Asenath. It was a century old when Joseph came into Egypt. Herodotus refers to it. It is lonely now; its companions are in exile. All about it are grain-fields, renewed in vegetable vigor by the inundations of the Nile. At the beginning of the century there was a battle on these fertile grounds between the French and Turks. The visible thing of interest here is apocryphal. It is a tree—an enormous and far-spreading sycamore. The tree itself is a marvel, but the other marvel connected with it is that it shaded Joseph and Mary, with the Child, when they fled hither from Herod! The tree is within an iron railing, and is surrounded with flowering jasmine. We plucked some "for thoughts."

Returning to our hotel, who should I meet but my old friend General Stone, now in high favor as the chief of staff and organizer of the Egyptian army. While relating to him the impressions of this elder civilization and its monuments and memories, he said:

"Would it astonish you to know that I have consulted a stone record forty-five hundred years old, to ascertain certain routes of travel in Upper Egypt, and that the metes and bounds, oases and wells, were all found to be accurately set forth in this record? This research became necessary for army and surveying purposes. It is an illustration of what does remain here of more moment than the mummies of Rameses and Pharaoh."

But why should one be astonished at the remoteness of that antiquity which antedates ancient history? When we remember that the Indus-Euphrates-Nile civilizations had their synchronous origins 5,000 B. C., their history becomes as nebulous as geologic eons, with its millenniums of cycles?

It was one of my delights to meet this sterling soldier, "Stone Pasha." Behind his fleet white horses, along the Shoobra road, we had the opportunity of seeing the *élite* of this mixed viceroyalty. Among them was the Khedive, out on a drive.

He is a man of the oriental type, and wearing the fez as the only sign, in his dress, of his Moslem faith. What a drive this is! While we were out two teams ran away. One landed a landau into a canal, and the other a carriage into a sugar-field. Dashing by us on the road are elegant equipages, with veiled Circassians within, whose eyes fairly flash like their diamonds. They are preceded by mounted janizaries, pistoled and scimitared. Strange attendants are on either side bearing wands. On each side rides a mounted eunuch, and behind the carriage are other eunuchs and other mounted janizaries. These women are wives of princes. While studying the phases of this Egyptian life, we visited old bazaars and streets. It is the old, old story here, which is of Arabic origin, that of the lazy, easy, smoking children of Mohammed and of the sun.

This morning we plan a trip to the suburbs. On our way we stop at the ferry and cross over to the isle of Rhoda, where we visit the palace of the former Khedive, now in disuse, and see the Nilometer, or basin in which the depth of the Nile is measured. "It is lower to-day than yesterday," says our guide. It indicates forty feet. Less than that is not accounted very fructifying, and much more is devastating. The walls of the garden are covered with the Nile water-lily, a plant that looks like our clematis, while the flower resembles our purple morning-glory. Professer Ebers pictures, in his romances of early Egypt, this isle of Rhoda as a second Paradise, with its gardens and shades; and such we, too, find even unto this day. We crossed and recrossed the river in a boat by sail, and landed with the current. At the pier, men were filling their hog-skin sacks with water; while women were washing soiled linen in delightful proximity!

I fail to see the ideal girl, referred to so rapturously by Warburton and others. The lustrous eye and plaintive voice are disenchanted by disease and dirt.

My wife was invited to go with our vice-consul's wife to call on an "Egyptian princess." A preliminary request had been made, and graciously acquiesced in. We of the sterner sex were not permitted. But it was a pleasant episode, when the Princess Nazlim, who is cousin to the Khedive, happened to be sister to the houris whom we met on the Bosphorus. She and they are not quite equal to the picture which the German Ebers makes of the Egyptian princess in the age of Pericles; but, with their refinement and French, they would make good heroines for any romance of the Nile.

After a pleasant dinner with General Stone at his residence, we were gallanted about by himself and our consul. As it happened, we met and were introduced to the prime minister. He has had many vicissitudes since, being supplanted by the new order. He was exceedingly affable, and hailed us as Americans with conspicuous cordiality.

Our first objective point is old Cairo. The streets grow more narrow, the walls that shut them in, rise high above us, and dirt and filth reign supreme.

"Can it be possible that such tumble-down houses are inhabited?" we ask.

"Only by two thousand or more," says the guide.

We seek the Coptic church, and, as we enter, an obstinate donkey is being dragged out of the passage-way to give us room! Quaint and old is the little church, far down below the level of the streets; but the priest shows, with laudable pride, the broken and patched columns of altar and doorway. The vestments and priestly emblems of his religion look like battle-worn flags. The church is much like its surroundings, impoverished and pitiful to look upon; though, after all, it may bear fruit suitable to the wants of this people. We cross to the synagogue. Small boys quarrel as to who shall be our guide. But there was less to be seen here than in the Coptic church. We drive to an old mosque, now in ruins. The sheik gladly opens to our knock. We hesitate to enter. It is too filthy. Standing on the threshold, we perceive many columns still remaining, which remind us of the mosque of Cordova, and with that glance we are content.

There is a good deal of politics going on in Egypt since the revolution by the military. It was a quiet revolution, but still it revolved out one prime minister, and put in a new one, pledged to—what? It is said that he is pledged to a new Egypt, without the Anglo-French influence. Indeed, we have heard much of the autonomy of Egypt, especially since the Sultan has sent a commission hither; and the English and French men-of-war have answered it by anchoring in Alexandria harbor. I am inclined to believe that there will be a new order here. Egypt is not lacking in native ability. It irks Egyptians to see officers and rulers *de facto* of other nationalities. The Khedive has summoned a sort of Congress, which meets on the 1st of January. It is not a very representative body, as we understand the term; but it is to be, nevertheless, though selected by the sheiks of provinces, a body of an Egyptian patriotic quality.

CHAPTER XXIX.

THE ANCIENT AND MODERN LAND OF THE PHARAOHS—VISIT TO THE SPHINX AND THE GREAT PYRAMID OF CHEOPS.

> *Still through Egypt's desert places*
> *Flows the lordly Nile,*
> *From its banks the great stone faces*
> *Gaze with patient smile;*
> *Still the pyramids imperious*
> *Pierce the cloudless skies,*
> *And the Sphinx stares with mysterious,*
> *Solemn, stony eyes.*
> —LONGFELLOW, *Hermes Trismegistus.*

NEXT to Judea, Egypt is the most interesting of all lands. Judea gave us Christ; Egypt sheltered him from Herod. Before Christ, Egypt had sheltered the fathers of Israel; for Egypt was even before Abraham. Although Africa, geologically, may be a younger continent than America, and although Asia may be older than Africa, still the human record of Egypt antedates all others. It is a record of interest to human nature, for it is the first and most trustworthy testimony of our kind about our kind. Doubtless other nations learned art and culture from Egypt. Greece was taught by her, even as she taught Rome. Our Biblical knowledge is after that of early Egypt. All its old people have gone to the abysm except the Coptic race, whose features we see upon the ancient monuments and in the market-places and Christian churches. These remaining Copts seem to be as foreign to Egypt and its Arabs and Bedouins as the Jews to Judea.

Turkey ostensibly rules Egypt. Much of the olden power of the Ottoman, however, has departed. When it arose in Asia Minor, with a capital at Broussa, it swept from Ispahan to Vienna, upturned the throne of the caliphs in Bagdad and of the emperors in Constantinople. It seized the sacred control of Moslemdom. Its population is said to be thirty or forty millions, including about eight and a half millions in Egypt. Of these, eight millions are Arabs, who mostly till the ground. They are called fellahs. Seventy thousand are Bedouin Arabs of the desert, fifteen thousand are Turks, and two hundred thousand are Copts.

The history of Egypt under the viceroys, the frail rope of sand which binds her to its suzerain on the Bosphorus, and the strange relations of France and England, politically, economically, and judicially, to Egypt, are not less interesting than the influence of the Suez canal on commerce, the Nile overflows on agriculture, the recently proclaimed representative body of Egyptian notables on democracy, the *quasi* revolution of a few months ago by Colonel Arabi Bey, in favor of native rule upon patriotism, and the general unrest of the Mohammedans in North Africa with respect to the encroachment of the Christian nations upon the Moslem world.

Continually since we arrived in Constantinople we have heard Pan-Islamism discussed. Events with reference to Egypt and its relations make the discussion interesting. With such numbers at present, and with the old zealotry of the Moslem aroused,—is the Jehád or war of extermination against the infidel probable? Islam rose in Arabia. Its early devotees were brave and hardy. Their patriarchal system and manners have changed but little. They began, and still live, by raids or *ghazu*. The Prophet was their war-cry. They spread and were absorbed. Persian, Turk, and Tartar were at once conquered, yet became leaders. The central elemental power, once established by the Caliphate, has had various centres; but, after all, Mecca remains most potential to-day as a religious nucleus. It is a long story, that of Mohammed and his relations and traditions. The schism made in the ranks of Islam affected its power. The great Haroun Alraschid combined it for a time; but when the last of the Caliphs at Bagdad, El Mutawakkel, was carried to Constantinople by the Sultan Selim, the Caliphate in its title and privileges was transferred to the Ottoman. There it remains. This is indeed a power; and from it, or from those who do or may wield it, will come the Jehád.

Accordingly, we see that the Mohammedan world is agitated over the expectation of the advent of the Mehdi, or Mohammedan Messiah. It is thought that he will appear on the 12th of November, 1882. He will be forty years of age, of fine figure, and with one arm longer than the other. He will have sacred names in his family—Mohammed and Fatima. Already such a one appears in North Africa. A fanatical following may make trouble in India, Egypt, Tunis, and Algiers, in fact, among the devotees of Islam the world over, from the Ganges to the Danube. Another one appears in Bombay. He is asked to assume the Caliphate.

While at Constantinople it was said that the Grand Shereef of Mecca had revolted against the Sultan, and claimed the olden Caliphate. If an authentic "green flag" should be raised, and the Holy Jehád should begin, it could not run long or far without arousing rivalry; for the Ommiade family at Damascus, and the Abbasides of Bagdad, and that of Ali of Persia, would so quarrel as to enable the Sultan to re-establish his rights. It is the more likely that Arabia, Egypt, and Syria would rebel against the political power of Turkey, than against its religious power. There are so many descendants of the Prophet, that the Moslem mind would become confused and the Jehád become localized. What if the Sultan, to compensate for losses in Europe, should himself proclaim the Jehád and resume an efficient suzerainty in Africa! May not the ambition of European powers hasten such a Moslem alliance? Mohammed Ali—viceroy and conqueror—put down the Wahabees of Arabia. May not the present Sultan, who has shown so much energetic individuality, and who leans toward the Ulemas, and cultivates a court where sheiks, khans, Circassians, Egyptians, Persians, Kurds, Albanians, and nondescripts from all Moslemdom are wont to congregate for a gigantic Pan-Islamic federation, hold in his grasp the power of Caliph and the prestige of the Messiah? May he not reunite the Caliphate of Mecca, Cairo, Cordova, Bagdad, and Damascus, upon the Bosphorus? Armed with the small guns of precision and the big guns of Krupp, and with the elements of this new age, and while Austria and Russia are embroiled over the Sclavonic question in Europe, may not the Moslem become a greater power than ever? If so, the new order now rising out of the chaos of Egypt may make many organic changes in this ancient land. Already the Sultan, chafing under foreign guarantees, has resumed many privileges granted to the predecessors of the present Khedive.

The Khedive Ismail, who preceded the present one, was educated in France. He was reckless in his desire for improvements. He pursued the policy of his father, Mehemet Ali, to whom Egypt is said to owe so much for her regeneration, innovation, and enlargement from Ottoman rule.

Certainly great changes are taking place in Egypt since the present Khedive, Tewfik, has attained power. General Sherman, who was here a few years ago, kindly permitted me to read his unpublished journal. In it he paints the political picture then and thus:

"Egypt is still subject to the Porte, or Sultan of Turkey—pays tribute and is liable to have laws and orders set aside by that power—but the thing that gives the Khedive most trouble is the fact that all strangers coming to Egypt from England, France, Austria, America, etc., to engage in business, retain their national character, subject to the jurisdiction of their respective consuls-general, and not to the local laws and authorities. It is for this reason that nearly all the enterprises of Egypt must be kept in the name of the Khedive himself; for if a stranger gets an interest in any enterprise, he will pay no tax, and any question that arises must go to his consul-general, instead of the local courts. This grew out of the old mistrust of Christian nations toward the Mussulman; but now, at all events, so far as we can observe, the old prejudice of religion is gone, and a Christian can go safely to any part of Egypt without being hooted at and pelted at as a Christian dog."

Perhaps this was so then; but it is also true that the rich lands have been taxed inordinately and mortgaged worse by their improvident owners. In the last result, the fellahleen have to make up in labor for the impecuniousness of the proprietor. This is the old story; and Egypt is no exception. Hence much of its unrest.

Remarking to an American here engaged in business upon this condition of affairs, he attributed much of it to the improvidence of the natives and the inertness caused by the climate.

"Think of it," said he, "our wintriest days are full of sunshine. They are as lovely as a pleasant dream. We have a lazy sort of weather here anyhow. Every one appears to think that Providence will take care of them whether they work much or not, and He generally does. 'Malesh' (Never mind), is constantly on the tongues of the Arabs, and they don't mind. It is 'Allah-ker-sem' (God will provide). This furnishes the code of their lives, and they live up to it."

These are the new phases of the oldest of nations. They are worth a visit to the Nile for their elucidation.

But as the politics of the Orient, including Turkey and Egypt, are in a transitory condition, and as not much of certainty can as yet be crystallized, the chief interest of Egypt for the tourist centres in its climate and position, and its history and monuments.

Its climate is balm itself. It is dry. The mud huts survive all its changes. In winter its mildness is a salutary luxury. These features of the climate result from the position of Egypt. It is in the north-east corner of Africa; yet it is not African in its ordinary meaning. It is a small corner of Africa physically; but neither are its people nor is its position African. Egypt is the Nile. The Nile made it the cradle of human thought and progress, and the Nile plays for it even yet an important part in civilization. The Nile has created its limits and gifted it with opulence. The delta, whose apex is near old Memphis and modern Cairo, is the creature of the river. The northern side of the delta country made by the river is 160 miles along the Mediterranean. From its southern boundary on Nubia, where the templed isles of Philæ and Elephantine divide the waters of the foaming river, you have a sweeping stream 550 miles in length; but the fruitfulness it engenders is straitened within a valley, seldom more than seven or ten miles wide. Mountains, or hills of sandstone or rock, shut in this strip from the invading sands of the desert.

I did not go even up as far as the first cataract at Assouan, but I know that there is a sameness in the scenery—a broad river, greenish when low, reddish brown when high, running within a fertile belt, between herbless, grassless, desert hills. Now and then a plumed palm and a dirty Arab town diversify the plain, where ox and camel, donkey and fellah, do the work of cultivation and transportation. Along the stream native women wash or fill their water jars, and naked men fill the furrows by means of baskets or shadoofs, which, like our primitive well process, lift the water from the river. The villages look like old Mexican adobe houses, and are not clearly distinguishable from the ground.

Before the steamers ran up the river, crocodiles

used to bask in the warm sun in secluded places. A few cranes and many pelicans are seen occasionally. This is the aspect of the river and its banks from Cairo to the first cataract. Its fields and riches are sugar, maize, wheat, barley, cotton, and dates.

The river runs nearly parallel with the Red Sea, and the Suez gulf, and the mountain ranges west and east, until about twelve miles from Cairo, when it divides into two principal streams. The mountains still follow by diverging east and west. Within the delta, in various forms, there are rich plains. But all there is of Egypt is sixteen thousand square miles—double Massachusetts, and but little over one-third of the size of Illinois, which is fifty-five thousand square miles.

Omitting, therefore, the excursion above the capital, on the river, all of Egypt can be seen, as we saw it, by landing at Port Said and Alexandria, and taking a railroad run over the level land to Cairo. From Cairo you may see the most interesting ruins and monuments, including the Nile and its most luxuriant islands and plains.

There is seldom any rain in Egypt. The Nile does it all. Its waters hold in solution infinite quantities of fertilizing elements. The farmers sow their seed in the oozy soil, which needs no other stirring than that of a wooden one-handled stick of a plough, three thousand years older than Abraham! There is little grass and no pasturage. It is agriculture which the Nile brings. The fellahs reap with a hook what the pigeons leave of the grain. Oxen thrash, and sometimes a winnow or fan is used in the breeze.

There are as many palms as there are people, and a pound of dates per palm a day is reckoned a good provision of this richest of food. Egypt has few roads. The Nile does it all, except the two railroads and some pathways to and from the desert for the pilgrims to Mecca, and the caravans to the remote lands of Arabia and Ethiopia.

Egypt is rich in clay, as the Hebrew slaves found out when they were compelled to make brick. Fine marbles, granite, and other stone are convenient to the river, and were used to build the temples and monuments.

This is the Egypt of to-day. It is soon seen; Arab towns of mud huts, long lines of loaded camels and of donkeys, and their naked or half-naked drivers, and lazy Arab boys and women begging for backsheesh; the fields of the Nile and the great river itself; the mosque and minaret; the hooded women, and turbaned, long-robed men; the acacia and palm; and in the two great cities luxury along with poverty, dirt with despotism; all the plagues, including an abnormal government; sugar-mills and palaces, and an equable temperature, with a sunset that never fails to allure and detain the eye.

The history and monuments of Egypt are its special marvels. We are accustomed to read the Bible account of the land of Egypt as connected with the bondage and exodus of Israel. We think this account very old. So it is in one relation. When Joseph was sold into Egypt it was B. C. 1728. Jacob removed there twenty-two years later. He died there B. C. 1689. Fifty-four years later Joseph died there, and thirty-six years later still, Moses was born. There lapsed one thousand four hundred and ninety-one years after he heard the voice of the Lord in the burning bush at Horeb before the Saviour was born at Bethlehem; just the time, plus one year, after Christ to the time Columbus found himself in chains for sailing into sunset!

These dates faintly express the antiquity of Egypt. Its monuments along the Nile are more expressive. There are various groups of temples and pyramids, and more are coming to light every year. They are as numberless as the old gods. The great pyramid of Cheops, near Cairo, called Ghizeh, was built one thousand nine hundred years before Abraham, and nearly three thousand years before Christ. It is five thousand years old. A pyramid at Maydoom is a century older. It is fifteen miles south of Ghizeh. It is a landmark on the Nile, and seems to stand on a hill made of its own débris. It is the oldest and best built pyramid in Egypt. Attempts have failed to enter it, although evidence was found to show that it was built in the third dynasty, almost B. C. 4000.

At these early epochs Egypt had a splendid, massive architecture and sculpture; a religion of wonderful beauty, complexity, and awe; a literature whose evidences I have seen on papyri (the original paper); mathematics, astronomy, music, agriculture; and factories of ivory, gems, and glass, not to speak of fabrics of various hue and texture.

After that time its armies ravaged Judea, Syria, and Assyria; the exodus of the Hebrew captives took place through the Red Sea into the desert and into Moab, and over Jordan; Asiatic hordes overran the delta, and Greek philosophers came thither to learn, and Alexander to conquer. Learning lighted her torch in Alexandria. A library was organized, whose manuscripts are said to have been so numerous that in the seventh century enough remained to heat the baths of Caliph Omar's time for six months.

After the Greeks took and ruled Egypt, Rome came. Christianity followed, and creeds began their diverse propagandism. Then came Saladin, whose scimitar flashed along the Nile; then, long after, Napoleon and his generals, less than a century ago; and then Mehemet Ali and his slaughtered Mamelukes. And now, with the canal connecting the East and West, stands England, with her foot upon the ancient river, leaning forward, as she says, to protect, through Suez, her dominion in India.

The placid Sphinx looks upon all these vicissitudes, and makes no sign of revealing its mystery. Thirty years ago Eothen looked upon the Sphinx and made a prophecy. The recent advent of ironclads, which I saw entering Alexandria harbor as they turned about the illustrious Pharos, and the joint note of England and France since, give significance to this prophetic view of Egypt by the Sphinx:

"Laugh and mock if you will at the worship of stone idols, but mark ye this, ye breakers of images, that in one regard the stone idol bears awful semblance of Deity—unchangefulness in the midst of change—the same seeming will, and intent forever, and ever inexorable! Upon ancient dynasties of Ethiopian and Egyptian kings—upon Greek and Roman—upon Arab and Ottoman conquerors—upon Napoleon dreaming of an Eastern empire—upon battles and pestilence —upon the ceaseless misery of the Egyptian race—upon keen-eyed travelers—Herodotus yesterday and Warburton to-day—upon all, and more, this unworldly Sphinx has watched, and watched like a Providence, with the same earnest eyes and the same sad, tranquil mien.

"And we, we shall die, and Islam will wither away, and the Englishman, leaning far over to hold his loved India, will plant a firm foot on the banks of the Nile, and sit in the seats of the faithful; and still that sleepless rock will lie watching, and watching the works of the new race with those same sad, earnest eyes, and the same tranquil mien everlasting. You dare not mock at the Sphinx."

Notables may note, Colonel Arabi Bey may declaim, Tewfik may temporize, and the Sultan may assume, scold, and coax, but the powers have a golden collar about the Egyptian neck, with the word upon it, "Thrall." But will Egyptian darkness or light prevail?

But for Napoleon, or rather one of his officers, the early history of Egypt would be a blank, except so far as a few Greek and Hebrew chapters are concerned. Making a redoubt near Rosetta, in 1799, Bouchard came upon a stone with a three-tongued inscription. I have seen it in the British Museum. It was the key of the hieroglyphics of old Egypt. It unlocked the chambers of the dead. It gave meaning to philosophy and religion, and dates to events and dynasties.

It was a small tablet of black basalt, three by two and a half feet, and a foot thick. It appeared fragmentary. It was set up in the temple of Tum by priests in honor of one of the Ptolemies. It was a recital of events, such as inundation, taxation, and rebellion. It was a lithographic order for a shrine to the king for his virtues. It was written in the hieroglyphic, the Egyptian, and Greek languages. The first was a language of sounds. When Alexandria capitulated, it was sent to England and presented to the Museum by George III. Not for the history it contained was it a precious stone, but because it enabled De Sucy, Akerblad, Young, and Champollion to decipher the sacred glyph. Greek scholars like Porson interpreted the broken Greek text. Afterwards, Brugsch Bey, in 1851, and Chabas, in 1867, completed the translation. Another stone, a cast of which we saw in the British Museum, was discovered in 1866 by Lepsius. It was three-tongued, and had a power almost pentecostal. It has thirty-seven lines of hieroglyphs, seventy-six of Greek, and seventy-two of the Egyptian. This stone was more complete; it confirmed the Rosetta inscription. It was found at San, and forms one of the interesting relics in the Boulak Museum, which we hope to visit. Still another monument was found of similar method and purport, at Kom-el-Hamadra. It is eight feet high, with pendant serpents. Its record is more full than that of the stone of San. It is in the Boulak Museum. Another notable advance in recent Egyptology is the interpretation of demotic writing. It was the handwriting of Egypt, used in daily business. It is unlike the hieratic and hieroglyphic. No less than seven thousand demotic papyri have been collected in the museums of the world. They are the key to old laws and institutions, and furnish themes as well for the daily habits and history of Egypt as for the science of its jurisprudence.

When these touchstones were applied to other inscriptions—as those upon the obelisks—the scroll of Time was unrolled and the papyri received new, real meaning. Then out came—carved, painted, and written—the materials for history. From Philæ to the sea, the old capitals—Thebes, Memphis, Abydos, and Elephantine—were reinvested with their ancient splendors. Temples and tombs, the pyramids themselves, became luminous under the new light which shone from the Rosetta stone. The Sphinx did not altogether withhold her sign, nor did the heart of the mystery of Egypt wholly refuse to be plucked by the ingenious courage of man. Such Egyptologists as the Frenchman Mariette, and the German Brugsch, gave their scholarship to verify and correct chronology and rewrite the list of kings, princes, and dynasties. Even the court architects came forth from their tombs, and the portraitures of men in life five thousand years ago were marked as though in the annual catalogue of the salon of Paris. The coats of arms of soldiers, priests, and kings, from forty-four and fifty-seven centuries before Christ, even back to the founder of the first dynasty, Mena, down to the time of Alexander the Great, B. C. 332, became illuminated missals, to be known and read of all men.

CHAPTER XXX.

THE PYRAMIDS AND TOMBS.

I cannot tell you the intense pleasure with which I look forward to seeing Egypt—that strange, mutilated form of civilization. For years nothing has excited me so much.—JOHN HENRY BUCKLE (1861).

ALAS! One week was, after all, too brief to see this wondrous land! Three chapters are too brief for the summary of the delightful experience. Therefore, omitting much of interest which I saw upon the coast, from the Suez canal at Port Said to Alexandria, and more of old and rare renown which was observed at Alexandria and Cairo, I have taken you, in the familiar way of the East, as in a story, from point to point around Cairo. The pyramids are now the main object of my observation.

To the pyramids! From one of these, the chief and eldest but one, of the monuments of Egypt, and its mysterious companion, the Sphinx, learn all. Upon the way thither, learn all the ways of this Egyptian daily ugliness of life. Is it a hard trip? The guide-book says it is twenty-eight miles, and seven hours in time; but guide-books are fallible. It is but a few years since the tourist to the pyramids had to ride these twenty-eight miles, following the canal dike, by donkey. The direct distance is but six miles. It is done by carriage and donkey, taking the donkey ride over the sand to the Sphinx, especially if the day is hot.

Our guide is selected. He is Dionysius, a Greek; but he has eliminated the Greek, and his card is truly Celtic. It says, "Dennis Cominos." He dresses with European neatness, and wears the fez cap. The Nilometer need not be consulted to tell that the river is up. By its color, it holds Nubia and Abyssinia in solution. We pass the "hosts of Pharaoh" bronzed. We cross the bridge to the island Ghizeh, which appears opulent in vegetation. Everywhere Egypt holds out her palm. The bridge under which this oriental Missouri marches to the sea is crowded with people of all shades, from the excessive black to the daintiest camel color. We pass some dozen of the forty palaces built for the family of Mehemet Ali, and his sons, successors, and relatives. We pass without the gates. We enter the precincts of a tax market, as Dennis calls it. It is really a customhouse out of doors, to collect the octroi duty. Under the shadow of the great lions upon the bridge here, which look wistfully toward their home in the desert, Egypt collects its mite for municipal matters, and the sellers of all kinds of truck and stuffs make their modicum of moneys. The market is a medley of men, women, and children. There is a lively trade going on in corn and cucumbers, dates, donkeys, and melons. Sore-eyed, one-eyed, and no-eyed people, as badly off in their optics as those of Judea, jabber in an unknown tongue. The flies and fleas are as lively as the customers and venders. Egypt has never had a rest as to insects since Pharaoh hardened his heart. It is painful to see the young Rameses, fresh out of a revolution against a complicated government, fighting insectivora. The flies light on the blind or sore-eyed children and cling as though at home; while the other insects, those of Pharaoh's time, give occupation in by-places for scrutinizing mothers.

One would think that here there was no emergency, under the very flow of the Nile, which furnishes a "top-dressing" for the exhaustless loam, for the people to gather manure from the streets and roads. But they do. We are soon in the avenue of acacias, which leads us to the pyramids. This shade is grateful, as the sun is tropical. All along the road people have their little booths for the sale of fresh dates and other vegetables. These are brought in on the heads of fellahs, or on donkeys. Sometimes we pass Egyptians driving and even riding the shaggy-headed buffalo, with ram-like horns. Along the road are sugar-cane fields, partially under water, for the Nile is very high now. We are told that they are now using the American seed for sugar-cane. Why not? The mummies handed down in their coffins Egyptian wheat, four thousand years old, for our American planting. Let us reciprocate. It will be a month before the cane ripens. As we turn to look upon the Nile, we see how it is here protected by walls, and how it is fringed with bananas and palms. We pass the ex-Khedive's palace. It is now empty, as he is residing with his many wives in Naples. In his enforced exile he must smile at the recent revolution.

As we turn to look back, Mount Mulcattem shows charmingly under the hot sun in the eastern horizon. Its sides are scarred. The scars are old and honorable, for out of them came the stone for the pyramids of old and the mosques and palaces of recent times. The mount and its hills make a pretty picture near Cairo. They remind us somewhat of a setting of silver for the emerald vale of the Nile. The land between is low. The smoke of steamers and the movement of sail-boats, with slanting masts, show where the bed of the river is.

Along the road to the pyramids, as in all these hot countries, we see bundles of rags lying in the sun. Under them, completely concealed from flies, are the weary descendants of the Pharaohs taking their siesta. Let them rest. They were born tired. Our guide points out Memphis due south. We are disappointed. It is under water, as the Nile is over forty feet deep. But there is not much to see in Memphis when there is no inundation. It has been rifled to build Cairo and other places. It was the second capital of Egypt, and must have been beauteous in its prime, in its circle of hills and plain of green.

There are intervening sand-hills and water on either side of the acacia avenue. The water broadens into a vast lake. We are out of the range of the noisy drivers and venders on the road. We are approaching the pyramids, and become naturally and silently eager for the first glimpse. Shall we be disappointed? A range of trees intervenes, and then some mad camels on the route distract our attention. The sugar-cane in the adjacent fields, with its tops above the water of the lake; bamboo hedges, which line the road, and a beehive-looking tomb of a sheik are passed, and then, lo! the pyramids! They do not look large at the first glance, but they do look as large far off as near. That is a curious optical illusion; but so it is. You cannot, however, estimate their immense size by being either far off or very near. If you stand by them, or at their corners they do not seem so lofty and huge as when you are one hundred yards away.

But what a desert beyond! It leads far off to Algiers, through Tunis, and nothing but sand, tawny sand. It furnishes the best sample of Egyptian scenery, in its "vivid contrast of Life and Death"—desert and green fields. As we come nearer, some rock on the edge of the sand shows white, for it is of limestone. The lake of water—the overflow of the Nile—enlarges on either side of the road; and when it subsides, as it will in December, the alluvial soil remains, and, with repetitious richness, remains perennial.

Two villages, like those of all the Eastern countries, are seen across the lake under the rocky rise on which the pyramids stand. The houses are built square, and some of stone out of the ruins of old Egypt. Indian corn of a peculiar kind, the "corn of Egypt" in the Bible, is seen growing like our own maize, except that only one ear grows at the top. Between December and May two crops are made, and another in June or July.

The people we meet are like the Arabs, in their long robes, but they generally wear the white turban. We see some of them at prayer along the road. The Egyptians are much devoted to Mohammed. They send out caravans and pilgrims to Mecca every year with much ostentation. These carry a new carpet for the holy place, and bring back the old one, which is cut into shreds and divided among the faithful; for be it known that the carpet is a sacred thing to Islam. The children, on the route to the pyramids, are good afoot. They run after us clamoring for backsheesh.

I confess that the surroundings of the pyramids are not my preconception. My ideal was rather too romantic. I had it from Dean Stanley's description of the grand platform, with its maze of pyramids and tombs,—a vast cemetery-city, extending along the western ridge for twenty miles behind Memphis,—a grand Appian Way out of which the Grand Pyramid arose like a cathedral above smaller churches, with the Sphinx couched at the entrance! This was the scene which sand and time have destroyed.

After we pass several bridges, and see some evidence of the road having been inundated and torn up, we perceive in the lake, and on the right, as we pass the last bridge, and a mile from the pyramids, some green isles, quite pretty, with palms and cultivation. When the water falls they will be isles no more. The water seems to be nearly up to the white cliffs upon which the pyramids repose, or rather to the sand-hills which almost hide the cliffs. Buffaloes are cooling and feeding in the water, and naked men are wading and camels trudging through it. The buffaloes look like hippopotami, with their big, black, ugly heads protruding from the water. Although a mile away from the cliffs, the sand begins to show in ridges and paths. We approach the monumental wonders; and as we are seen, a race takes place between a dozen or more natives, who expect to aid our archæological researches. More camels are seen across the lake, for this is the road to the desert which the caravans take, and their heavy load and tawny color are silhouetted under the cliff against the rock and sand. Now we see that the water is very high and spreads over a vast space, for wells are being used and houses appear in the midst of the lake. Many of the people we meet are very black, and, being dressed in white robes, are quite a picture. We steal glances at the pyramids, and see birds circling round their tops. This gives more seeming elevation to the solid structures.

"What is that white object on the further shore, on the right?" we inquire of our Greek.

"Pelicans"—by the hundred. We see two groups of them, enough to furnish rhetoric for Louisiana orators for a half century. There is a smaller pyramid, not far from the two large ones, on the horizon toward Memphis. We cannot as yet arouse the romantic sentiment which surrounds our own picture of them at home, with the palm group in the foreground and the pink and saffron haze of the Egyptian sunset on them and the sky.

Turning to practical matters, I inquire: "How do people know their own farms when the water settles? Does not its subsidence destroy the landmarks?"

The guide answers that the land is so valuable that it is well marked with metes and bounds. Monuments are one of the specialties and evidences of title in Egypt. There are villages in, and sometimes under, the water. They are left full of rich mud, and that is a comfort to the inundated.

As we approach the hill, my wife observes more pelicans in the distance. She is willing to make affidavit that pelicans are domestic and tame. As we approach, she sees a flock feeding in or near one of the little towns. They turn out to be—

geese. It is ever thus. We discuss no more birds, but proceed straight toward the pyramids, and mount the donkeys in waiting, for the half-hour's jaunt to the Sphinx, before we enter the pyramid.

Much has been written as to this mystic god of the ancient cradle of civilization, the Sphinx—which is the name for Egypt. I am puzzled to express my idea of it and its temple. We alight amid the sandy heaps, and look down into the rock-cut caverns, and up to the half-hid genius of the Unknown.

The Sphinx is sunk in the lime rock. It is a part of it. The tombs about it are lined with immense granite blocks, laid in perfect courses, and with joints as true and handsome as any modern masonry. These blocks came from the cataract, 800 miles above. They form an antique cemetery, covered by forty feet of sand. The temple is thirty feet beneath the level of the sand. From it a roadway, paved with white flagstones, leads up to the pyramids. They seem to have been connected, religiously. The nose of the Sphinx is broken or worn off. It detracts from his dignity. It is a mistake to call the Sphinx *her*. His head-dress is partly demolished. Once the head was crowned with the royal helmet of Egypt; but his feet and form remain—for solution. Let its Œdipus stand forth! There is no satisfactory guess yet as to any of these gods of Egypt. Only one thing is surmised, that in the gods we see the men who made them. We read in their calm features aspirations after the other world—Immortality!

The pyramids are resolvable into tombs, or, if you please, by a stretch of fancy, into astronomical edifices; but this Sphinx has been from the earliest days as much of a dumb enigma as the protoplasm. An intelligent and metaphysical writer, who was here, regards the Sphinx as more wondrous than the pyramids, because so awful and lonely. He even finds comeliness in the thick lips of the Sphinx, and regards him as a forgotten mould of beauty. To my thinking he or it is simply a monster, begotten of the wild imagination of a sunny people, who, after running out of the animal creation for their deities, framed this miscreant. It is said to be an image of the Deity, because unchangeable, having the same will and intent forever! But it has changed. It is not inexorable. It is dead rock, and subject to mutilation and wear like any other piece of limestone. I have seen in Corsica forms almost as whimsical, bearing resemblance to birds, beasts, and creeping things, and to men and devils. The impression, however, which this Sphinx and its problem produce here, on this lonely, shifting edge of the unknown desert, is owing as much to its age as to its insolubility and monstrosity. I cannot connect, with it, except nebulously, the idea of Deity or of immortality. Nor can I feel the same sense of vague, nightmarish horror in contemplating its sister monuments.

Remounting our animals we return to the base of the pyramids. We are pointed out, in a hole in the sand a rod off, the old corners before they were stripped. We look up to the apex of the large one, that of Cheops. Now its massiveness and height are felt. It is simply enormous. It is specific and general gravity. No room for levity of any kind. Made on a square, and with angles geometrical, and with immense stones—and these piled by the aid, likely, of mounds of earth, or, as some suppose, built from the inside—the impression deepens till the head is dizzy and top-heavy with solid substance, acres of stoniness. One feels, in a finite way, a sense of the labor and load by which they were made. Shall we go in, or on top? We resolve first to enter. It is no holiday work, especially for a lady. My wife tries it, and I follow. Three Arabs for each; but Dionysius, the Greek guide, fails of heart. He has been in once. Once is enough for him. These bronzed Arabs dance about, with fragments of bad English on their tongues, and are rather too ready to help us up to the opening. The day is hot. It looks cool inside; but to reach the northern entrance is not to be done in a hurry. Before diving into these acres of piled stone we rest for a farewell glance at the country around. Cairo looks as though half under the water. The majestic river, in reddish yellow, swings through its green banks on, on to the sea. Forty centuries—yes, likely forty times forty—have looked down from these cliffs, half hid in sands, upon this stupendous stream. Less devastating in its overflow than our Father of Waters, the Mississippi, it makes fat the fields, till they laugh again! "*Viridem Egyptum, nigrâ fœcundat arenâ.*" What contrasts are painted under our eye by the chemical forces of water and sun! How beautiful are the green fields of corn and sugar, compared with the tawny infinite upon the west!

Let us enter; not without hope! The slippery path inward slopes downward until it meets a greater gallery, which runs upward at an angle of forty-five degrees. Then, on a level, it runs to the Queen's Chamber. Returning on this level,

SECTION OF PYRAMID AT GHIZA.

and at the same angle, and about half-way up the inside, you enter the King's Chamber. But it is no time or place for photographing this picture. Nor, if I were a poet, could I set a single airy sentiment in time, under the yawning, cavernous gap which opens as we enter.

"Take care, head!" I hear the Arabs say to my wife. She bows to Cheops. I do the same. We go up and down, sliding on polished stones, and in peril of tumbling into dark vaults. Our tapers give a sort of "clear obscure" Rembrandtish aspect to the stony horror about us. After much lifting, pushing, and tugging, relying upon the prehensile grip of the naked Arab foot, and the grasp of the steady Arab hand, now being carried and now pulled, now groping along perilous and slippery edges, we come to the Queen's Chamber. Its sarcophagus has been removed. But where is the queen? Doubtless the soothsayers told her, five thousand years ago, that she would be safe forever in this grand mausoleum. Her fear of death may have been thus soothed. When she was wrapped up in her mummy cloths, embalmed, with her papyri biography in her hand, she bade fair for a long, long survival of the millions of the human race, who soon mingled their dust with the common soil. Now she is in some museum. If a Zulu prince may exhibit himself alive in a museum for money, why may not a dead Egyptian queen? A brass band, perhaps, plays for her dead ear in some caravan, where she is a part of a show. Her chamber is below that of the King. But we must go further and up to the King's Chamber. Here we are, surrounded by seven Arabs, with lighted tapers, which make the gloom worse and worse.

Then begins the diabolism of these fiendish-looking Arab genii of this centre of the largest tomb ever made. Cut off from the world by thousands of tons and thousands of square feet of solid stone, we begin to feel that we, and not *Cheops et uxor*, are the entombed. The Arabs now begin to coax, threaten, grimace, and jabber for more money. I say to them: "We have contracted for so much. If more is to be paid, it will be paid outside—not here."

I thought of our situation, and hinted that if they were ever so good as to get us out safely, we would consider the matter in the open air, not in committee of the hole! One of these gentle genii said that he would touch off some fireworks if I paid him two francs.

"Go it! and let us see."

Whereupon he lit a match, and whiz! off went a magnesia light! It gave a ghastly look to the King's Chamber. Sparks flew around, like miniature stars; and I knew what Professor Proctor meant when he proved, in Steinway Hall, that the pyramids were built for astronomical observations! Cheops did not get up from his sarcophagus. He, too, had emigrated to a foreign museum.

On our way to the large chamber of the king, we stop to look down the well, as best we can in the terrible darkness, only illuminated by a candle. One of the venturesome Arabs, with a taper, crawls down the black void some five feet, and another holds my wife up as she looks down. I shudder, and call a prompt retreat. The man in the well loses his hold and slips. His light goes out. Just then my footing gives way, and but for a prehensile grip on the voluminous trousers of my Arab, there would have been trouble. I took in a dozen yards of fragile blue nankeen slack, "as some men count slackness." Had that cotton given way—a yard or so more—there would have been a vacancy in the Sixth Congressional District of New York. But I am pleased to say I survive Cheops, and helped to organize the Congress, though it may be on a basis as dark as the cavernous depths of the Cheops pyramid.

When we reach the outside some twenty Arabs are on hand, although only seven went in with us, to claim their reward. The fireworks artist was the most importunate. Two francs did not satisfy his greed. Water was brought to us in classic urns, and money asked. The lame and blind were pushed forward to us for charity. Our guide was powerless in the hubbub. It looked like regular highway robbery. Pulling me one way, and my companion another, and with all the infernal cries of which the Arabic tongue is capable, these Arabs kept it up until a tall, gray-haired sheik appeared. In a hoarse voice he howled them all down. The stipulated price was paid to this sheik. Whereupon a dozen cried out: "Sheik never pay us. He keep all the money. He don't divide nothing."

I endeavored to sing the "Star-Spangled Banner" to drown the clatter, but my breathing was all too short after our extreme exertion in entering the pyramid. I told them I would leave them all a hundred francs apiece when I died. This was too remote. One fellow said: "Yankee Doodle come to town." Where he got the phrase we did not stop to inquire. Our horses started amidst a terrific howl for more money. We took refuge and coffee in a house near by, erected, it was said, for the Prince of Wales when here; but when we emerged the same crowd was there. The man who came near going down into the well seemed to be loudest now, and, considering his real peril, we compensated him. We had to buy some antiques from the pyrotechnist. Then we turned our faces Cairo-ward, wondering that out of the good sense prevalent even here in Egypt, they could not provide a decent police system for these monumental wonders.

The pyramids have three groups, and are about sixty in number. They are all within a circuit of twenty miles. I heard Professor Proctor declare that they were astronomical observatories, or stony telescopes. This has just this much truth, viz., that the opening is on the north side, and out of the dark tunnel in daytime the polar star can be seen. Others regard the large pyramid as a standard of measurement; that the angles of its passages indicate latitude, based on the circumference of the earth, and the seasons and time. Some · regard this pyramid as the result of inspiration, inasmuch as it squares the circle and has no element of idolatry; that its measurements, on the basis of the English mile, are right to an inch, and that the infant eras of our world were more scientific than our maturer eras. It is even said that the temperature of the King's Chamber is 68° Fahrenheit, which is the mean temperature of the earth. We found it *mean* in many ways. Others hold that Job had this pyramid in his mind when God spoke to him about laying the measures of the earth, and that it was over this corner-stone of the universe that the morning stars sang together. Some have calculated that exactly one thousand million pyramids piled on each other would reach the sun. Of course this is absolute nonsense. The angles were made for rest to those who buried the king and queen, and who visited them after burial. The truth is that the pyramids are tombs, royal and gigantic, and nothing more. There were two places for ventilation. They are now closed.

The labor and expense bestowed by the ancient Egyptians upon their dead, make our monuments seem flimsy toys. The tombs are full of armlets, bracelets, rings, necklaces, and other varieties of handicraft. Out of the cerements, preserved by the bitumen, come flowers thousands of years old —so old that some of the species are lost to our world of botany.

Like Thebes and Heliopolis, this pageantry of death passes away. It leaves nothing but a few mouldering ruins—"like sea-shells where the ocean has been—to tell that the great tide of life was once there!"

After seeing these six pyramids in a group, and the other three groups in sight, one becomes as silent and thoughtful as the Sphinx seems to be. The immensity of the larger ones would not seem so great if they were Alps, or Atlas, or Lebanon mountains—God's handiwork. The largest one, the one we entered, is only 460 feet high and 15 feet square on its top. It covers thirteen acres. It employed 100,000 men ten years to make the causeway to transport the material for building; and to build it 360,000 men twenty years! It does not, however, compare with "Nord Cap" even, nor with the Cathedral Dome in the Yosemite. But the pyramids are man's work. God works geometrically in the petals of the flower, in the laminated foldings of the pearl, in the strata of the mountains, and in the evolution of the constellations; but here, this simple big square, or triangle set on its larger end, now rough with rugged stones, though once glossy and smoothed by the same manual dexterity which lifted them in their geometric order, because man made it, becomes sublime by its work and its permanency. No demi-gods, no giants, piled up these honors to dead royalty; but the ambition to be remembered made the kings of Egypt confiscate and press the labor of hundreds of thousands of slaves for a score or more of years; and all that their mummies might be handed down for transportation among subsequent nations.

These monuments indicate the slavery of Egypt to the mysteries of royal and priestly control. Every Egyptian ruler began to reign by building his tomb. What chattels men and their muscles must have been, the Israelitish history demonstrates. Call it necromancy, witchcraft, spirit-causes, or the beginnings of science, it is certain that the masses of men in old Egypt were dumb cattle, driven by their rulers to build monuments to perpetuate royal glory. Even as late as the Ptolemies the social order of Egypt had its symbol in the pyramid. The whole structure was based on the labor of the many, with a "royal priesthood" as the apex! Then, the child was owned by the mother, the married man by his wife, and even every corpse belonged to the priest. There was no individuality except at the apex! Egypt was ruled by creeds whose mystery was in sacred keeping. To the profane vulgar this mystery was as awful as the features of the Sphinx, and as Delphic as the Greek letters over the portal of Apollo. They reverenced most who understood least.

CONCLUDING CHAPTER.

BOULAK MUSEUM—FAREWELL TO THE NILE.

And what a series of history it is! In that long defile of ruins every age has borne its part, from Osirtasen I. to the latest Ptolemy, from the time of Joseph to the Christian era; through the whole period of Jewish history and of the ancient world, the splendor of the earth kept pouring into that space for two thousand years.—STANLEY'S *Sinai and Palestine,* Introduction, xxxix.

ON returning to our hotel we sought the celebrated Egyptian collection in the Museum of Boulak. It is the most interesting in the world. It has five times as many Egyptian monuments and hieroglyphs as all other museums. It has a recent acquisition of the old kings. We found these kings arranged in order. Although the room is small, it contains more thousands of years of interesting human antiquity than one could study in a lifetime. We gave to it only about at the rate of ten minutes to a thousand years. Statues in black marble of priests and kings, with curious beards and headgear, and *outré* animals—gods, I suppose —appear, with bas-reliefs of men and women in wood. There is a statue in sycamore from Sakkarah, five thousand years old, and sarcophagi covered over with writing about the lamented Ra-fer. Prince Ra and his relative Nefert, in the fourth dynasty, sit serenely on stony seats, with their hair of formal cut, and a smile over their countenances, quite child-like and bland. Horus, Osiris, and Ammon, with beards, and looking serious, are top-heavy with head decorations of various significance. A goddess of the twenty-sixth dynasty, Thoueris, is as curiously shaped as the fancy of the sculptor could make her. There is a sphinx-like mystery about her head, which is half hog and half elephant; and her ears, like the wig of an English judex, give her a comic aspect.

One of the handsomest of the statues is that of the Pharaoh of the Exodus, Meneptha. He wears a head arrangement of lofty height, topped with a big bottle. Fancy meeting the Pharaoh who "would not let my people go."

The builder of the second pyramid is here, and he smiles also, as he sits with his hands on his knees in supreme content at having his stony immortalization. So is Queen Amenintis, from Karnak, a very beautiful and graceful woman; and near by is a cow goddess, Hathor, and various funereal and other symbols, enough to make one ponder, if not smile, over the preparations civilized folks make for permanent monuments.

Here are rings and bracelets of the early queens. Hair-combs, eggs, seeds, fish-hooks, cribbage-boards; hair-pins, not unlike those now in use, are here, in interesting profusion. The glass eye of the royal mummies follows you around, in a suspicious way, as you look at the decorations which they once used to astonish, please, and awe. Comparing these relics with the writings of the Egyptians, my vote was in favor of the latter as most interesting; but history is not made up of writing merely, and here were evidences of this elder world in its daily routine from life to death.

We were accompanied in this visit by our consul,

Mr. Simon Wolf, a Hebrew of the Hebrews. To him we were indebted for an introduction to the learned Egyptologist, Mr. Brugsch, who was quite communicative, especially over his new and wonderful acquisitions. As we came out of the chamber where they were arranged in order of rank, he said: "I wonder, if these old dynastic Egyptians could talk among themselves, what they would say?"

I took the liberty of answering that a portion of them would give Meneptha some good round Egyptian rhodomontade for his silly hardening of heart and wasting of time in following the Jews into the Red Sea.

But it has since occurred to me that they would rather have sermonized on the condition of their native land under foreign domination, and would have referred the problem to the Sphinx to solve, whether the suzerainty of the Porte, the intermeddling of the French, or the intervention of the English, or all combined, made as good a government as when they commanded abject thousands to work on their monuments, and kept them good-natured on onions for their work. Or would they wonder what had become of the Egyptian race, which Prof. Ebers has rescued from oblivion by his fiction and facts, since the only representative left of their old worship and kinsfolk are the two hundred thousand Christian Copts, who, in their devoted way, have found in the issue of that race of which Joseph was a type, a Saviour more potent than Osiris or Isis? Whatever their converse might be, they could not imagine the interest which an age that has its steamboats on the sacred Nile, its electric congress on the Seine, and its telegraph all round the world, could take in such dead and dried specimens of their kind as they themselves now are. With the image of the strange tombs and coffins, some of them opened within a few weeks, and the lotos flowers and papyrus leaves almost as fresh as when, five thousand years ago, they were laid upon these embalmed and swathed bodies, a sickly sensation followed me as I left the chamber of mummies:

> "It smelt so faint, and it smelt so sweet,
>   It made me creep, and it made me cold;
> Like the scent that steals from the crumbling sheet
>   Where a mummy is half unrolled."

This was the last of the objective points of our travel from pole to pyramid. It is supererogation to attempt to describe a museum which has such an opulence of relics, and such interpreters as Germany, France, and America have given. To my fancy, nearly all these kings, queens, and princes of Egypt are only brown bituminous bodies, to illustrate the weakness of human control and the vanity of human ambition!

My first objective point of travel has been described in a volume of "Arctic Sunbeams." I reached it, at the North Cape, amid the snows of the Arctic, where there was no night. My last ends in the land of the sun, where Egyptian darkness throws its shadow over millions of our race. My first began amid the pines; my last ends amid the palms. Not far from the unseen, undiscovered, and undiscoverable pole, to the seen, undissolvable pyramid, in a land of eternal summer, "where all except the sun is set"—this rounds our travel!

The little light I have thrown over these dark places of the East by these "Orient Sunbeams" is not unlike the electric light in its worst condition. The current is from rapidly moving magnets. It depends upon the uncertainty of horse, steam, water, air, or other forces, and the slightest variation in the revolutions, or even a ripple of a wave or a joint in the harness, causes that uncertain tremor in the light whose sensitiveness has not and will not be allayed.

Heine once wrote a love poem about a noble pine in the far, far north, which slept and dreamed of a graceful palm beneath the tropic sun, and waved in the rich luxuriance of her beauty. It was a poetic analogue of divided hearts. We have more than realized the analogue; for we have not merely dreamed, but, by traversing three zones in which pine and palm have doubled our delight, enjoyed one delicious summer of real romance and experience!

www.ingramcontent.com/pod-product-compliance
Lightning Source LLC
Chambersburg PA
CBHW051724300426
44115CB00007B/450